T0293692

Your AI Roadmap

Actions to Expand Your Career, Money, and Joy

DR. JOAN PALMITER BAJOREK

WILEY

Library of Congress Control Number: 2024946268

Cover design and image: Sehyun Jeon and Jennie Stenhouse
Author photo: © Lynn Bajorek

Disclaimer

This book is designed to provide readers with a general overview of careers and finances. It is not designed to be a definitive career, personal coaching, personal finance, or investment guide or to take the place of advice from a qualified financial planner or other professional. Given the risk involved in investing of almost any kind, there is no guarantee that the investment methods suggested in this book will be profitable. Thus, neither the publisher nor the author assumes liability of any kind for any losses that may be sustained as a result of applying the methods suggested in this book, and any such liability is hereby expressly disclaimed.

Names and Pseudonyms

All the names of people referenced in anecdotes are pseudonyms unless specified otherwise. This is done to protect the privacy of friends, family, and colleagues.

To A and L, for the joy and love you bring to my life,
my cup floweth over—
and for showing me that heaven on Earth is a place
of Earth, sea, and sky and with the freedom
to chase our hearts' pursuits in laughter and love.

Contents at a Glance

Contents

Part 2 Beyond the Day Job: Future-Proofing Your Income and Entrepreneurship 101

Choose Your Own Adventure: How to Read This Book

This book is a labor of love, and I hope you read every word. However, if you are as desperate as I have been before, here are quick answers to the common questions I get asked often in my DMs and in person.

Frequently Asked Questions (FAQ): Where to Find the Answers to Your Questions in This Book

1. **Jobs in AI:** How do I get a job in AI?

   Build a network and have people connect you with jobs. This is the best way. Read Part 1, "So You Want a Job in AI? Let's Accelerate Your Career," of this book and all its data. Take the steps outlined in Chapter 4, "People, People, People: Weak Ties Will Help Me Rise, 80% of Effort on Your Network." Follow my recipe "80% People, 15% Projects, and 5% Skills." Craft a list of 50 to 100 professionals and 20 to 50 companies that you'd love to learn more about and begin your outreach plan. Reach out to them asking to meet for coffee. People are your ticket into the job market. That's the short version. Don't want to go it alone? My team and I host Your AI Bootcamp, which is highly popular: **YourAIRoadmap.com/Bootcamp**.

2. **Skills: Do I need to learn how to code to have a job in AI?**

   No, you do not need to learn how to code. You really, really, really, really don't need to learn how to code. Do you want to be a software engineer? Then, yes, you need to learn how to code. But there are so many other roles than being a developer! What will you need to do? You will need to craft your path and build your portfolio and network, and for that, check out Chapter 8, "Actions Speak Louder Than Words: Skills, Projects, Portfolios, Degrees, and Certificates."

3. Job in AI: Do I have to get a job in AI to future-proof myself?

No, but you will need to future-proof your income to make it through this turbulent time of AI. Check out Part 2, "Beyond the Day Job: Future-Proofing Your Income and Entrepreneurship," for more about that.

4. Job Loss: I've lost my job in a layoff or believe I will lose my job soon. Any advice for me?

Hey, that sounds stressful. You're going to get through it. Get support from your personal and professional support system. Work out to avoid burnout,[1] and go to therapy if you need to. Invest time heavily in your network. Save money for an emergency fund. We'll cover more about finances in Chapter 9, "B*tch Better Have My Money: Beyond the 9 to 5, Finances, and My 22 Income Streams." Document your work for the projects you can speak to. Build your network and connect with the coworkers you like on LinkedIn who might provide you with references in the future.

5. Will AI Give Me Money?: How do I make money in AI? People keep saying there is money to be made. It doesn't seem clear. How do I connect the dots? Where is the money?

AI doesn't make money in any legal ways I've found. What you need is a project that can be monetized. Whether you leverage AI to make something profitable or people buy AI you build, you need to connect AI to something monetizable. Did that sound too vague? Want more depth and concrete answers? Good news, we'll cover this topic in depth extensively in Part 2, "Beyond the Day Job: Future-Proofing Your Income and Entrepreneurship."

6. LinkedIn: I've heard I need a LinkedIn profile. How do I make a "good" one?

It depends on your goals, but 98 percent of the time, having a profile is helpful. A strong LinkedIn presence can be a crucial part of your

---

[1] Burnout is out of the scope of this book, but check out the amazing research that talks about how 30 minutes of cardio can help you flush stress out of your body: **https://www.burnoutbook.net**.

professional and personal brand. To learn more about this topic, check out Chapter 5, "Personal Brand: Get Credit for Your Work and Hone Your Brand," and Chapter 8, "Actions Speak Louder Than Words: Degrees, Portfolios, and Getting Credit."

7. **Certificates and Degrees:** What degrees and certificates do you recommend I pursue?

It depends on your goals. Don't waste your money on just any degree or program. Check out Chapter 8, "Actions Speak Louder Than Words: Skills, Projects, Portfolios, Degrees, and Certificates."

8. **Up to Date:** How do I stay up to date about what's going on in AI?

There are many resources out there for this, and they keep changing! I recommend the *Your AI Roadmap* podcast. As of the writing of this book, my production team and I have dropped Season 1 and gotten 600 downloads in a few weeks and more than 10,000 impressions on YouTube. On the podcast, I interview leaders building in AI from Microsoft, Google, Intuit, Adobe, and more who talk concretely about their projects. Check it out at **YourAIRoadmap.com/Podcast.**

9. **Audiobook:** Why didn't you read your own audiobook?

I sure wanted to! Regardless, please know that my heart is in every page of this book even if you aren't hearing my voice on the audio version. You can hear my voice on the *Your AI Roadmap* podcast at **https://YourAIRoadmap.com/Podcast.**

Want to get personalized Your AI Roadmap ideas? Take the Your AI Roadmap Personality Quiz at **YourAIRoadmap.com/Me.** I hope these FAQ answers your pressing questions. The rest of the book has examples and explanations of modern advice about all these topics. Let's dive into why I wrote this book for you.

Introduction: Why I Wrote This Book

A pesky truth of the age of AI is that everyone's day job is at risk, but we all still need money. This book has one job: to provide you with practical, data-driven tools to equip you with the ability to future-proof your career and income. I dare say we can have fun, too! If you have the desire to develop your career, expand your career opportunities, and make more money, you're in the right place. This book is all about the agency you have in your life to take action, upskill, and expand your life and income. But before we get there, I need to address the elephant in the room: fear.

No one's job is safe. Shifting sand under our feet and an often small safety net can be scary. Large-scale layoffs at companies fill our new feeds almost daily. Almost 50 percent of Americans report lay-off anxiety.[1] About 28% of Americans have already been laid off since 2021.[2] While the COVID-19 pandemic played a role in these layoffs, the anxiety continues today. Does working in AI keep you immune to being laid off? Nope! Even the chief executive officer (CEO) behind ChatGPT, Sam Altman, lost his job in 2023 when the board tried to oust him. Luckily for him, he was reinstated a few days later.[3]

That's truly the age we live in. The age of AI brings both high volatility and opportunity. These types of opportunities did not exist even as recently as 2015, when I was in graduate school. In the age of AI, it is estimated that "69 million new jobs are expected to be created and 83 million to be eliminated," says the World Economic Forum in their 2023 report.[4] "The report finds that nearly a quarter of all jobs (23%) globally will change in the next five years." That is a loss of 14 million jobs eliminated internationally. Even large companies previously

---

[1] https://www.harvardbusiness.org/wp-content/uploads/2023/03/2023_01_managing-your-emotions-after-being-laid-off.pdf
[2] https://www.harvardbusiness.org/wp-content/uploads/2023/03/2023_01_managing-your-emotions-after-being-laid-off.pdf
[3] https://www.axios.com/2023/11/18/sam-altman-greg-brockman-openai-board-timeline
[4] https://www.weforum.org/agenda/2023/05/future-of-jobs-in-the-age-of-ai-sustainability-and-deglobalization

considered relatively stable have had layoffs: Amazon, Meta (formerly Facebook), Google, Microsoft, Salesforce, SAP, Dell, Cisco, IBM, Uber, X (formerly Twitter), Xerox, VMware, Peloton, PayPal, Shopify, Indeed, Zillow, Airbnb, Wayfair, and Yahoo, among others.[5]

I myself have been in two large-scale layoffs. It's painful, but so common for folks working in the tech sector. When we look at the individual to the societal level, do the folks whose jobs are eliminated have the experience for the new jobs being created? Not necessarily. So begins a great time of upskilling to get new jobs, make pivots, and reconsider our life paths. This book is especially for you if you're at the crux of these career decisions.

Why do we have jobs? For some it might be a vocation that is meaningful for us personally. I know doctors and scholars who feel truly called to their work. For most people I know, jobs are about money. We work for a paycheck. We need to pay our rent, mortgage, student debt bills, childcare, and grocery bills, to name a few. We need money to live our lives. For people who were used to a world of stable jobs for 30 years, this is a pretty big change for so many to have such high amounts of job and career volatility. One interpretation from this is, "We are doomed! There is no more job stability! Gahhh!" Things are changing for sure. Doom and gloom is one way to look at it. I see this as a time of reimagining—a time when you question if a 9 to 5 job is what you want or need.

I'm wildly optimistic about your future. Yes, it's true that the age of AI is a time of great volatility. With great change comes great opportunity to democratize power and wealth. This is especially true for people previously excluded from wealth and agency in their lives and careers. You can build wealth today fast, ethically, and legally for you and your family. This is especially powerful for Black and Brown folks, women, gender expansive, caretakers, LGBTQIA+ folks, people with disabilities, veterans, and other marginalized folks in our world. Lucrative opportunities are now readily available to anyone with a computer, Wi-Fi, and enough time to take action. I am not saying this to diminish the digital divide and those who do not have the time or access to tech, which often are in marginalized communities. For those who do have access, my goal is to show how they can use these tools for good, for themselves, and to lift others up.

---

[5] **https://layoffs.fyi**

In this book, we will explore answers to the following questions:

- **Resilience in the Age of AI:** How do we build resilience during the turbulent and opportunity-filled times of AI?
- **Careers:** How do we future-proof our careers in the modern age of AI?
- **Income:** How do we future-proof our incomes?

This book is a collection of answers. These answers have changed my life and the lives of those around me, and are bolstered by data-driven research and exemplifying stories. I'll share my own story in these pages, as well as the journeys of others who have different identities from mine.

Goal of the Book

This book provides robust answers to these questions as you craft your AI roadmap through the age of AI. Frankly, I'm really jealous of you! You have this resource that distills more than 30 books worth of career and finance content in what I hope is a clear and openhearted way. This book is about 200 pages. Roughly 100 pages are about careers, and 100 pages are about finances. Wow, do I wish I'd had this book even two years ago! I had to chart many decisions that were hard and scary alone. I'd love it to be easier for you! This book can provide actionable shortcuts.

As the author, I hope you can view me as a friend, rad cousin, or ridiculously bold niece/granddaughter who talks about careers and wealth in an open, inclusive, and modern way. I would love for this book to cheer you on and equip you with practical tools to be resilient and live in joy, freedom, wealth, and fulfillment.

Do you talk openly about careers and money? My family doesn't. I'll be honest with you, some of my family members can't stand how openly I talk about these topics. It can be deeply uncomfortable. Words akin to, "How dare you talk and post about how much you get paid?" In fact, "Oh, you know that other people are going to see this?!?!" is a heated discussion my mom and I have had at least five times across the years. I love you, Mom. Agree to disagree! I frequently get told at family dinner tables to quiet down and change the topic. People say that influencers are stupid, not realizing my friend, who is an influencer, brought in $3 million in revenue last year.

Pressured to work long hours? Are you pressured by others to work wild hours and never dream of alternate paths? Is it taboo to talk about side hustles? I have worked a job where I was pressured to work 7 a.m. to 7 p.m. six days per week. Life is too short. I definitely didn't stay at that job long. There are still people I know who work there more than half a decade later. That's a choice! Not what I want.

Some people in my life are indifferent to ambition. They blink at me when I mention negotiating large contracts, raising $500,000 for my nonprofit, or semiconductor stocks. They say, "That's nice, dear, so about our recent trip. . .." To protect my tender heart from shame and disinterest, there are some folks I choose to never talk with about money or careers. We instead talk about the weather and our current favorite show on Netflix. That's okay!

Is it a taboo for you to talk about your ambitions? To explore how you could expand your income? Perhaps you're from a family and community that openly talks about stocks, portfolios, and entrepreneurship. Lucky you! If you have ever felt like the odd duck out, I want to let you know: you are not alone.

You and Me

You and me, though? I bet you're here because *we* are on the same page. We are ambitious. We have goals to build our careers and bank accounts. We want to lead meaningful and fulfilling lives. Not all of your family and friends may feel comfortable with these topics. Your boss may work from 8 a.m. to 10 p.m. every day of the week. That's their choice. That's their journey. But there are *other* options. There's never been a better time to make a plan, take action, and make a change. Let's make it easier! I've got a great map to help you chart your way—this book!

Will all of it be easy? If I said "Yes, all of it is easy," then I'd be lying to your face. It may be even hard if folks in your life aren't supportive. My advice? Create and enforce boundaries as a strategy for the haters and doubters. Prioritize friendships and people who cheer you on. Consider therapy (it's been awesome for me!). Keep eating your vegetables, working out, and increasing your wealth. It may be safer to build wealth in stealth! It sure has been for me! No one is coming to save you but you. Let's build that roadmap and achieve these goals.

My Story

Who am I to be talking about careers and wealth? My name is Joan.[6] I am an entrepreneur, influencer, and investor living in Seattle. Before I share my story, please know that despite these accolades I'm about to share, I really don't have a big ego. In real life, I often get mistaken as Sarah, that brunette from yoga class, or Rachel, your mom's friend's daughter. Let me share my story.

I have always loved languages. But no one was sure whether that passion would ever pay the bills. I grew up in Portland, Oregon, to parents who have advanced degrees and a love of exploration and travel. In college at the University of Washington, I remember being around a table where people were saying their majors: computer science, pre-med, and chemical engineering, and when the question came to me, I said my dual degrees, "French BA and photography BFA." People laughed and said, "Wow, I thought you were smart." Ouch! I now have a vibrant career where I am thoughtful and persuasive with the language I use daily to communicate and have beautiful visuals across my work. These degrees helped!

After college, I moved to France and worked for the French Ministry of Education. I taught at underprivileged middle schools, working with more than 300 students in Toulouse. I applied and was accepted into graduate school and moved back to the United States. While working on my master's degree in linguistics at the University of California (UC), Davis, I came across the field of phonetics and natural language processing (NLP). This is the field that evolved into large language models (LLMs) and multimodal AI systems. Computers attempting to process human language was a comical idea back in 2015. People gave me the advice "Don't go into that part of the field; we're not going to solve those problems any time soon." Yet, at the same time, products that used text, speech, and sounds were becoming more ubiquitous. I was enchanted by companies like Duolingo that were building language products with tech used by millions worldwide. How cool! This technology was incredibly powerful, and I longed to be in those rooms building impactful projects.

As I navigated my next steps, I knew I wanted to go into tech. Tech was a place where I could have impact, live wherever I wanted, and be paid a good salary. To prepare myself to work in research and

---

[6] My name rhymes with the word *stone*.

development, I earned a PhD. I applied and was accepted in the top 2 percent of applicants and the only one awarded a first-year fellowship in my program. In an interdisciplinary PhD program at the University of Arizona (UArizona), I thrived in a supportive environment. In my research, I worked on defining how we optimized multimodal products and did consulting for tech companies.[7] Yet, it was clearer and clearer to me that the same biases of the white dudes around me were the same biases being built as default into these powerful, unregulated products deployed to millions worldwide. I grappled and processed my experiences of being "othered" with my PhD advisor. Dr. Mike Hammond[8] gave me helpful advice: "If you lead with bias, people shut down and won't listen. If you lead with money, opportunity, or something else that everyone wants to listen to, then you might be able to talk to them about bias." These words of wisdom have been invaluable. This book follows this advice, which I recommend you follow when it comes to the impact you may want to make in your communities and the world.

As I began to apply for jobs, there were very few women and Black, Indigenous, and People of Color (BIPOC)[9] people in the room. In one interview loop, I wasn't sure there was another woman in the building. Yikes! I realized either I was complicit in normalizing this, or I needed to do something. At the time, I became more active on academic X (formerly Twitter). My tweets got noticed. So many people post, but few have the technical creds to show they know their stuff. It wasn't long until I was publicly listed as a voice AI Influencer in 2018.[10] Becoming an influencer wasn't something I aspired to; it simply was a product of being public about my work. I founded the nonprofit Women in Voice in August 2018. In just a few years, I raised $500,000, expanded the number of chapters to 20+ globally, and built a brand with more than 56,000 followers worldwide. I published one of my PhD comprehensive papers in *Harvard Business Review*. By the end of 2018, I signed my first six-figure contract in AI (Nuance was acquired by Microsoft for $16B in 2021). I began to get invited to speak at fancy tech events and podcasts

---

[7] Check out ImmerseMe, the company I collaborated with for my PhD research!

[8] Real name, not pseudonym.

[9] The appropriate terms for talking about these communities keep changing. Today, the term BIPOC is common but may not be tomorrow. I use these terms with respect and acknowledge that they may have changed by the time you are reading this book. To learn more, check out https://www.thebipocproject.org.

[10] https://www.soundhound.com/voice-ai-blog/top-15-voice-ai-influencers-to-follow-on-twitter

such as Dashbot and Voice Summit. In 2019, I spoke at the annual VentureBeat Transform conference as the CEO of Women in Voice.

Along my journey on the technical side, I secured jobs with titles such as "Senior," "Head of," "Advisor," and "VP" at companies working on the backends of AI and data projects for companies like Verizon and Boeing. My base salaries ranged from $100,000 to $250,000 and more per year. Contracts I've signed include much more than just base salaries, including equity, paid national and international work travel, signing bonuses, annual bonuses, fundraising cash bonuses, and more. My net worth is more than $1.5 million as of the writing of this book. I have 22 income streams, which shocked even me when I documented them for you for this book—see more details in Chapter 9: B*tch Better Have My Money: Beyond the 9-5, Finances, and My 22 Income Streams. I'm not telling you this to brag. I want to share with you big milestones that I'm proud of. You can achieve big things, too!

Layoffs have come my way also. I was laid off in two large-scale AI company layoffs. Imagine how it feels when 30% of the company is laid off in a day. My coworkers messaged each other asking who got cut and who still has a day job. Yikes! I've been knocked down, and I've kept getting back up. I've learned how to be resilient. I grew my personal brand, network, and close group of friends and mentors. As an influencer and person who has cultivated my personal brand for years, that journey has paid off in spades. My network and entrepreneurial endeavors have been crucial to my successes.

One of the keys for me is entrepreneurship. After layoffs, I've taken coffee chats with people who wanted to hire me on the spot. Some offer me jobs, connections, and contracts. I have closed six-, seven-, and eight-figure contracts in my own name. Over time, I founded a company and became the CEO at Clarity AI.[11] I decide what products we make, when I work (flexible), where I work (mostly my home office), and how much I pay myself. I hire people I want to work with, choose which businesses to partner with, and decide which customer projects to take on.

I keep my financial house in order. I have no credit card or student debt. My credit score is in the 800s. As an influencer, people DM me on social media with life-changing opportunities. I am flown around the world to speak on international stages and company campuses. I am a homeowner in Seattle in a beautiful, central neighborhood. I am on track to financial independence and to retire in my early 40s, or sooner.

---

[11] Check out examples of all the cool stuff my team at Clarity AI builds at **https://hireclarity.ai**.

Today, I have a portfolio career. I'm a CEO and founder of an AI company. I'm the founder of Women in Voice,[12] a nonprofit organization. I'm an advisor to startups and companies, such as CleanAI,[13] a company at the intersection of climate tech and AI innovation. I am an investor. I have invested in a dozen startups and am eager to invest more in the future. I'm a podcast host of *Your AI Roadmap*, where I interview my friends and connections who are leaders at Google, Microsoft, Amazon, and more to discuss their projects and how they are shaping the AI landscape. You can listen on Apple Podcasts or Spotify and watch on YouTube: **YourAIRoadmap.com/Podcast.**

Honestly, I'm confident you might struggle to take my technical chops seriously because I'm a woman, I'm playful, and I'm writing you a book about careers and income. I am working to come to terms with that. For years, I've wanted to be taken seriously in technical spaces. I have worked to prove myself my whole career, and even after every gold star, people continue to question whether they might want to work with someone who looks so feminine and young. Woof, misogyny and ageism don't look good on ya! Since my first year of grad school, I was given the feedback "Your presentation deck is too readable. People won't think you're smart." The world may not be ready for technical women who can create modern, readable, practical content. I won't be sitting on my thumbs waiting. My goals have shifted. I have goals beyond people acknowledging my technical chops. I feel called to share with you the powerful things I've learned along the way. I'm hopeful you can see I'm multifaceted, too.

Another thing we've got to talk about is privilege. I am a white woman in a white patriarchal capitalist society. My parents and grandparents have greatly supported my career and finances. This intergenerational support ripples through my life and career. I have privilege. I have a different kind of safety net than other people. I started in a different place from other folks. This is one of the key reasons I am a founder and investor. I own a company that has a primarily female staff. Clarity AI has staff members who are parents, women, BIPOC, caretakers, and neurodivergent, and who are based all over the world. I invest my money in companies founded by Black women and men

---

[12] See our work at **www.womeninvoice.org.**
[13] Learn more at **https://www.cleanai.com.**

(CurlMix, PuffCuff, Runner, The Cru, Audios), built by white women (ViralMoment, It's By U Flowers), and established by female founders building amazing products the world needs (RuthHealth, Intentionalist). When I look at the missions of these companies, their work policies, and their ethos, I find these are workplaces that align with my values. They are new types of workplaces. I want to fund companies that are building better worlds. When I consider my legacy, this book is part of that. I want to help you build your career and achieve financial independence. If you have doubts about someone like you becoming wealthy, please know that Black women and men, Asian wealth influencers, and white female multimillionaires agree with me that anyone can build immense personal wealth. This includes:

- Arlan Hamilton, author of *It's About Damn Time* and *Your First Million*
- Julien Saunders and Kiersten Saunders, authors of *Cashing Out*
- Tori Dunlap, author of *Financial Feminist*
- Rachel Rodgers, author of *We Should All Be Millionaires*
- Vivian Tu aka *Your Rich BFF* and author of *Rich AF*

I continue to learn from their work and advice. As awards and opportunities keep piling up, people have been asking me how I did it. My DMs are exploding! "What advice do you have for me? What do you recommend I do?" This book is a direct answer to these questions. I'll be sharing with you my best strategies about crafting your career and finances throughout this book.

Scope of the Book

There are a few things that this book doesn't cover, such as an overview of artificial intelligence and venture capital investment. If you are looking for how to raise investor and venture capital money, that is not this book. This book also is not a comprehensive tome on artificial intelligence. I would love to write you a vibrant, inclusive, clear, and plain-language book about what artificial intelligence actually is. Please let me know if that's the next book you'd like me to write! The purpose of the book you have in your hands is to deepen your understanding of modern careers and money.

This book doesn't cover venture capital and raising investor money. It's out of scope for this book, primarily because it is a route only truly viable to white men who attended Harvard or Stanford.[14] Please read that sentence again. More than 70% of startups that raised venture capital between 2015–2020 have a white male cofounder who went to Stanford University and/or Harvard University.[15] In 2023, 98% of all venture capital in the United States went to startups with a man as a founder.[16] Please read that sentence again. That's such a tiny sliver of the population! It's also many people who look the same and have a whole lot of privilege. I would like to work on changing this in my lifetime. Female investors can help change the game. For today, though, raising investor money is not the route for most folks in the United States. What about a path for the rest of us? Good news! You can build wealth and never need to speak to a venture capitalist. We're looking for paths that are realistic and data-driven.

Your AI Roadmap is not just an advice book—it's a modern blueprint for your career and income. You and I are going to talk in modern, inclusive, and data-driven ways about your career and income. I'm not satisfied by just building wealth for myself. I want to help to democratize wealth and power. I have learned so much along my journey. I want to share it with you as you chart your own AI roadmap. Where are we headed? Let's look at an overview of this book: The first part is about modern careers. In the second part, I'll give my broad recommendation about finances in this modern age. Ideally, your next steps are way easier than mine. Hurray! Let's do this!

---

[14] https://www.techstars.com/blog/pov/why-do-white-men-raise-more-vc-dollars-than-anyone-else

[15] https://www.techstars.com/blog/pov/why-do-white-men-raise-more-vc-dollars-than-anyone-else

[16] https://pitchbook.com/news/articles/female-founders-vc-year-in-review-2023

PART 1

So You Want a Job in AI? Let's Accelerate Your Career

"Having a personal brand is no longer a choice; it's a requirement."[1]

—Aliza Licht, podcast host of *Leave Your Mark*, and bestselling book author

"Your network is your net worth."[2]

—Porter Gale, board director of Reddit

[1] https://alizalicht.com/on-brand
[2] https://www.amazon.com/Your-Network-Net-Worth-Connections/dp/145168875X

CHAPTER 1

Let's Future-Proof Your Career and Income: Volatility and Opportunity in the Age of AI

"We don't have the money to pay you anymore," said my boss. I knew the writing was on the wall when my boss asked me completely out of the blue for a one-on-one meeting. My heart sank, and I knew I would be in an AI layoff. He seemed genuinely sad as he told me how I would get my last paycheck. My termination was immediate. It was the first time I'd ever been let go from a company. It really hurt.

Just months before, I had been on top of the world! I spoke on one of tech's glitziest stages in the world, the Consumer Electronics Show (CES) in Las Vegas. I had been flown to Australia to meet with the team and international customers. I had a gorgeous wardrobe. I got tech gifts in the mail regularly from Amazon and Google. Google's teams tried to poach me. They even did so in person in front of my boss at a meeting (awkward!). At the time, I had been happy with my manager and compensation. To be so wanted and seen! Wow, I felt like a high flier!

But then things changed. What had once been a growing company now lost contracts and enterprise clients that fell out of the sky. The CEO was transparent that the company was in financial freefall. There were regular meetings with a graph that showed a cliff. I was on the innovation and international expansion team. I spoke with customers about conversational AI projects. I collaborated with teammates on reviewing data and designing data-driven AI products. While my team pitched new companies regularly, the financials did not drastically improve. I can't say that this was a surprise, but that didn't mean I was completely ready for it. Then the layoff came. I was not alone in losing my job.

Thirty percent of employees lost their jobs that day. It was the first time I had been let go from a job *ever*. It was a huge hit to my ego. My team wrote me recommendations and offered to make me intros. I was a ball of shock and sadness. I was the only woman on my team, and now my team would be all men. My job was a huge part of my identity, and I lacked the vocabulary to talk about it. When family and friends heard the news, some blamed me. I felt the desire to hide my head in my turtle shell. As I went to therapy and worked out, I realized that this was more than just me.

It dawned on me that I could lose my job in a second. It didn't matter how hard I worked. It didn't matter that my boss appreciated my work. It didn't matter about work achievements. I could lose my job in a day. Talk about volatility! This is the reality in the age of AI. We see layoffs daily. No one's job is safe. Sadly, this can happen to you. So what comes next? How do we future-proof our careers and income? My answer: expand your horizon and income.

What happened next for me? My entrepreneurial skills kicked in. I scaled my side-hustle. I had been building my personal brand and network. I was passionate about supporting women in conversational AI and voice technology and scaled my community Women in Voice. The global community that I built on the side of my technical career flourished, even more so now that I had a lot more time for it. My team and I filed and made Women in Voice an official 501(c)(3) non-profit. Within a few months, I closed my first six-figure sponsorship. It was with Google for a summit that co-promoted programming. In this book, I'll talk a lot about the paramount importance of people in careers and business. Although many may think of business as a corporate engine, the truth I've found is that for every contract, there needs to be a signature from both business entities. A signature from a person. A piece of paper and two humans.

At the end of the day, so so so so much is about people. During this time, I upskilled in contract business negotiations. I closed big deals and set up a business bank account. I began to pay myself and my team from money I closed. I took on other technical work along the way and scaled both my entrepreneurial chops of how to manage a team and cash flow in addition to working on incredibly innovative AI projects in the field of medicine, customer service, agriculture, waste management, and many more! My own career took more twists and turns before I got to where I am today.

I'm excited to share with you my best advice to future-proof your career and income. Some of the advice may sound counterintuitive to advice about getting degrees and polishing your CV. Some of the advice I bet you've heard before, but maybe through explanations and humorous stories I can convince you to finally take action. As mentioned in the introduction, I would love for this book to cheer you on! I want to equip you with practical tools to be resilient and live in joy, freedom, wealth, and fulfillment, and to help with that, I'll share some of my stories with you as well as those of other Black, Brown, LGBTQIA+, and female leaders and entrepreneurs in AI and beyond.

Future-Proofing Your Career Steps Overview

In the next chapters, we will cover the following steps of Your AI Roadmap to future-proofing your career:

1. Resilience, Mindset, and Thought Work
2. Goal Setting: WOOP Method
3. Job vs. Career, Paycheck vs. Income
4. 80% of Effort on Networking and People
5. Professional Glow-Up and Personal Brand
6. Own Your Story and Share It
7. Mapping Your Work to AI Jobs (If You Want)
8. Professional Stories and Getting Credit with the STAR Method
9. Taking the Next Small Steps: Prototyping
10. Get Ready to Talk About Money

That's your AI Roadmap for careers! Let's start the first step on this journey by talking about your mindset.

Resilience and Mindset

Fear is a common emotion right now. Many people are worried about losing their job, they already have lost their job, or they might be supporting someone going through this. More than 517,554 jobs in the United States have been lost to layoffs in the past three years.[1] You are far from alone! Frankly, your fears are totally rational. But hiding in your turtle shell isn't going to make it better. Doomscrolling TikTok isn't going to save you. In this first part of the book, we'll talk about resilience and mindset, goal setting and meaning, jobs versus careers, people, personal brand, owning your story, chasing an AI job if you want one, and building a robust portfolio of things you've tried and charting your own roadmap through the age of AI. I hope it will be a fruitful, practical, fun, and detailed journey that we can go on together. I've done this work myself. It has worked for me to hit my goals and milestones *years* ahead of schedule. I have helped others achieve their goals, too. If you're in a rut, I want to speak directly to you about resilience and to stop beating yourself up.

What is stopping you from the life of your dreams? Yes, there are structural societal barriers such as disability, misogyny, exclusion, overwhelming caretaking responsibilities, sexual abuse, toxic environments, and more. Call me naive, but I truly believe in you. I believe that if there's a will, there's a way. Something between all and nothing where you can get your foot in the door and pry it right open! Mindset is crucial to resilience. I've fallen hard. I've gotten back up. As Cardi B says in her song "Get Up Ten," "Knock me down nine times but I get up ten."[2] Join Cardi B and me and keep getting back up. If you believe you can learn and grow and work at it, or you believe you can't and don't strive, ultimately you'll prove yourself right Throughout the book, I'll be sprinkling in a few of my hot takes for you that are my quick responses to important topics. Here's the first one!

---

[1] **https://layoffs.fyi**
[2] **https://genius.com/Cardi-b-get-up-10-lyrics**

Joan's Hot Take: Proving Yourself Right

> If you believe you can, you can. If you believe you can't, you can't. Ultimately, you'll prove yourself right.

When I told one of my mentors that I'd been laid off, he was thrilled for me! "Congrats on being liberated!" He said, "What do you want to do next?" I was stunned and laughed. This type of expansive thinking is crucial. He saw my job loss as an opportunity where I had the freedom to chart my own course. Having supportive outside perspectives on big transitions in your life can be helpful. Since I'm the family member and friend who loudly talks about her career, I'm often the family member who people call and text for help when it comes time to negotiate that big contract. I'll admit to you that some of my closest friends have told me about "channeling Joan" before taking an important negotiation meeting or asking, "What would Joan do in this context?" However, in the last few years, my DMs have been overflowing! I don't have enough time in a day! This book helps me share advice at scale. I want to be helpful to more people. Thus, I wrote this book for you, my dear reader.

Mindset is crucial. If you are currently beating yourself up right now, let me be clear. Believing in yourself is crucial. When I've looked back at my career, I see that believing in myself is not something everyone else had. When it comes to my peers from the past, we differ in this. I am not more talented. I am not more brilliant. I'm not more hardworking. I believe in myself and my potential. If you don't believe in yourself, let's talk about it.

The Inner Saboteur and Thought Work

Do you struggle with imposter syndrome? Do you beat yourself up internally? Do you have an inner saboteur? Some people call it lack of self-confidence, and others call it imposter syndrome. RuPaul, the internationally acclaimed drag queen and drag contest show host and winner of 12 Emmys,[3] talks openly and regularly about the saboteur

---

[3] https://www.hollywoodreporter.com/tv/tv-news/rupaul-host-emmy-win-streak-seven-1235210588

we all have in our heads. RuPaul says the term is used "to identify that little voice in your head that is also nagging away at your confidence and feeling your insecurity."

Do you have a little voice in your head that says nasty things to get you down? "One of our biggest tasks in lives is identifying our inner saboteur and then basically telling it to shut up all the time,"[4] says RuPaul. I agree. Talking openly about these inner thoughts that affect us is crucial to moving past them. I mean talking openly to our support network, as well as talking to yourself. Many folks have recommendations of how to get out of this mindset as well.

"I was a horribly mean b*tch to myself. My thoughts were vicious," writes Rachel Rodgers, "So how did I change the tape that was playing this 'you so ugly' song in my head every day? I did thought work."[5] Thought work is about reframing our internal thoughts and eventually adopting the narratives we choose. Table 1.1 shows examples of thought work on careers.

TABLE 1.1 Thought Work Examples

Topic	Initial Thought	Reframed via Thought Work
Losing my job	I'm scared of losing my job. Will AI take my job?	AI will transform the workplace as we know it today. While women's jobs could be more disrupted by AI and automation in the short term than men's jobs,[6] I have agency to future-proof my income and build a big career of my choosing.
Identity	I've lost my job. I'm a failure.	With layoffs every day, many people will lose their jobs. I am not a failure. I have fallen, but I will get up and figure out my next steps.
AI jobs	How do I get a job in AI? Isn't that the only way I'll be safe?	I can work to get a job in AI, but it might be like running after a rocket ship. I'm going to work to future-proof my income and career and keep upskilling in AI so I have options for the short and long term.

---

[4] https://www.wmagazine.com/story/rupauls-drag-race-season-10-episode-11-power-rankings-evil-twin-inner-inner-saboteur
[5] https://www.amazon.com/We-Should-All-Be-Millionaires/dp/1400221625
[6] https://www.cnn.com/2023/06/21/economy/women-employment-ai-disruption/index.html

TABLE 1.1   (*Continued*)

Topic	Initial Thought	Reframed via Thought Work
Networking	I'm not good at networking. Isn't that sleazy?	Networking is a skill like any other. It's a skill I can learn and get better at. (TONS of tips on this one in Chapter 4.)
LinkedIn	My LinkedIn sucks. I don't know what to post, and I'm stuck.	LinkedIn is a powerful social media platform. I can learn how to build a profile and grow my network there. It will take time, but I am committed to figuring out my career's next steps.
Tongue-tied	I don't know what to say in professional settings. I don't want to sound stupid!	I will be prepared with the STAR method story examples and an elevator pitch. I can get support from family and friends (Chapter 8 will go into this in depth).
Work portfolio	My work should speak for itself. People should already know that I'm awesome. Why don't they? Why am I still a nobody?	For people to know me and my work, I need to package it and share it. I can curate a portfolio of work using the STAR method and a few visuals to make it easier for people to know my work and for me to get credit for the work I've already done.
Money	I am bad with money. I don't know what to do.	I can learn how to use money as a tool. Maybe I didn't get the best financial education, but I can expand my income and build a flourishing, rich life.

These are some examples of thought work related to this book. Our thoughts are influenced by many things—our larger society, our particular culture, our family and friends—but it is also, thankfully, something that we ourselves have the power to influence."[7] In a different approach, multimillionaire and media juggernaut Alex Hormozi says, "You don't become confident by shouting affirmations in the mirror, but by having a stack of undeniable proof that you are who you are."[8] We'll talk later about the STAR method and how to talk with hiring managers, recruiters, or anyone else who needs to be reminded of exactly what you have *already* accomplished in your career. Everyone starts somewhere!

An investor who came from humble beginnings, Arlan Hamilton tells herself every day, "I deserve to be here. I worked my ass off. I will

[7] https://helloseven.co/the-book, p. 16
[8] https://www.threads.net/@hormozi/post/CutGMaLN5vg

not shrink myself to make someone else more comfortable. I deserve to be in the room."[9] We'll dive more into Hamilton's story in a minute. There are many ways to deal with these doubts and insecurities. I prepare myself for these rooms psychologically. I remind myself of what I contribute to rooms and that if an event is free and open to the public, that means everyone. There is a list of recommendations about how to prepare yourself for networking events. Check out the "List of 10 Ways to Prepare for Effective Networking Questions for You" in Chapter 4.

In addition to the tactics I recommend there, I also text my friends anecdotes about microaggressions and inappropriate behavior so we can commiserate and heal together. To deal with trauma and anxiety, I work out and go to therapy. Therapy is one of the most powerful tools I have leveraged across the years to heal myself and navigate my career. I can't recommend it enough. While there are people in my life who don't believe in therapy and shame people who do, you don't need to get permission from anyone else to get clinically validated professional support to help you live your healthiest, happiest life.

Imposter Syndrome

In 1978, Georgia State University psychologists Drs. Pauline R. Clance and Suzanne A. Imes researched 150 "highly successful" women who despite their achievements deeply questioned their own abilities. In the paper they published entitled "The Imposter Phenomenon in High Achieving Women: Dynamics and Therapeutic Intervention," and later, the term *imposter syndrome* was popularized.[10,11] The authors of the paper wrote that "[d]espite their actual achievements, some successful people believe their abilities have been overestimated and that they will eventually be unmasked as impostors."[12]

I've met people who struggle with this. As they rise, they somehow don't believe their accomplishments and believe they'll be uncovered.

[9] https://www.penguinrandomhouse.com/books/617251/its-about-damn-time-by-arlan-hamilton-with-rachel-l-nelson, p. 163
[10] https://asm.org/Articles/2020/August/Imposter-Syndrome-The-Truth-About-Feeling-Like-a-F
[11] https://impostorsyndrome.com/uncategorized/impostor-phenomenon-or-impostor-syndrome
[12] https://psycnet.apa.org/record/1985-31379-001

My take on this is that the air we breathe in our society predicates itself on patriarchy and white supremacy. There is constant pressure being put on folks who are not white and male. I believe that imposter syndrome has a lot to do with internalized white patriarchy. Just as I mentioned earlier that people doubt my technical credibility because I'm feminine, this is not something I can change. Imposter syndrome may simply be related to feeling "othered" because of white patriarchy and supremacy. Can anyone feel imposter syndrome? For sure! But I believe this sinister mind game isn't by accident. Who would benefit from you never believing you're good enough, despite your list of accolades getting longer and longer? Wealthy white men who pay you less than the value of your work. We'll talk more about pay equity in Part 2 of this book. If you experience imposter syndrome, know you're far from alone. You might be surprised to see that a list of famous people who have publicly talked about imposter syndrome includes Tina Fey, Maya Angelou, Emma Watson, Joshua Jackson, Bella Hadid, Lupita Nyong'o, Ellie Goulding, Wolfgang Puck, Tom Hanks, David Bowie, Lady Gaga, and Sonia Sotomayor.[13] To my knowledge, all of these folks absolutely deserve their accolades.

The *imposter syndrome* term was coined in 1978. Framing this in a cultural context, "Women were joining the workforce and entering spaces that were historically only reserved for men. And they were joining a space full of men who were raised to believe those spaces were exclusively for them."[14] The hostility I have felt in workplaces as a woman feels just as sexist as 46 years ago. There are male colleagues and bosses of mine who were just as sexist as folks in the 1970s. They were just hiding it better. As women, we're just supposed to figure it out. Put your head down and do the work. Just get used to being one of the only women in tech. It is the air we breathe.

To illustrate the point of the tech environments, let's see some photos of AI events hosted in Seattle in the last few months (Figure 1.1).

When you walk into these rooms and there are almost no people who are female-presenting, it can be "othering." If the bulk of the people in the room appear to be men and mostly presenting as white or East and South Asian men, I don't always feel physically and

---

[13] https://www.entrepreneur.com/leadership/12-leaders-entrepreneurs-and-celebrities-who-have/304273
[14] https://bookishbrews.com/overcoming-imposter-syndrome

psychologically safe. In one job interview I had a few years ago, in the warehouse lab where I interviewed, I saw only one other woman in the entire building. But this doesn't mean I'm not worthy of being in those rooms. I was offered that job and am frequently asked to speak at tech events near and far.

FIGURE 1.1   Rooms full of male-presenting people at AI events in Seattle in 2023 and 2024[15-17]

I'm not the only one who recognizes that these spaces were not built and curated for me as a white woman. Hamilton writes, "If you're trying to break into an industry from which you've been excluded, it's important to remember that the prescribed ways of doing things won't always work for you. As a queer Black woman trying to hack my way into Silicon Valley, knowing that it was built around the lives and

---

[15] https://seattle.aitinkerers.org/p/ai-tinkerers-seattle-april-2024-meetup

[16] https://seattle.aitinkerers.org/p/ai-tinkerers-seattle-august-meetup

[17] https://www.canva.com/design/DAGB2C1U9Kw/dsG57jAUlObL1MTo2AaeEw/edit?utm_content=DAGB2C1U9Kw&utm_campaign=designshare&utm_medium=link2&utm_source=sharebutton

experiences of straight white men, I had to be innovative, and I had to trust myself."[18]

You must trust yourself. There are ample opportunities to learn, grow, connect, and network in these rooms. Let's acknowledge that these industries and spaces weren't made for us by design. Now that we have acknowledged the thought work and inner work we might need to do, in the next chapter, let's talk about those big goals and dreams that can help us live lives full of purpose and meaning.

Questions for Reflection

Questions for You

- ☐ Are you scared of being in an AI layoff? Have you already been laid off? Has someone close to you lost their job? How are they experiencing it?
- ☐ Have you experienced imposter syndrome? How does that feel to you? Who do you talk to about your fears?
- ☐ Do you go to therapy? Are imposter syndrome and extreme anxiety some of the explanations you give for why you don't take strides in your career?
- ☐ Do you have an internal saboteur? Do you do negative self-talk? Have you tried doing thought work, starting affirmations, or creating a list of your proven track record for you to review?
- ☐ Do you feel comfortable in networking environments? Are there people there who look like you? Do you feel safe physically and psychologically?
- ☐ What tactics do you use to help yourself navigate those rooms to go after opportunities?

---

[18] **https://www.penguinrandomhouse.com/books/617251/its-about-damn-time-by-arlan-hamilton-with-rachel-l-nelson**, p. 150

Want to get your personalized AI roadmap ideas? Take the Your AI Roadmap Personality Quiz:

YourAIRoadmap.com/Me

Want to follow along with all the checklists in the book? Download the checklists, frameworks, and resources from the book:

YourAIRoadmap.com/Resources

Scan the QR code to go directly there:

CHAPTER 2

Goals, Dreams, and Purpose: Craft Your Goals with the WOOP Method

*W*hy do you wake up in the morning? No, seriously. What does a meaningful life look like to you? Where are you? How do you pay your bills? No one can decide what your goals are for your life, apart from you. In this chapter, we're going to talk about a meaningful life by setting goals and taking the next steps to get there. No big deal, right? Just your life.

You have agency in this life, and you don't need to take my word for it. In a research study of 2,872 pairs of twins,[1] researchers found that longevity of life is "only moderately heritable." In plain language, the study "established that only about 20% of how long the average person lives is dictated by our genes, whereas the other 80% is dictated by our lifestyle," writes Buettner of the acclaimed Blue Zones research, books, and documentary.[2]

---

[1] https://link.springer.com/content/pdf/10.1007/BF02185763.pdf
[2] https://www.ncbi.nlm.nih.gov/pmc/articles/PMC6125071

Blue Zones: 9 Lifestyle Habits for Living Long

In the Blue Zones research, nine lifestyle habits were documented from the places in the world with the largest populations of people who live the longest. The "Blue Zones Power 9"[3] include:

1. Move Naturally
2. Purpose
3. Downshift
4. 80% Rule
5. Plant Slant
6. Wine @ 5
7. Belong
8. Loved Ones First
9. Right Tribe[4]

Several of these are about exercise and what you eat and drink.[5] Since we're here to talk about your career and not your wine and plant consumption, let's focus on Purpose. Purpose is all about how we spend our lives. Large populations of people over the age of 100 were found in Okinawa, Japan, and on the Nicoya Peninsula in Costa Rica. The factor of Purpose is described in Blue Zones as, "[t]he Okinawans call it 'Ikigai' and the Nicoyans call it 'plan de vida'; for both it translates to 'why I wake up in the morning.'" According to this research, "Knowing your sense of purpose is worth up to seven years of extra life expectancy."[6] Holy moley! Almost a decade more of life!

---

[3] **https://www.bluezones.com/2016/11/power-9**

[4] The term *tribe* is used by the Blue Zones researchers but is not one I would use. The term *tribe* has been used by white people to delegitimize nations of indigenous people. See **https://www.wellandgood.com/spirit-animal-native-american**. I use it here only to accurately represent the Blue Zones research.

[5] Learn more about Blue Zones via the mini-series on Netflix with the same name. I find it charming and visually attractive.

[6] **https://www.ncbi.nlm.nih.gov/pmc/articles/PMC6125071**

Ikigai: Sense of Purpose

My favorite visual representation of Ikigai is an interlocking diagram you may have seen on social media (see Figure 2.1).

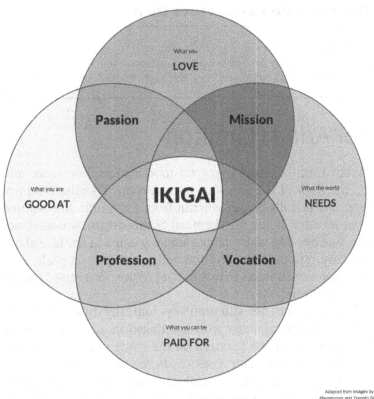

Adapted from Images by
@emmyzen and Toronto Star

FIGURE 2.1   Ikigai overlapping Venn diagram with four concentric circles[7]

The gravitas of this research feels quite intense to me. You probably didn't think we were going to talk about death and the meaning of life in this book, but here we are! What we see from this research of hundreds of centenarians from around the world is that having a purpose is key to living a long life. I see this research paired with the research about twins and 80% of your life being about lifestyle choices.

---

[7] **https://uxmastery.com/your-design-ikigai**

To live long and to live well, I take these studies to mean that you have so much agency about how you want to live your life. I envision a sign that says, "Your life, your choice!" You can design the life you want! Is that freeing or terrifying? For me, it's definitely a bit of both.

Joan's Hot Take: Your Life Is Your Own

Free yourself. Release your mind. Your life is your own.

Again, I sense you may be in disbelief reading this section if you're in a rut in your life right now. Let's consider a story that might knock your socks off.

Investor Arlan Hamilton

In 2015, Arlan Hamilton was living on food stamps, homeless, and sleeping on the floor of the San Francisco Airport. Hamilton did not go to college. She is a Black, gay woman from the South. She wanted to become an investor. If you are skeptical of this dream, you were not the only one. She has had many people actually laugh in her face about her goals and aspirations. But Hamilton had a plan. She set goals, educated herself, got herself into venture capital rooms, and raised capital for her investment fund.

Just a few years ago, her situation was radically different. Today, Hamilton is a venture capitalist who has raised more than $30M, is a multimillionaire, has been featured on the cover of *Fast Magazine*, has an ABC TV mini-series *Our America: In the Black Conversations*,[8] and has invested $20 million across 200 startups.[9,10] One of her biggest investors is famous *Shark Tank* investor Mark Cuban.[11] Named one of the best books of the year by *Fortune*, her book *It's About Damn Time: How to Turn Being Underestimated into Your Greatest Advantage* discusses how she had no background in finance but also saw a huge gap in the investment community. Investors kept investing in the same

---

[8] https://abc7ny.com/post/multimillionaire-rachel-rodgers-talks-financial-freedom-our-america-in-the-black-conversations/14940478
[9] https://www.yourfirstmillion.live/about-arlan
[10] https://time.com/6155039/arlan-hamilton-crowdfunded-vc-firm
[11] https://dallasinnovates.com/mark-cuban-talks-about-pickleball-pharmaceuticals-and-his-addiction-to-helping-entrepreneurs

demographic. They were missing huge, lucrative investment opportunities founded by other people.[12]

I'm grateful to have taken an investment course with Hamilton in 2021 called "Investing as a Catalyst," where a cohort of people from all around the world paid to take a video-based course with PDFs and Zoom sessions to discuss investing, startups, branding, funding, and more.

How did Hamilton do it? In a *Time* interview in 2022,[13] Hamilton said,

> *I kicked my way in. I didn't know what a venture capitalist was in 2010. I learned about startups around that time while I was on the road with musicians as an assistant and a production coordinator and fell in love with the startup ecosystem because I always felt like an entrepreneur. I just didn't know exactly what to call it or who my people were. And so I had this grand plan that I was going to go to Silicon Valley, start a tech company. I started doing research in order to do that. I didn't have much money, and I didn't have any connections in that world, but I knew it was for me. [. . .]*
>
> *During my research, I found out that 90%-plus of all venture funding and angel funding goes to white men in a country where they make up one-third of the population. That caught me off guard as a gay Black woman in the South with no connections. I thought, 'That doesn't seem like that's going to end well, if that stays the same.*
>
> *So instead of going out and teaching myself how to raise money for a company, I taught myself how to raise money for a fund by diving into any book I could get my hands on and any interview I could get my hands on. I started making phone calls, sending emails in the dozens at a time, and little by little started making breadcrumbs and finding my way. And then, you know, overnight five years later, I got a check for $25,000 that would kick off my investing career."*

While you may or may not aspire to become a venture capitalist in the tech ecosystem, Hamilton's advice mirrors the Five Career Tips you'll find next.

---

[12] **https://www.yourfirstmillion.live/book-tour**
[13] **https://time.com/6155039/arlan-hamilton-crowdfunded-vc-firm**

5 Career Tips

Here are my five career tips:

1. **Goals:** Create big goals (Chapter 2 we're currently in).
2. **People:** Find the people who can help you make it happen, whether that takes emails, phone calls, meetings, etc. See more in Chapter 4.
3. **Personal Brand:** Create a personal brand and flywheel for continued successes. See Chapter 5.
4. **Resilience:** Be resilient and don't give up easily. Check out Chapter 6.
5. **Finances:** Know the difference between a paycheck and income. Grow your wealth. Be in control of your finances. See Chapter 3, and we'll go in depth into this in Part 2 of this book.

Hamilton had big goals, and you might also. In the next section, we'll talk about how to structure goals so they actually come to life. For setting and achieving goals, many people have pointed me to the SMART method,[14] yet there is little research evidence that this method is actually tied to statistically significant outcomes.[15]

Specific: Know exactly what you want to accomplish.

Measurable: How will you know you met your goal?

Actionable: Make your goal challenging but attainable.

Realistic: Link it to important things to you that fit in your life.

Timely: What is the timeframe for this goal? When will it be met?

Being able to define, measure, and set a timeline for your goals are great, but there's a better formula than the SMART method.

WOOP Method: Clinically Validated Framework for Goal Setting

What I love about the WOOP method is that it explicitly addresses those pesky obstacles in your way. It's the kickoff of getting your goal

---

[14] **https://www.forbes.com/advisor/business/smart-goals**
[15] **https://www.ncbi.nlm.nih.gov/pmc/articles/PMC5785177**

from ideation to action. Then it charts out how you'll tackle those obstacles in the framework. Here's an overview of the WOOP method. WOOP stands for the following:

Wish: A goal or dream you have

Outcome: Vividly see the biggest and best version of your dream's outcome

Obstacle: Deciding how you are going to address the obstacles to this dream

Plan: Acting on your plan to go for your dream and tackle the inevitable obstacles

Sounds simple enough, right? The WOOP method is based on 20 years of scientific research pioneered by Dr. Gabriele Oettingeng.[16] Across the 37 years of 1985 and 2022, Dr. Oettingeng has authored 223 publications, listed on her website, on topics related to goal setting and motivation.[17] This is a startlingly prolific list of publications. Go, Dr. Oettingeng, go! Simply scrolling down the list induces exhaustion in me. She's been doing this research since before I was born. While the acronym "WOOP" might sound a tad comical, it is usually examined under the scientific terminology "Mental Contrasting with Implementation Intentions, abbreviated MCII."[18] Gracious! Now you understand why WOOP is a more attractive title for this research.

Still don't believe me about the WOOP method? Check out this list of a subset of 13 studies:[19]

Health: WOOP helped people to be healthier:

Exercise and diet: People doubled their physical activity and had a healthier diet (Stadler et al., 2010).

Exercise: Pain patients became more physically active in their everyday lives (Christiansen et al., 2010).

Well-being: People with type 2 diabetes took better care of their well-being (Adriaanse et al., 2013).

---

[16] **https://woopmylife.org/en/home**
[17] **https://woopmylife.org/en/publications**
[18] **https://woopmylife.org/en/home**
[19] **https://woopmylife.org/en/science**

Depression: Depressed patients became more active and found it easier to pursue their goals (Fritzsche et al., 2016).

Stroke patients: Stroke patients engaged in more physical activity and lost more weight (Marquardt et al., 2017).

Social behaviors: WOOP helps people to improve their social behavior:

Overcoming prejudice: People with prejudices became more tolerant and socially responsible (Oettingeng et al., 2005).

Couples: Couples strengthened their bond and decreased anxiety-related behaviors (Houssais et al., 2013).

Negotiation: Negotiators found more integrative and fairer solutions (Kirk et al., 2013).

Overcome negativity: People who struggled overcame disappointment, regret, resentment, and other negative feelings (Krott et al., 2018).

Academic Performance: WOOP helps people to improve their academic performance:

Academic performance: Students exerted more effort in test preparation and improved their time management (Duckworth et al., 2009).

Improve grades: Students from underprivileged backgrounds went to class more regularly and improved their grades. (Duckworth et al., 2013).

Homework: Children at risk for ADHD found it easier to do their homework (Gawrilow et al., 2013).

Studying in medical school: Future anesthesiologists were better able to study (Saddawi-Konefka et al., 2017).

Did I mention this WOOP method works? Incredible, thank you, Dr. Oettingeng.

Let's check out an example. From Hamilton's example discussed earlier, let's see what the WOOP method may have looked like based on Hamilton's books and interviews:[20]

Wish: I want to become an investor.

Outcome: Raise millions of dollars and invest in startups.

[20] https://time.com/6155039/arlan-hamilton-crowdfunded-vc-firm

Obstacle: Money, connections (in interviews Hamilton said, "I didn't have much money, and I didn't have any connections") and white patriarchy ("90%-plus of all venture funding and angel funding goes to white men").

Plan: Raise money and build a network regardless of white patriarchy—"I taught myself how to raise money for a fund by diving into any book I could get my hands on and any interview I could get my hands on. I started making phone calls, sending emails in the dozens at a time, and little by little started making breadcrumbs and finding my way."

Hamilton's goals were big, and it took her years, but she now has made her dreams come to fruition.

Let me share my journey to get my first dog:

Wish: I want a dog! I've wanted a dog since I was 8 years old.

Outcome: Have a dog that I can spend time with, love up, and work out with.

Obstacle: My parents don't want a dog. I have to be old enough to have my own place and time enough to spend with the dog. In Seattle, I need to rent a place that allows dogs or buy a home with a yard. I also need to have finances for any unexpected five-figure vet bills that might arise.

Plan: Build my finances to be robust enough to support unexpected vet bills and make sure a dog is logistically an option for where I live.

Tricolor Corgi Luna (Figure 2.2) joined my life in the last few years as you might well know from her photos on my social media feeds. Having her join my life has been even better than what eight-year-old Joan could have imagined!

Pretty fabulously happy having accomplished my goal! Here's another one: "I want to get a job in tech." During my PhD program at the UArizona, my WOOP method might have looked like this:

Wish: I want to complete my PhD and get a job in tech.

Outcome: Have a job in tech, earn a PhD, live wherever I want, and be well-paid.

Obstacle: Paperwork and degree requirements, professors who block you from completing your degree, connections to people in

FIGURE 2.2 Joan holding Corgi puppy Luna

tech, resilience to keep working hard across the years, a CV that is accepted by tech companies so I can have the freedom to get a tech job that pays well in the city of my choice.

Plan: Foster a relationship with an advisor who can help along the way, know the paperwork and degree requirements like the back of my hand, create a plan to tackle each and every degree requirement with a proposed timeline for each milestone (course completion, exams, manuscript deadlines, etc.), keep eating vegetables and working out, iterate a CV and get feedback from people about it, go to tech events, and follow up with people you meet to build a tech network.

You know from my story that I successfully completed this outcome. It also took me several years. As related to the tech job, my north star of a goal is one you might have also. Knowing the obstacles and having a plan to navigate through them is crucial. I believe the "Obstacle" part of the WOOP is the most potent part. If we can acknowledge the hurdles and fears, we're more likely able to conquer them.

Let's consider the WOOP method for other goals and dreams. While I'm not with you right now because you are reading or listening to this book, there are two big goals you may be looking to work on. Let's talk about them.

Job in AI: I frequently get asked "How do I get a job in AI?" Here's a WOOP version to achieve that goal.

> **Wish:** You may wish to get a job in AI. This means by definition that you do not yet work in AI.
>
> **Outcome:** Have a title and project that are in AI and get paid to do it.
>
> **Obstacle:** You might have imposter syndrome. People in the rooms might not look like me. These AI jobs might be hard to get. You may need a new network of people. You might need projects and a portfolio to demonstrate your skills. You may need new skills you do not yet have. You may need to learn how to tell your story to connect the dots for professional opportunities.
>
> **Plan:** Build a personal brand, cultivate a strong network, document the skills you need for a specific role, educate yourself and get the skills for that role, create projects that demonstrate these skill sets, share them widely on social media and with your network, leverage the second-degree connections in your network to get the job.

This book can help you with this goal! Another topic I hear about often is about stability and resilience.

Future-Proof Income: Many people are worried about their job stability. Here's a WOOP version of this:

> **Wish:** Future-proof my income. I am concerned I might lose my job or already have lost my job.
>
> **Outcome:** Have stable income.
>
> **Obstacle:** With widespread layoffs and economic instability, a traditional 9-to-5 job on a W-2 contract may not be a stable way to have income in the 2020s and beyond.
>
> **Plan:** I will build several income streams to diversify my wealth. A W-2 contract can be an aspect of building wealth, but not the only

means of building wealth. I can build up these income streams to be robust enough to fulfill my goals and may not require me to have a day job.

We're going to dive into income streams and your finances in Part 2 of this book. Perhaps you have other goals! Let's begin mapping out WOOP versions of your goals:

Wish: I wish: _____

_____

Outcome: The outcome would look like: _____

_____

Obstacle: Obstacles in my way are: _____

_____

Plan: If the obstacles _____ happen, **then** I will _____.

The WOOP method is incredibly powerful. When I've done this exercise with people, they say that many emotions bubble up during the "Obstacle" part and that it's helpful to really define the problem and talk through solutions.

If you'd like to learn more about the WOOP method, check out Dr. Oettingeng's website "WOOP my life." Great title, right? There is an app, PDFs, groups, and many more resources.[21] While I have just provided you with examples about investors and tech jobs, I will remind you that there are many types of goals in this world. When I talk to people at tech conferences and happy hours, their goals are typically far more practical. They aren't thinking about their higher purpose in life. Ikigai is not something they've heard of. They're figuring out their job and career next steps. They might be singularly focused on how they're going to pay rent and groceries for the next few months. This is practical and reasonable, especially in a country with great opportunity but no real safety net. We'll talk about jobs, careers, paychecks, and income in the next chapter.

---

[21] **https://woopmylife.org/en/home**

Questions for Reflection

Questions for You

- ☐ What does a fulfilling life look like for you?
- ☐ How much agency do you feel like you have? What do you want to do that you're not doing yet?
- ☐ What things are you grateful for that get you out of bed in the morning?
- ☐ What emotions are brought up when you think of Hamilton's story? Do you know people who have gone on a similar journey? What can you learn from her story?
- ☐ Have you heard of the WOOP method before? What about it resonates or doesn't fit for you?

CHAPTER 3

On Lily Pads and Rainbows: Job vs. Career, Paychecks vs. Income

I once had a friend who worked from 9 to 5. He clocked in at 9 a.m. He got offline at 5 p.m. He didn't talk about his work outside of work. The job didn't bring him joy. He got paid. The job was *just* a job. I found this exceptionally odd. "He really didn't care at all?!" I found myself thinking. I met him when I was in graduate school working voraciously toward my goals. I was maximizing everything I could in order to prioritize my career's success and was exceptionally passionate about my work. It wasn't about our age; it was about our mindsets. I was eager to have a career that I was passionate about. He had a day job and cared about his paycheck. In this chapter, we'll talk about jobs versus careers and paychecks versus income.

Some people use the term *job* and *career* interchangeably. Though related, they are not the same thing. A job is a specific project you do for money.[1] A career is "a field for or pursuit of consecutive progressive achievement."[2] I think of careers as the journey crossing of a pond with a rainbow overhead and a job as one of the lily pads used to hop on as

---

[1] https://www.merriam-webster.com/dictionary/job
[2] https://www.merriam-webster.com/dictionary/career

you continue your crossing.[3] Jobs are helpful, for sure. But don't stagnate chilling on just one lily pad—unless it's a really great lily pad. The rainbow is the career: the overall path you want to take that matches your goals, values, and mission. In this metaphor, getting laid off or fired is being booted off the lily pad so you're in the water treading and floating until you get on your next lily pad. . .or create your own.

When is it time to take the leap to the next lily pad of a job? Well, if you get a job offer, then that's a moment to reflect. My formula is to see if what you're giving is more or less than you're getting. Either the job pays you in a strong paycheck, pays you in what you're learning, or both. If you are neither being paid well nor learning in your job, make a plan and leave.

Joan's Hot Take: Rule About Jobs and Paychecks

> For a job, make sure you are earning, learning, or both. If you aren't learning or earning, it's time to find a different path ASAP!

If it is sucking your soul, turning into a toxic environment, affecting your mental and physical health, etc., it's also time to make a plan for your next lily pad. It often takes energy to decide the trajectory and launch yourself from one lily pad to the next. Sometimes, even if you're a top performer, you will get laid off anyway. Sometimes layoffs are personal, and sometimes it's just 30% of the company that gets laid off.

Remember that the entrepreneurial route is an option also. You can create your own pond with your own lily pads! A whole new exploration. Entrepreneurship isn't always comfortable for everyone to try, but it can be a helpful option for upcoming turbulence in the job market due to AI layoffs. I hope to support you in this if it's something you'd like to explore. In the second half of this book, we talk concretely about how to know, grow, and be in control of your finances. I also have simple frameworks to build your first offer and scale to $1 million in revenue. I'm here to help if this is something you'd like to explore. Why do we work a job anyway? For some of my friends and family, it

---

[3] Unless you're doing a really corporate path, ladders are archaic. I've heard about the metaphor of jungle gyms (**https://www.forbes.com/sites/deborahljacobs/2013/03/14/why-a-career-jungle-gym-is-better-than-a-career-ladder/?sh=7ffb0ab71248**) but didn't really like those as a kid myself.

is about helping others and pursuing what we love. Typically, though, it's about money, that thing called a paycheck. To be resilient in the time of AI, you're going to need to future-proof your income and think beyond the paycheck.

Paychecks and income aren't the same thing. A paycheck[4] is a wage or salary from a job. Income[5] is money and wealth that comes across time usually derived from money and labor. Some people live off the money their money is making through investments and do not have day jobs. They have an income and don't bring in a paycheck from a day job.

Why I Focus on Careers and Income

I focus on the topics of careers and income because they are expansive. Careers can take many twists and turns. There might be low points; there might be high points! You are on a career adventure. I love stories. Who doesn't love a good story? Similarly, income is talking about all the different revenue streams. Income can be money from the robust financial portfolio you've made. A paycheck is a single payment from a job. It's good, but it doesn't yet speak to the fabulous things you can do with your wealth and income overall. If you're craving to talk more about money and incomes, good news! That's the topic of Part 2. When it comes to planning out your next few hops, it's good to look both at the next lily pad and the greater arc of where your rainbow is headed.

Questions for Reflection

Questions for You

☐ What jobs have you had in the past? How do you talk about them? Were they part of a career path?

☐ How do you frame the topic of money? Do you have a reliable paycheck?

---

[4] **https://www.merriam-webster.com/dictionary/paycheck**
[5] **https://www.merriam-webster.com/dictionary/income**

☐ When you think about your overall career trajectory, where do you want to go?

☐ How have people been helpful to you along your job and career journey thus far?

CHAPTER 4

People, People, People: Weak Ties Will Help Me Rise, 80% of Effort on Your Network

"I want to hire you," said the CEO on the Zoom call in August 2019. My jaw dropped to the floor. I had thought this was just an intro call! "Wow, I'll need to think about it. Gosh, I would have worn something more formal if I thought this was the conversation we'd be having!" The CEO laughed.

This was a follow-up call from a follow-up call. After I'd met a friendly human at the VentureBeat conference, he introduced me to his colleague who he thought would be a wonderful person for me to meet. That person referred me to this CEO and this fortuitous Zoom call. I was looking for a job, and she was hiring. A few weeks later, she and her coworker met me for coffee downtown. "Your offer is one of my top three choices," I said, playing hardball and not committing to their job offer. This apparently inspired laughter later from the CEO who was used to having people grovel for jobs. A few weeks later, we confirmed the job offer details via email. When it came down to my two favorite options, I negotiated with both to get the best contract terms by leveraging the fact that I had competitive offers. I was excited by both and ended up taking the one the CEO verbally gave me on the spot. I increased my base salary from my first tech job to my second tech job by 90% in four months.

In this chapter, we'll talk about people, networking, and my best tips to move from common reasons or excuses for not networking into tactics to network effectively and cultivate a robust network for your short- and long-term goals. "Relationships, relationships, relationships" was the piece of advice my mentor Gary gave me years ago about career success. He gave me a book that had chapters detailing the importance of goal setting and people who support you. Honestly, I thought he was being sentimental. It took me only two years to realize the brilliance of this advice. Wow, he was right!

My DMs have been inundated with requests for coaching and support. My team at Clarity AI has put together a Your AI Bootcamp. We work on goal setting, a personal branding glow-up, storytelling, and networking. You can learn more at **https://YourAIRoadmap .com/Bootcamp**. This book version is the detailed explanation of how you can do it cheaply and at your own pace. Let's dive in!

My 80% Networking Rule for Career Building

When it comes to preparing the next few lily pad choices and the launch to the next job, spend 80% of your effort on your network.

People-First Career Building: The 80% People, 15% Projects, and 5% Skills Recipe

When people ask me about building a career and how to spend their time, I have a pretty clear recipe for job and career building called the "80% People, 15% Projects, and 5% Skills Recipe."

- **80% People:** Spend 80% of your time working on the people and networking category.
- **15% Projects:** Dedicate 15% on projects and honing a portfolio of how to show people rather than tell them about your accomplishments, ambition, and work to date.
- **5% Skills:** Allocate 5% of time on skills, but ONLY if people give you feedback about improving them.

My rule is that if you're actively looking for your next job, spend 80% of your time working on the people and networking category. Why are those numbers so aggressively skewed to "People"? Because it's the thing that's truly going to move the needle for you. My guess is that you've heard this advice but are still not doing it. While it's all over social media, it is not often taught at school. How many years did I go to public and private schools? This definitely was not covered! In the next few chapters, we'll go through all the actions I recommend that go into that "80% People" bucket of time: going to events online and in person, hosting coffee chats, honing your personal brand, curating your LinkedIn profile and email signature, owning your story, and having STAR method stories ready to tell folks. The STAR method is a framework for how to tell your story effectively. We'll go over this in detail later.

By spending time on the "People" and networking aspect of your career, you'll create a robust network. You'll get feedback on your work from the people who you could collaborate with and ultimately build a career alongside. We'll spend the rest of this chapter on the steps to do that more effectively. Spend 15% on projects and honing a portfolio that can show people rather than tell them about your accomplishments, ambition, and work to date. Spend 5% learning skills you don't yet have, if you get feedback from people and networking about those skills. For the folks in the back: stop spending all your time on "skills" and spend your time making real connections with real humans.

Sadly, I often find people fastidiously taking assorted certificates and add "skills" to their LinkedIn profile, but they do little else. They hide in sadness wondering why someone else got that cool job they applied to four months ago. They watch their LinkedIn feed full of other people's job announcements. Please don't doomscroll passively watching the work of others. Take action!

Invest in your LinkedIn profile to create content about your own work and stories, go to events, and follow up via email and LinkedIn. Give out your phone number only to people who you want to become your close friends. Turn off your notifications at night. Email and LinkedIn can stay professional. Depending on their own time zones, people can send you messages at 2 a.m. there while you sleep blissfully. Respond to them when it works for you, or not at all! Build relationships professionally for the short and long term. In this chapter, we'll look at empirical research, my journey, and your next steps to level up in this department. This chapter is arguably the most important chapter in the whole book because of how it can impact your life and move your career forward. Please grab that bubbly water or coffee and pay attention!

Strength of Weak Ties and LinkedIn Research

I've found "people" to be a key factor in my career successes. I'm far from alone. Let's look at the research. In 1973, Dr. Mark S. Granovetter published the famous paper "The Strength of Weak Ties."[1] You may have heard of it— it has more than 15,000 citations. The paper was a piece of influential social theory about societal structures. Dr. Granovetter talks about "strong ties," such as your best friend or coworker, who talk to you every day and are people you have strong relationships with. These could also be first-degree connections. They are close friends in your network.

By contrast, "weak ties" are relationships with people you don't know well. We can consider these as second-, third-, and fourth-degree connections. For example, you have a friend named Morgan. Morgan is your close friend you see all the time and is an example of a "strong tie." Morgan has a friend named Sehyun who runs a successful design studio. Sehyun is a "weak tie" for you. If you're interested in learning more about design studios and prototyping about career steps in the design field, you could ask Morgan whether they would be open to asking Sehyun if she'd be open to a coffee chat. Double opt-in intros are key! We'll talk more about coffee chats, intros, prototyping, and what to talk about in the next few chapters.

---

[1] https://www.jstor.org/stable/pdf/2776392.pdf?casa_token=4z7EOjge_IIAAAAA:B-LLAYesAEGWLN_izUcy28j8Vd28TkNrBlQevHGUmPRfOUtzmQzllmNl8QjVl3Vm54hLxpe3UR1ICpjBEYFl6SbsQtQpMIfPmhRiCkhm_WJw5SPOcyg

In the 1970s, Dr. Granovetter's concept of "weak ties" and "strong ties" was a hypothesis. It was hypothesized that "weak ties" are more likely to lead to new job opportunities and job mobility compared to strong ties, as they have less overlap in their social networks. Almost 50 years later, researchers decided to put the theory to the test! They leveraged LinkedIn data to test these hypotheses with real people and jobs (see Figure 4.1).

The Strength of Weak Ties

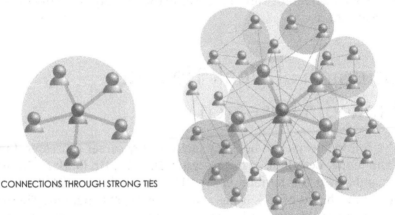

CONNECTIONS THROUGH STRONG TIES

CONNECTIONS THROUGH WEAK TIES

© 2012 CHESS MEDIA GROUP

FIGURE 4.1   Strength of weak ties[2]

Analyzing two billion new ties across 20 million people across five years, researchers saw 600,000 jobs were created.[3] This is an impressively large dataset. The data was pulled in chunks during 2015 and 2019. Was the hypothesis from the 1970s right? Yes! Indeed, even more than expected! The researchers found that the data reinforced the idea that your second-degree connections and your ability to leverage your network's network is exceptionally powerful. The paper says that the term *weak ties'* is actually paradoxical, since these can be some of the most *powerful* ways to land that next job and take huge leaps in your career. After the height of COVID layoffs in 2020, LinkedIn research said that 73% of people reported landing their next job based on intros

---

[2] **https://onepager.vc/blog/the-strength-of-weak-ties-and-how-companies-can-accelerate-their-hiring-process**
[3] **https://www.science.org/doi/abs/10.1126/science.abl4476**

and connections.[4] Networking and asking for help are what got them the next job!

Joan's Hot Take: People-First Networking Is Backed Up by 2 Billion Data Points

> People-first networking is not just advice. This is a data-driven and powerful strategy based on 20 million people and 2 billion connections. Modern careers require people! Don't believe me? Read this chapter again.

Weak ties are powerful! How about I make up playful slogans to help us remember this phenomenon from the data from 20 million people's career paths. How about something like, "Weak ties will help me rise!" or "The rando is the key that binds!" Decent? Solid C+? You can fire me as your slogan writer; I have many revenue streams, so I don't care! (In fact, I'll be sharing all my revenue streams with you in a few chapters, my dear reader.) I hope it's a memorable slogan though. Okay, that was a lot of jargon. Let's look at a real example.

Taylor's Dad

My friend Taylor got his next job using the paradoxical strength of weak ties. Taylor works in finance and worked at the same job for five years. He won awards and was a top performer on his team. During the pandemic, his company who he had previously loved working for started to pressure him to work longer and harder hours, without increased pay. Some of his coworkers were working more than 70 hours per week. They weren't taking care of their mental and physical health. People normalized that this is what everyone was expected to do. When it came time for annual reviews, the only feedback Taylor was given was "just take on more work." Oooof! Taylor was already the top performer on his team. With a huge mountain of work he plowed

---

[4] https://news.linkedin.com/2020/october/helping-job-seekers-take-their-next-step

through daily, he was already maxed out. He began looking for his next job. After exhaustion daily, he applied via uploading his résumé cold on company websites and was able to interview at a few places, but it didn't pan out.

Taylor was scared to share with *anyone* he was looking for a new job. He barely wanted to admit to himself that he needed a change. His partner supported him, but often his extended family was hard on him. But he was close to burnout and figured it was worth asking for support. When he mentioned it to his mom and dad, it paid off! A few weeks later, Taylor's dad was at an event and saw an old friend. The old friend knew that her company was hiring in the finance department. Taylor's dad passed along her contact information. Taylor followed up, interviewed, and landed the job. Talk about a weak tie that is so tenuous! What if Taylor never had the courage to tell his dad he needed a change? Sometimes it's safer to make career changes in stealth, but the power of your network can yield incredible results.

Taylor changed companies, is paid 25% more, is a valued team member with a full but balanced workload, feels more appreciated by his boss and coworkers, and loves playing sports with the company team. I know that Taylor really dislikes putting himself out there, but this new company is a breath of fresh air. Networking by talking to his people and asking for help was great. Following up and showing his skills sealed the deal. It's not just Taylor. This people factor is beginning to click, right? I hope so! But not everyone loves networking. Let's check out more data and examples.

My Biggest Professional Opportunities and the Person Who Helped Me Get Them

To continue to hammer home the point of how important people are to your career and in case you are the glum reader like some of my friends who hate networking, Table 4.1 addresses some of the grumpiness I anticipate you might be feeling. It shows how I got some of the biggest opportunities in my life, what the opportunity was, who helped me get it, and the contact method that connected me to the opportunity.

TABLE 4.1		**People and Contact Method: Examples of My Biggest Professional Opportunities 2006–2024**	
Year	**Opportunity**	**Person Who Helped Me[5]**	**Contact Method**
2006[6]	First official job with paperwork, art camp counselor	Close friend Kate	Friend told me about it; I emailed to follow up and asked for the job.
2013	French Ministry of Education	My mom	Mom emailed me a link; I applied.
2014	French tutor	Just me posting online	I posted on Craigslist; I followed up via email, text, and phone calls.
2015	Graduate Student Association gig	Acquaintance Maddie	I heard about the job at an event verbally and followed up via email.
2016	UArizona PhD Program acceptance and fellowship	Mentor professor Ralph; recommendations from professors Tania, Paulo, and Ralph	I sent several emails to UArizona faculty to learn if it was a good fit of program, got yeses, crafted an application, got recommendations, and got accepted.
2017	Assistant to the Director job	Acquaintance Lisa	In a meeting I mentioned looking for a campus job, Lisa emailed me about it, and I applied.
2018	Graduate student award	Professor Jason	I strategically took a class with Professor Jason. I asked him in person and had the materials prepared. I followed up via email and applied for the award with his support letter.

(Continued)

[5] Reminder, all of the names in this table are pseudonyms to protect people's privacy. They are all real people.
[6] While researching data in this table, I even found the email I sent in 2006 asking to get my first official job in Portland, Oregon, as an art camp counselor. I had this skill set of following up and asking for the job I wanted even as a high schooler. I was not coached to do this. I wanted the job, and the steps of how to get it had been laid out for me. I followed up and sent the email.

TABLE 4.1 *(Continued)*

Year	Opportunity	Person Who Helped Me	Contact Method
2018	First $100,000+/yr tech job	Acquaintance Daniel	I met him at a conference after-party. I followed up via LinkedIn, and he contacted me via email to the hiring manager. I interviewed and was hired.
2019	VentureBeat speaking opportunity	Total stranger Alissa	Alissa reached out via the Women in Voice website and sent an email. I followed up.
2019	Agency job	Acquaintances Tom and Ron	I met Tom at a conference. I followed up with Tom via email. Tom introduced me to Ronald. Ronald introduced me to a CEO. The CEO wanted to give me a job offer on the spot. I met the CEO and Ronald for coffee before finalizing the offer on paper.
2019	Published in *Harvard Business Review*	Total stranger Cindy	Cindy emailed me after seeing my Twitter or LinkedIn.
2020	Spoke at CES conference	Total stranger Luciana	Luciana sent me cold emails, a Twitter DM, and a LinkedIn message inviting me. She was persistent!
2020	Lucrative tech consulting	Acquaintance Gary	Gary messaged me on LinkedIn, he met up with me at CES, and we scheduled email and follow-up calls.
2022	Startup job $250,000+/yr	Acquaintances Charlie and Ian	I met them on LinkedIn. I had intro meetings and phone calls with them.
2023	Biggest customer deal	Me at an event	I met my customer at an investor event. I followed up via LinkedIn and email.
2024	Book deal	Book connector Nathan	We connected via LinkedIn, had a meeting, and emailed. After four years, I circled back. We met, and I submitted paperwork.

Notice how many times in this table it was about a person. Stanford professors Bill Burnett and Dave Evans[7] wrote the book *Designing Your Life*[8] about building a career and life you love. One of their book's chapters is humorously entitled "How Not to Get a Job," and it talks about cold applying for a job into the abyss of CVs. "Don't look for job listings online or on a company's website, don't make a decision from a description, don't submit a résumé, and don't wait for a call from a manager. This is what we call 'the standard model' and it seldom works."[9] I agree. Talking directly to the team on LinkedIn and meeting them on Zoom or for coffee is a better strategy.

Despite all this evidence, I always get pushback from folks about networking. I've just presented you with both anecdotal data as well as a robust study of LinkedIn data. But our lives aren't primarily driven by data. Also, if you already are convinced that networking is important, feel free to skim the following list and go to the section about effective ways to prepare and maximize your networking. The following are the common pieces of pushback I hear about networking and building a professional network.

Avoid Networking List: 11 Common Reasons and Excuses People Tell Me About Why They Hate Networking

1. Introvert: I'm an introvert. This isn't my strong suit!

My dear reader, it may be obvious to you, but I'm an extrovert. Networking comes more naturally to me than some of my friends.

---

[7] One of my biggest pieces of constructive feedback about this book is that it was clearly written for a young, white man, despite its authors saying the content is for a general audience. For example, there is an anecdote about a man downgrading his career and still having enough money to own a house in Berkeley, California. The average home price in Berkeley is $1.4 million (**https://www.zillow.com/home-values/16992/berkeley-ca**). This advice doesn't apply to me and more than half the population of America. Exactly to my point, the Designing Your Life brand has come out with "for Women" new content, directly addressing the women demographic it wasn't accounting for initially: **https://designingyour.life/dyl-for-women**.
[8] **https://designingyour.life**
[9] **https://ericsandroni.com/book-summary-designing-your-life-by-bill-burnett-dave-evans/#Chapter_7_How_Not_to_Get_a_Job**

Is this fair? Nope! However, the evidence still remains that you need to network also. These days, networking can be in-person, hybrid, and online. Figure out what is most effective and works best for you. Make sure to build in rest time and get support. I also have been the wing-woman to my best friend who sometimes asked me to support her at events she was obligated to attend in the past. Got a bubbly friend you could ask to join you? Or meet up with someone cool there.

Practice icebreaker statements about the weather, parts of the event you're excited about, a piece of news about the field to get people's opinion about, etc. Give yourself ample time to rest before and after events and conferences. For events in person, take breaks in the bathroom or other third spaces to recenter.

Networking is a skill set, like any other. Typically, you're not going to get better at a skill if you don't work on it.

2. Energy: Networking takes so much energy!

That's true, it takes energy! But so did your degree that took you years to complete, that sport you played for hours for years after school, or that video game you have been honing your skill in for years. Networking takes energy but is a worthwhile use of your energy. Doom-scrolling LinkedIn and sending your résumé into the black hole abyss of some job portal sounds more like a recipe for loneliness than for landing the next job.

3. Tongue-Tied: But what do I say? I'm not sure what to do!

Prepare before the event. Don't freak out the few hours before going to the happy hour. Decide your goals of *why* you're going in the first place. Prepare some small talk to break the ice. What are relatively safe topics that you might bring up that people going to the same event might also be interested in? Get some professional stories together and ready to share. We'll cover more of how to structure professional story-telling in the STAR method in Chapter 8.

Imagine if you happened to be in an elevator or with someone you deeply admire. What would you ask them? What might you want to know?

4. Waste of Time: Networking and events can be a waste of time. What if I don't meet anyone?

Research the event. Write down your goals for going. Do the opportunities match your goals? If not, don't go. You can't guarantee you will meet amazing people; there are no guarantees in this lifetime!

However, I can guarantee you that sitting at home in your fuzzy socks and watching HBO won't get you to your next fabulous job opportunity.

5. **Feeling Othered, Rooms Full of White People:** I feel othered in many professional spaces. There are few people who look like me.

As a white woman, I feel this keenly about being one of the only women in many rooms. For you, it might be an intersectional aspect such as your race, sexuality, disability status, and more. For example, there are very few Black professionals in tech. According to McKinsey research, "Black people make up 12% of the US workforce, but only 8% of employees in tech jobs."[10]

Another way to say it is, yes, many networking opportunities nationally might be full of white men. I encourage you to get support from friends and family. If it's not safe for you to go, prioritize online networking. Reminder of my silly slogan, "The rando is the key that binds!" The people outside your current network or are secondary connections can be the most powerful right now in getting you from where you are to where you want to be. Identify awesome local meetups that have women and people who look like you as a component of your networking process.

Consider also asking a wing person to join you! Could your friend come in tow? Who could you meet up with? Who do you trust, and who can you giggle with at or after the event? Make it happen!

6. **Sleazy:** Networking is so sleazy. I feel uncomfortable.

When I talk to people about networking, they often think I'm talking about ill-fitting suits and handing out business cards. I vehemently disagree! I often hear from people that they feel sleazy and salesy in these types of environments. The ideal networking is authentic.

If you are pitching a fake version of yourself, I would argue that you're doing it wrong. No one likes to meet fake people who are using each other to get ahead. There is a reason for the icky Chad stereotype of the bro who would talk your ear off about Bitcoin, NFTs, and golf. The type of person who would sell out his own grandma just for a few bucks is not the person I recommend you keep in your network.

---

[10] **https://www.mckinsey.com/bem/our-insights/how-to-close-the-black-tech-talent-gap**

Obvious, right? A better way to phrase this, as Arlan Hamilton famously says, "Be yourself so that the people looking for you can find you."[11] The most successful people I know are *themselves* in professional contexts and set boundaries.[12] They are clear about what is personal and what they are willing to share publicly and in professional settings.

At the same time, present yourself as well as possible. Embody the professional you want to be and where that person is headed. It's your Sasha Fierce moment![13] This is a multifaceted topic. We'll discuss more in the Personal Brand chapter.

7. **Boasting:** I was always taught not to boast! Is talking about my accomplishments wrong?

Fundamentally, telling your professional story is not boasting. It's sharing, connecting, and educating. If you are rude and talk over people while listing your accolades, then you need to change your course of action.

I struggle with this one because my parents, who I am very close to, don't agree with me. My parents and I have had several long, heated discussions on the topic. It's a strange truth of my world as an international influencer who gets flown to international conferences. My parents are not comfortable with how publicly I talk about my work and successes. For all the ways I have been pushed by my family to succeed, they are not always ready for me to talk about my work and successes.[14]

One of my mantras is "Get credit for the work you've already done. Play big. Tell your story and help others." By contrast, my mom and dad's versions might sound like "Work hard, work for years, be the best in your field, and don't talk about it." I get where they are coming from, but keeping quiet and hoping people notice your work is a *terrible* plan. You need to *own* your story and career.

Part of me wants to chalk this one up to age, but it's not that. I've met people old and young who are totally comfortable or *deeply* uncomfortable sharing their professional journeys. Race and gender definitely play a part. Back to that annoying white patriarchy rearing its head. For whom is it acceptable to talk confidently about careers?

---

[11] **https://dallasinnovates.com/arlan-hamilton-be-yourself-so-that-the-people-looking-for-you-can-find-you**

[12] I used to think one of my aunties who has incredible boundaries and clear expectations was selfish. Now, I realize that she's brilliant and happy.

[13] **https://www.oprah.com/own-oprahshow/beyonc-on-her-alter-ego-sasha-fierce**

[14] This is not a joke.

Who consistently gets told "Quiet, we don't want to hear your voice"? Typically, BIPOC folks and women. Overall, you can live your best life by crafting and owning your own story.

8. **Condescending:** What if people talk down to me?

People can be condescending. I can't guarantee people will be nice. If people are rude, they're not your people. Thank you, next!

9. **Bro-Culture:** How long do I have to listen to Chad mansplain about blockchain?

People hogging the microphone and sound space is poor manners and ultimately antisocial. Typically, I find this happens when people are *craving* external validation, they word vomit on others. If people are long-winded and boring even after social cues giving them feedback of disinterest, you can always exit the conversation. Sometimes people aren't great at social cues. You can say aloud that this topic doesn't interest you and ask to explore the edge technology and architectures instead, for example. You can interject and change the topic. Do not let yourself be steamrolled.

Is there anything redeemable you can salvage? Could you pivot the conversation to digital transactions in Thailand? What topics could you both find interesting to discuss? Tactics I use include excusing myself to use the bathroom, get water, or see a friend, say you're feeling sick (sick of them perhaps!); and physically moving myself away from the person or people who aren't great to be around. If the people are truly inappropriate and endangering you or others, document the behavior, report it, block them in person and digitally, and leave the situation.

10. **Talking and Pitching Yourself:** Why do I have to talk about myself? I feel uncomfortable.

Communicating effectively is a skill set that will take you far. If you truly are uncomfortable talking to other people, this is a skill set you might need to develop with professional support. This might take the shape of professional coaches and therapists.

If you also don't feel comfortable owning your story, this may be something you would find helpful to discuss with a certified therapist. I adore my therapist! I have worked through and navigated some of the hardest parts of my life with her support and guidance about how to navigate hostile work environments, mean-spirited people, and defining what a meaningful life means to me. Storytelling is crucial to your life internally and for your professional career.

11. **Underdog:** What if I'm not as accomplished as other folks at the event? Am I good enough?

Everyone starts somewhere. I started in the tech environment by being a PhD candidate who didn't know the jargon and didn't know how to play the game. To meet people and find opportunities, half the battle is showing up. Wherever I do yoga, they say a similar phrase, "Give yourself credit for just showing up at the mat today."

With time it will get easier—like a muscle you flex after getting better at weightlifting!

In the next section, we'll move beyond this list of fears and reasons people hate networking to my strategies to effectively prepare for networking opportunities.

Okay, so we've established that networking opportunities can be powerful and addressed some of the reasons you've already told me you might dislike these environments.

Let's talk about strategies on how to build your skill set and network effectively. I've honed this list over the years. This isn't rocket science. It's about physical and mental preparation.

Effective Networking List: 10 Ways to Prepare for Effective Networking Questions for You

We've established that networking is super powerful and some common reasons people hate it. How can you be prepared for networking? How can you hit your goals and make the whole process easier? Here are some of my common tips for effective networking. Feel free to use whichever ones float your boat.

Set Your Goals: What Is Your "Why"?

Define what your goal is for the event. Do you want to reinforce a relationship? Are you really interested in robotics and want to see some tech demos to learn more about it? Be clear and consider writing down three to five solid reasons to remind yourself.

Here are some examples: Go to the booth for X company and meet people who work there. Support my friend at her speaking thing and take pictures. Work to make genuine connections with three people. Find swag for my roommate that isn't a hideous, branded T-shirt.

Do Your Research: Identify Key People and Companies

Instead of just showing up willy-nilly, do your homework. Who would you love to meet? Where will the best food be? What companies might be in attendance, and where could you find their booth?

You don't need to be creepy, but it would be helpful if you have those goals in mind so you can make sure you meet that person and hit those goals.

Choose Your Outfit

In many professional spaces, there is often a dress code. RuPaul says, "We're all born naked and the rest is drag."[15] We are all in these body suits, and we get to decide what to put on them. You could wear whatever you want like a purple hoodie like Arlan Hamilton, bejeweled dresses like multi-millionaire Liz Elting, or blue moto jackets like me.[16,17]

Consider wearing a shirt or outfit that can be a helpful professional conversation starter! Is there an organization that you participate in that has a logo you can add to your blazer?

If it's not clear what the dress code is, ask the organizers, look at past images from events, and pick outfits that can be dressed up or down. If there will be lots of standing and walking, consider keeping comfortable shoes handy. We'll talk more about your personal brand in the next chapter.

---

[15] https://www.oprah.com/own-supersoulsessions/rupaul-explains-were-all-born-naked-and-the-rest-is-drag

[16] https://www.linkedin.com/posts/dr-jpb_aisummit-ai-activity-7180606080647925760-3LSH

[17] I've been wildly overdressed to events where Seattleites wear shirts and jeans. I've also been underdressed at a posh event in Southern California, where I was the youngest person and the one not in designer clothes and dripping in $15,000 worth of jewelry.

Figure Out Logistics and Transportation

How will you attend the event? Is it as easy as jumping on a Zoom call? Do you need to get a hotel, transportation, and more? Will you need to coordinate with your current work or school schedule? Do you need to set up plans for childcare or your elderly dog who loves to bark in the background?

Create a plan related to logistics and transportation so that you know how to execute your game plan on the day of the event. Consider meeting up with a friend outside the venue and walking in together.

Post on Social Media Before, During, and After

If you didn't post about it, did it happen? Joke, but not a joke. If you want people to know that you will be at an event, it is a wise idea to post on social media that you will attend; post during the event, especially with photos of your face; and post after the event and make sure to tag people and companies that you met so they could more easily follow up with you if they are also on social media.

On your personal and socials, you need to document where you have been and show people the professional you are and where they can meet you.

Have Your Elevator Pitch Ready

While the concept of an elevator pitch may sound trite, I have literally been on elevators where people who are influential and high up on the food chain ask me what I do. Be ready with your answer to this question. Consider practicing it in the mirror, on a phone, or with a friend to practice how you discuss your professional experience, think about a really, really short version that could intrigue the right person who also might be looking for you.

Have Your Call to Action and Follow-Up Materials Ready

Let's imagine that at the networking event you meet the person you have been dying to get in touch with. What are the next steps that you would want? Are you hoping that Morgan could make you an introduction? Are you looking for feedback on your AI project? What is the specific call to action and follow-up you are looking for? This is crucial, so do not let it be haphazard.

Be prepared! Link your project to a website and have the link ready. Download the LinkedIn app on your phone and allow people to scan the code in the querybar so you can connect with them there. Have a QR code that links directly to a project. Consider having a slide deck or prototype of the product you would love someone to look at if they consent to discussing it with you.

Just a few minutes to hours of preparation time could be the difference between you awkwardly fumbling on your phone versus getting specific, actual feedback from a phenomenal professional, who could help you greatly as you both grab coffee at an event.

A common blunder I've seen is that people get nervous and don't share the sound space. They aren't in tune with their audience. They come off as sleazy and long winded. They do not pick up on social cues. They hog the microphone and do not check in if the person they are talking with is actually engaged. Have you met these people? Do you also feel a desire to run away? Exactly. If you are a motormouth and people aren't truly conversing with you, they won't do business with you. They won't make that crucial introduction. They will be *dying* to get away from you. Make sure that the conversation is going back and forth.

Be Gentle with Yourself

Sometimes you will not always hit your goals. Sometimes you will not get to talk to the two people you were hoping to meet at the event. Sometimes you will be exhausted and need to go back to your hotel room before a major event. Sometimes you may say something you wish you had not, and you are embarrassed. Sometimes you will not get the job or someone will laugh. Please be gentle with yourself and know that you need to be resilient regardless of painful experiences.

Drink water, take breaks, text a friend and share your story, use the restroom, and take care of yourself.

Follow Up!

If you do get the contact information for someone or connect with them, make sure that the connection is both via email and LinkedIn.

Send them a message to document that you met and send any follow-up material that you can share. While it seems extremely obvious, many people ask me for things at conferences that I say yes to and then they never send the email. Following up is crucial. Always do it.

Rest and Get Support

Even as an extrovert, I can find conferences and meetings extremely taxing. Make sure to take care of yourself during and after the event.

Tell your close friends and family about the experience, get feedback from how you can do better, thank all the people who supported you as you took the courage to build your career.

This list is part of the method I use for almost all events I prepare for. With just 20 minutes to 2 hours, you could be much more prepared than you initially were. The goals don't have to be complex! The more you do these networking events, the easier it will become. This is a skill that will pay dividends.

The Power of a Cup of Coffee: Informational Interviews and Coffee Intros

Coffee meetings are crucial to bolstering your network.[18] In addition to attending networking events such as conferences, happy hours, meetups, and more, I recommend strengthening your network through informational interviews. The term *informational interview* was coined by Richard Nelson Bolles in the book *What Color Is Your Parachute?*[19] This term is misleading and clinical. It sounds as bad as daylight saving! Talking to people and building relationships is great!

When I first heard about the concept in 2014 from my friend, I thought it sounded like cheating. Stephen said, "I reach out to people at companies I like and ask them to get coffee with me." "You can really do that?" I responded incredulously. "Oh, for sure!" he

---

[18] You don't have to drink coffee at the meeting. Tea is fine. Or grab a scone. It isn't about the food and drink!
[19] **https://archive.org/details/isbn_9781607743620**

responded, "They won't always say yes, but for the price of buying them a cup of coffee, you can ask them about their work." Stephen would ask the people about their work, what inspired them about their projects, whether they liked their coworkers, what recommendations they might have for ambitious people who were interested in the field, and other researched questions tailored to the person he was having coffee with.

The #1 rule about these coffee chats is that you do NOT ask for a job. You don't want to grovel. Even if you *are* desperate for a job at this person's company, you want to be seen as a peer or someone who would be great to work with who is stable and ambitious. Listen deeply to what they are saying. Do they like their job? Is their work actually interesting? Does their job sound prestigious but they actually are miserable? Do they have to work such long hours that they have sleeping bags under their desks?[20] Would you want to be in their shoes in the future? Learn from their experience like a sparkly light in your dataset that becomes a constellation of stars. Have 5–10 questions prepared. Prepare a short introduction of roughly one to two minutes to say who you are. Make it clear why you are worthy of their precious time you are asking them to give for free, or the price of a coffee. Ask if they have any recommendations for resources to read, events to attend, and other people you could meet. Follow up with a personalized thank-you message every time. Ask them how you could help them as well. Relationships are two-way streets. Is there a cool article you recently read that they wanted to read? Do you know a yoga studio that specializes in the yoga they wanted to try? Follow up with those things also.

One of the key parts of informational interviews is that you bolster the connections in your network, especially ones on the periphery. You are supporting the magic of the paradoxical weak ties to work in your favor. I strongly recommend reaching out to people for informal meetings. They are even easier these days because people are so used to virtual meetings. When I want a meeting like this, I even use the phrase *virtual coffee meeting* to indicate a 15- to 30-minute Zoom meeting.

Before the pandemic, I recommended people rising and pivoting to reach out to 10–15 people in the field where they wanted a career. As the vaccine for COVID-19 is now readily available, I recommend job seekers reach out to 50–100 professionals in their field. Craft a list of 50–100 professionals and 20–30 companies that you'd love to learn

---

[20] Real the story from my friend who interviewed at a hedge fund.

more about and begin your outreach plan. The "50–100" isn't a range I pulled out of thin air; it's based on the job searches of my friends. Buckle up for a story that shakes me to my core.

Marion's Story: From Amazon Layoff to 55 Coffee Chats to Job Offer

My friend Marion Desmazières[21] worked at Amazon for 8.5 years before being in a large-scale layoff. The layoff came a few weeks before she gave birth to her second child. Her whole team got let go in one fell swoop. Her layoff was featured in the *New York Times* in the article "Portraits of People Living the News."[22] Marion is brilliant, hard-working, and extremely well-networked. When I saw her LinkedIn post saying she had been laid off, I thought it must have been a mistake. I was so surprised. The value of her rolodex of professional relationships is more valuable to any company than her base salary. Why didn't they just reorg her? Amazon's loss! I've worked with Marion on projects for Women in Voice and know the strength of her work. More than that, did I mention she worked at Amazon for more than eight years? Amazon is not an easy place to work. The tech giant has one of the worst employee retention stats.[23] The average Amazon worker leaves after only 12 months.[24] In 198,826 Glassdoor reviews, the phrase "no work-life balance" was written in 7,657 reviews.[25]

So the fact that Marion worked at Amazon for 8.5 years and earned three promotions directly is an objective metric that she's a really hard worker.[26] Despite her incredible work experience, she found it hard to find her next full-time job. During her job search, she and I would take walks around Seattle to discuss her approach and talk about how to be

[21] Real name.

[22] https://www.nytimes.com/interactive/2023/12/29/opinion/2023-people-living-the-news.html

[23] https://candor.co/articles/tech-careers/is-work-life-balance-the-reason-behind-amazon-s-turnover-rate

[24] https://candor.co/articles/tech-careers/is-work-life-balance-the-reason-behind-amazon-s-turnover-rate

[25] https://www.glassdoor.com/Reviews/Amazon-Reviews-E6036.htm

[26] https://www.linkedin.com/posts/mariondesmazieres_amazonlayoffs-amazon-microsoft-activity-7022251805052993536-hRoW

resilient during rough times. She showed me her spreadsheet documenting all her warm intros and coffee chats along the way. She did eventually land her next job! What did it take? She identified 70 listings, took 55 coffee chats, applied to 40 opportunities, went to 12 networking events (multiple with me by her side!), and finally signed her next full-time job offer.[27] Remember, this is how hard the job market can be even for a well-networked white woman with an overflowing portfolio of work examples from a prestigious tech company. For BIPOC folks and those with disabilities, it might be even harder. I'm not telling you this story to scare you; I'm sharing it so you can see the brilliance of Marion's dedication and organized process paying off. Being more organized can help you move through this faster.

If you are looking for a job, wanting to make a career pivot, or going after a big goal, I recommend you reach out to 50–100 people in your field for informational interviews and coffee chats. This is based on my network's experience, especially illustrated through Marion's story. This is a project sprint. Here's my recommended formula to leverage strong and weak ties toward your goals via spreadsheets and templates:[28]

- **Spreadsheet:** Get organized. Make a spreadsheet and write down the names of the people and companies you'd like to be in touch with. Do you have people in common who would be willing to make you the introduction? People who are connectors are very helpful for this purpose. Connectors are people who can connect you to resources and actually follow through.

- **Text:** Provide sample text. If someone makes you an introduction, be clear about why you want to meet the person and provide them with sample text. Here's an example: "My name is Joan, and I'm a researcher in linguistics. I'd love to connect with X to hear from her about research on multimodal interfaces."

- **Be Human:** Leverage any connecting material, no matter how small. If you're a student of the university of their alma mater, mention it! If you share the same hometown, you may want to drop that you also are from there.

---

[27] https://www.linkedin.com/posts/mariondesmazieres_jobsearch-jobseeker-linkedin-activity-7155314933025415169-2jCp
[28] Since I get asked for these exact materials often, we sell our templates and spreadsheets: YourAIRoadmap.com/Brand.

- **Be Friendly:** Personalize your message and show that you're a real human and not a bot trying to add yet another Zoom meeting to their already long work days. Go to all the networking events. Touch base with as many people as you can.
- **Be Diligent and Grateful:** Follow up with all of your leads and send thank you messages afterward.

Get organized and save yourself time. Create a template of the message you send to people. Make sure to customize it and state the ask clearly. "Can we meet up for coffee?" is less compelling than something more specific like "If you could find the time for just a 15-minute Zoom call, I have questions about your journey into AR projects for cancer patients. I completed a project testing different AR scenery for 20 elders in my community. Just a little bit of your time would be so helpful. I would love your advice about how to evolve the project." Know that many people may not reply or have the time to give you right now. That's fine! The people who don't have time right now also most likely won't follow up with helping you connect with a job opportunity. Let them simply be someone you admire.

Mentorship and Connectors

As we talk about people and networking, here's a note on mentorship. A lot has been written about mentorship, mentors, advocates, and sponsors. In many workplaces, there are dramatic power dynamics and people with two years' work experience collaborating with someone with 15 years' work experience. People who are more senior than you opening doors for you and providing constructive criticism can be immensely helpful. Relationships have to be two-way streets for them to be truly long-lasting. I find it disingenuous for people to send me DMs asking me to be their mentor. "Who is this person I've never met from the Internet?" I ask myself. Contrastingly, if you culti-vate professional friendships, mentors, people who advocate for you, allies, and advocates, these relationships will prove invaluable. The way you cultivate mentors, connectors, and people who advocate for you are invaluable.

Mentorship relationships *have* to be double-opt-in. Just like any good relationship, both parties find it meaningful. I foster relationships with my mentors by emailing them, tagging them on social media, messaging them when big life things happen, etc. I ask them for advice, intros, and favors, and I send great opportunities their way in return. I generally think of them as friends I am lucky enough to learn from. While you can certainly ask, my recommendation is to never expect things from people. Be delighted if people do you favors, but mostly expect that you will need to do almost everything yourself. Lastly, don't forget to give back and be a connector yourself. The more intros you take, the more you'll hear what people want and need to achieve their own milestones. Feel more and more comfortable letting people know your goals, and make sure to listen and give back. As I always say about the best types of luck, "We pay it forward, we pay it back." Be the key opener for others when they are looking for the intro that can help them land the next opportunities on the path to achieving their dreams! If you want good things to come to you, make sure you're also supportive of others in your life as well. Overall, these conversations will bolster your network and help you hone your story. Owning who you are will take you far. Being known for your work and honing your personal brand is the topic of the next chapter.

Questions for Reflection

Questions for You

- ☐ Do you think about your job in a "clock-in, clock-out" type of way? Is that what you want for the rest of your life? What are the benefits and pitfalls of this type of job?
- ☐ Do you find yourself making excuses and coming up with a litany of reasons why you don't want to go to events? Even if you need a bigger network? What of the advice in this chapter could you implement?
- ☐ Has a "weak tie" ever significantly impacted your career? How has focusing on relationships benefited your career?
- ☐ How do you own your professional story publicly? Do you have a LinkedIn or other social media account?

CHAPTER 5

Personal Brand: Get Credit for Your Work and Hone Your Brand

et's start this chapter with the story of a branding expert, Aliza Licht. Brand savant and innovator, Aliza Licht's life is a mashup of *Emily in Paris*, *Gossip Girl*, and *The Devil Wears Prada*.[1] Rising the ranks in the fashion world, she has worked at some of the biggest brands in the world such as *Harper's Bazaar*, *Marie Claire*, Donna Karan, and DKNY.[2,3]

One of the biggest inflection points for her career, though, was when social media and legacy brands collided. In 2009, she and her team created the Twitter (before it became X) handle "@DKNY PR GIRL."[4] The second season of *Gossip Girl* had just come out, and fashion brands did not yet have robust social media strategies. The team strategized that if they named the social media handle "Donna Karan," people would assume that it was Donna's real words, while someone else on the team actually was authoring tweets and responding to comments. The workaround was to create a handle for a fake PR girl who tweeted on behalf of the brand. As the SVP of Global Communications, Aliza was tasked as the person who solely tweeted on the account.

---

[1] https://alizalicht.com/about

[2] https://www.linkedin.com/in/alizalicht/details/experience

[3] https://podcasts.apple.com/us/podcast/aliza-licht-from-pre-med-to-fashion-the-making-of/id1481231734

[4] https://www.nytimes.com/2012/02/16/fashion/aliza-licht-unnamed-twitter-fashion-star-comes-out-on-youtube.html

"It was like the wild wild West when we first started,"[5] says Aliza about how brands wanted to leverage social media back in the early 2000s. In the next two years, the Twitter handle took off and garnered nearly 380,000 followers and 500,000 by 2015. With this new knowledge of how to grow huge followings on social media and create a persona from scratch, Aliza documented this skill set for herself and others.

After working at Donna Karen for more than 17 years, she next wrote a bestselling book, *Leave Your Mark: Land Your Dream Job. Kill It in Your Career. Rock Social Media* and launched an international podcast by the same title. The podcast has garnered more than 1.4 million downloads. "People have to have their own personal brands," Aliza implores, "to be able to really know who they are and what their value is without the companies they work for because those jobs won't always be around."[6] This certainly fits with the age of AI where layoffs are a daily occurrence. It's employed one day and laid off the next!

In her second book, *On Brand: Shape Your Narrative. Share Your Vision. Shift Their Perception*, Aliza covers how to craft a brand, amplify it, and sustain a brand. I'm a huge fan of Aliza's work, podcast, and book *On Brand*,[7] which I've found phenomenally insightful, helpful, and inspiring. Where her work needs to go farther, however, is how to monetize effectively. If you are interested in personal branding, Aliza's work is next level. I'd love to share with you about personal branding AND help take your financial acumen to the next level. We'll do that together in Part 2 of this book. So what is a personal brand, anyway?

Personal Brand

What is a personal brand? A personal brand is who people know you to be, your own brand. While I realize it seems counterintuitive that this is a professional brand, the concept is that this brand is who you are apart from the company you may work at. It's a relatively new concept that people are known as brands regardless of which company they are currently at. This personal brand is who you are known to be in professional spheres. Important note! Who you are online and who you are with friends and family is not the same. This is a common

---

[5] https://www.nytimes.com/2012/02/16/fashion/aliza-licht-unnamed-twitter-fashion-star-comes-out-on-youtube.html
[6] https://podcasts.apple.com/us/podcast/aliza-licht-from-pre-med-to-fashion-the-making-of/id1481231734?i=1000463054560
[7] https://alizalicht.com/on-brand

mistake I see people make. You have different personas when you are online on LinkedIn, at your grandparent's anniversary party, on a walk with your dog, and while giving a talk to thousands of people. I think of my two main personas as "professional Joan" and "personal Joan." While I endeavor to be authentically me in different spaces, it's healthy and extremely important to have boundaries.[8]

Joan's Hot Take: Your Online Self and Personal Brand

> Your personal brand is powerful. You can be strategic. It's worth the effort to future-proof your career.

Instead of throwing spaghetti at the wall and hoping things work for your personal brand, I recommend being strategic and thoughtful. As of the writing of this book, the most powerful platform professionally for my field is LinkedIn. More than 830 million people from over 200 countries around the world use LinkedIn.[9] As someone who has been building a personal brand online for years, I previously built my presence on academic Twitter (now X) and then transitioned to LinkedIn when content moderation decreased. By investing in my LinkedIn profile in 2023, my LinkedIn follower count grew 160%. But being on LinkedIn for me is far more than my follower count. People reach out to me with life-changing opportunities in my DMs and in the comments. I'm talking about a few hundred dollars to eight-figure contracts. Before I get ahead of myself, let's talk about how you build your personal brand. What's my recipe? Let's talk about personal brand construction.

My Personal Brand

Adjectives: My professional brand is ambitious, approachable,[10] authentic, celebratory, cheerful, confident, feminine, feminist, intentional, irreverent, modern, playful, professional, and technical. What adjectives might your brand use? Let's write down your versions in Table 5.1.

---

[8] I have had two stalkers. It is really horrible. I now work far harder to protect myself, my partner, and my dog by keeping my private life private. Boundaries are one of the most important things I work on as an adult. Thank you, therapy!

[9] https://www.forbes.com/sites/forbesagencycouncil/2022/06/10/linkedin-are-you-taking-advantage-of-the-worlds-largest-professional-network

[10] That being said, please ask before touching and hugging me in person. It can be overwhelming when people I don't know run up and hug me at conferences. Please ask for consent!

Color: My favorite color is yellow, which often washes me out. My second favorite color is blue. You'll see me wear blue or black in professional settings. Does this mean I'll never wear yellow? Nope! It means I have a preference for outfits and colors that fit my brand. What are your core brand colors?

TABLE 5.1 **Your Personal Brand Colors and Adjectives**

Your Personal Brand Adjectives and Colors	
Adjectives examples: ambitious, approachable, authentic, celebratory, cheerful, confident, feminine, feminist, intentional, irreverent, modern, playful, professional, and technical	Your Adjectives:
Color examples: White, teal blue, black	Your Colors:

Headshot: Figure 5.1 shows my professional headshot. It was taken on the University of California campus. In the photo, you see me with my brown wavy hair off to one side of my head. My hair is long enough to go a little over my shoulders. I am smiling with my mouth closed and looking directly at the camera. Behind me are some architectural columns. I'm wearing makeup, turquoise oval earrings, and a high-collared blue dress that has a lace pattern. My shoulders are visible with my pinkish, beige skin. This is the headshot I use on almost all social media platforms today.

FIGURE 5.1 Joan's professional headshot

This photo matches my personal brand. Across social media, this photo (sized big or small as an icon) has been seen hundreds of thousands of times based on analytics from my LinkedIn and Twitter (now X) handles. I prefer to choose outfits that are high-necked for two primary reasons. I don't like to show a lot of skin. I prefer people focus on what I'm saying rather than staring at my chest if I can help it. Second, I have acne that I find embarrassing. Showing less skin overall can help redirect people to listen to my loud, confident voice and jokes on stage.

These preferences may not be the same for you. What if you are a beauty influencer and you are really excited about showing off your curves? That could be a huge component of your brand and how you show up online. Similarly, what if you are the owner of a lingerie empire and the fit of clothes on your torso is one of the crucial things that you want to make sure is always on point? Truly, your online persona has to fit *your* goals. What does your headshot and persona online look and feel like?

Personal Brand via LinkedIn Profile

Spending time curating your LinkedIn profile can pay dividends. At the time of this writing, LinkedIn and email are the two most powerful networking tools I use. Let's look at the current version of my LinkedIn, shown in Figure 5.2. In a 2018 study, researchers found that recruiters spent just 7.4 seconds reviewing a single résumé.[11] You might get the blink of an eye from someone passing by your profile on LinkedIn. For this reason, you should spend a lot of time curating and honing the first things people see on your LinkedIn profile. First impressions are important. They can have a huge impact on how people think of you and consume your brand.

In my LinkedIn header, there is a banner image that is the imagery of blue mountains and sky with white puffy clouds above a sandy brown landscape. This is one of our main imagery items we use at Clarity AI, so it evokes our company. The banner serves a few purposes, it sets the tone, and provides the literal backdrop for my face. You want to make sure whatever banner you pick, you don't have key content behind your headshot! My headshot is on the left side overlapping the banner.

[11] **https://www.theladders.com/static/images/basicSite/pdfs/TheLadders-EyeTracking-StudyC2.pdf**

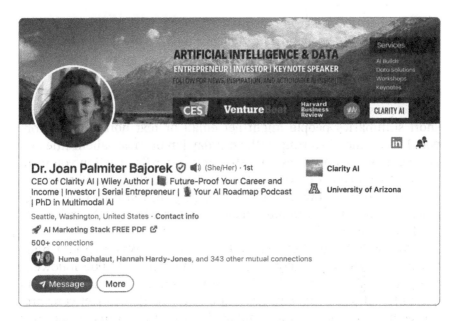

FIGURE 5.2   Joan's LinkedIn profile header, Spring 2024[12]

The banner has large text of the main words people know me and my career for ("Artificial Intelligence & Data" and "Entrepreneur | Investor | Keynote Speaker") as well as a call to action ("Follow for News Inspiration, and Actionable AI Insights"). On the right side, I have the services my company provides, including "AI Builds, Data Solutions, Workshops, Keynotes." Let's hope that by the time this book gets published, the words "Best-Selling Author" might be on this banner, also!

The footer of this banner includes the logos of the biggest stages I've been on, CES and VentureBeat, my most prestigious publication venue, *Harvard Business Review*, and the organizations I've founded, Women in Voice and Clarity AI. In that rectangle, I frame the professional perspective and top accolades of my career. I built this banner in Canva[13] where they have many free LinkedIn banner templates. Your banner doesn't need to be this involved, but you do need to have a banner. I recommend being strategic in what your banner says about you.

---

[12] **https://www.linkedin.com/in/dr-jpb**
[13] I love this tool and wish it had an affiliate program. It is such an easy to use and speedy tool that keeps rolling out product features I always wanted. So impressed. Even the free tier has amazingly powerful tools.

Below my headshot I've got my full name with "Dr." in front of it, cueing folks that I have an advanced degree and ideally not to underestimate me. I have my pronouns and also have added an audio file of how to pronounce my name.[14]

Your headline is a key part of your LinkedIn profile. The first few characters will show up when you post comments, and it'll be in the short summaries people might get email or text notifications from you. I recommend starting with your day job or most salient title and also using keywords, titles, industry, or other calls to action you want people on LinkedIn to know about you personally or professionally. Since my personal brand is peppy and playful, I also include emojis since that fits with my brand. I have had people in my DMs ask me to use fewer emojis, LOL!

On my LinkedIn, I say where I live, "Seattle, Washington, United States" and show publicly that I have more than 14,000 followers. I tag Clarity AI LLC and the University of Arizona as organizations I am affiliated with. Tag your geolocation. Correctly connect your profile with companies you are affiliated with. If you'd like a checklist of all my recommendations for an excellent LinkedIn profile, go here: **YourAIRoadmap.com/Brand**.

I recommend you create your personal brand and LinkedIn profile with intention. What are the goals of your LinkedIn profile? What is the biggest call to action you might have for someone on your profile? My goals for my LinkedIn profile include maintain and build my career, stay in touch with current and future professional connections, have a go-to place for people to review whether they want to work with me, get credit for the work I've already done, and share posts and insights with my network. Your network, your professional brand, and you will all change and evolve over time. You want to keep your work up-to-date so that people can know and find you.

I find that some people don't take LinkedIn seriously. You might encounter these folks, too. Some people have teased me profusely for my LinkedIn, that influencers are "stupid," and that spending time on social media is a waste of time. My influencer friend made $2 million last year. Does that sound "stupid" to you? Probably not. Feel free to tease me as my career soars. Being an influencer means I push my world to be more inclusive. My work on social media has directly translated into me getting paid more and doing work I enjoy. I've built my

---

[14] "Joan" rhymes with "stone" for those of you who are curious.

network so well that there are people who send me DMs about wanting to hire me. Projects we talk about pay four to seven figures. You don't have to make the same investment in your personal brand and network, but you don't need to give me flack while my investments continue to pay dividends!

If you are working hard to get noticed more on LinkedIn, be both a consumer of content and a content creator. Post content that fits your personal brand and goals at least twice per week. I recommend using imagery of your projects, work, and faces. Images of faces perform very well on LinkedIn. People love seeing other people and hearing stories! Isn't it lovely to resonate with other people?

Email Inboxes

Email is the other powerful platform I strongly recommend as you build your career trajectory. According to statistics, 99% of people with emails check it daily, and 58% check it first thing in the morning, don't you?[15] Research indicates that employed people receive an average of 121 emails per day and more than 20 instant messages, chats, and DMs. Of all those emails people get, only 10–40 actually require people's attention. They check their emails 15 times per day, typically between meetings. Thus, people are checking their email and having access to send them messages here is relatively intimate territory. Media moguls Dorie Clark[16] and Amy Porterfield[17] both swear by the power of an email list. If you have people's personal emails, that's an email they may have for decades. If it is a company-specific email, it may no longer be helpful when they change jobs. Make sure to connect with people both on LinkedIn and email, if possible.

You've heard across my stories the power of email. I recommend you boost your email writing chops as you evolve your career. I also strongly recommend you curate your email signature to have important information and a call to action. They are already in an intimate place and opening your email. Why not offer them options to connect with you on LinkedIn or sign up for a waitlist of yours? See my current personal email signature in Figure 5.3.

[15] **https://www.mailbutler.io/blog/email/email-statistics-trends**; the rest of the research in this paragraph also references this study.
[16] **https://dorieclark.com/entrepreneurialyou**
[17] **https://twoweeksnoticebook.com**

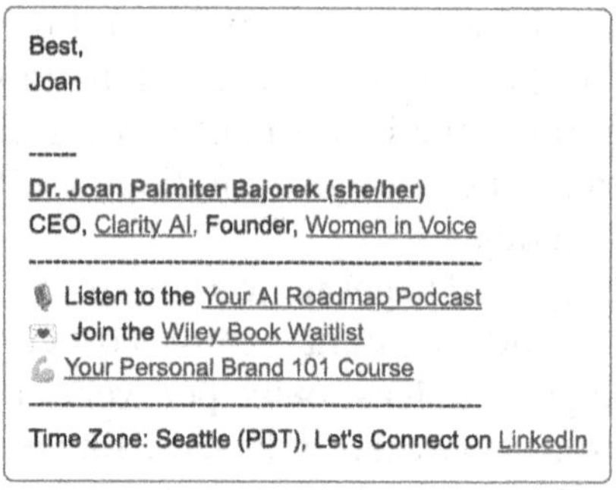

Best,
Joan

Dr. Joan Palmiter Bajorek (she/her)
CEO, Clarity AI, Founder, Women in Voice

🎙 Listen to the Your AI Roadmap Podcast
📷 Join the Wiley Book Waitlist
🔒 Your Personal Brand 101 Course

Time Zone: Seattle (PDT), Let's Connect on LinkedIn

FIGURE 5.3 Email signature

So those are my two cents on personal brand, LinkedIn, and email. These are all worthy uses of your time professionally that can pay off massively toward your professional goals! Remember, you can always make changes. I may not always be the CEO at Clarity AI. I might be offered another thing that I want to pursue. I may choose to radically change my hair style and color palette. All brands can change and pivot. Allow yours to also. Now that we've talked about your brand, let's talk about your storytelling. In the next chapter, we'll talk about pivots and how you own and share your story.

Questions for Reflection

Questions for You

- ☐ What do you want to be known for? What is your personal brand online and in the professional sphere?
- ☐ Do you have a LinkedIn? How do you own your professional story publicly?
- ☐ Do you check your LinkedIn profile and email daily? What brings you there? What content is most interesting? How much time do you spend there?
- ☐ Who are you inspired by? What do they do well on their online profiles?
- ☐ From this chapter, what could you improve on your profile? Do you poo-poo my recommendations as overkill? Where have your most powerful professional opportunities come from?

CHAPTER 6

Left, Right, and Center: Pivots, Resilience, and Connect the Dots via Storytelling

W hen Pinky got fired from her television job in 2018, it hurt.[1] She'd worked there for two years. She'd never been fired before, and her ego was bruised. While initially painful, Pinky says that it "was the best thing that could have happened to me, because it made me go all in on my business."[2] This wasn't the first time she tapped into her resilience. Riffing off the title of her 2023 book, *I Hope You Fail*,[3] Pinky explains about her journey that "If you know anything about me, you know I've experienced a lot of 'failures' in my life. "I've gotten a business that I lost. My car got repoed. I got kicked out of my apartment. My father served 22 years in prison. So by society's standards, I'm supposed to be a statistic." She continued

---

[1] https://www.cnbc.com/2023/10/31/slutty-vegan-ceo-getting-fired-was-best-thing-to-ever-happen-to-me.html

[2] https://www.cnbc.com/2023/10/31/slutty-vegan-ceo-getting-fired-was-best-thing-to-ever-happen-to-me.html

[3] https://www.amazon.com/Hope-You-Fail-Statements-Everything/dp/1400242851

playfully, "I've been an expert in the field of failure, I went to the Harvard's of failure. [. . .] Failing is not failing at all. It's about finding the aspirations and the losses and about rising above it. [. . .] Everything in life is modifiable."[4] So what is the business Pinky went all in on? A vegan restaurant empire. On the same day Pinky got fired from her day job, Snoop Dogg ate at her restaurant[5] which had been her side hustle. The restaurant serves vegan burgers, fries, and hotdogs, among other fare.[6] Talk about a roller coaster of a day for Pinky!

Pinky Cole is the founder and CEO of Slutty Vegan. Yes, you read that correctly. A pretty spicy name for a company! It's a memorable name, too. As a vegan living in Atlanta, Pinky struggled to find good vegan food.[7] She saw a gap in the market. She came up with the brand one night for the vegan restaurant. The "naughty"[8] branding was an intentional choice. Pinky explains, "I got this racy name that as a television producer, I knew people would pay attention to."[9] She said, "I knew that if I named it Pinky's Vegan, nobody was going to come, but Slutty Vegan had a ring to it because I merged the two most pleasurable experiences in life: sex and food."[10] It worked. People bought in droves. In her first six months of launching Slutty Vegan, she brought in $4 million of revenue.[11] In the first six months! The brand is now valued at $100 million.[12] In 2023, Pinky was listed on the TIME 100 Next List.[13] Slutty Vegan now has a chain of restaurants and opened the 14th location in 2024 in Brooklyn, New York. Whenever new locations open, the line is around the block.[14,15] Fans of the brand include Snoop Dogg,

[4] https://www.youtube.com/watch?v=8VWwhQ7XVL8
[5] https://www.cnbc.com/2023/10/31/slutty-vegan-ceo-getting-fired-was-best-thing-to-ever-happen-to-me.html
[6] https://vegnews.com/interviews/pinky-cole-slutty-vegan-empire
[7] https://vegnews.com/interviews/pinky-cole-slutty-vegan-empire
[8] https://time.com/collection/time100-next-2023/6308471/pinky-cole
[9] https://podcasts.apple.com/us/podcast/bossy-with-tara-katie/id1709498106?i=1000648338269
[10] https://www.yahoo.com/lifestyle/slutty-vegan-founder-pinky-cole-explains-her-restaurants-name-190150324.html
[11] https://podcasts.apple.com/us/podcast/hibt-lab-slutty-vegan-pinky-cole/id1150510297?i=1000604415092
[12] https://fortune.com/2023/01/27/slutty-vegan-founder-pinky-cole-100-million-dollar-brand
[13] https://time.com/collection/time100-next-2023/6308471/pinky-cole
[14] https://time.com/collection/time100-next-2023/6308471/pinky-cole
[15] Trust me, I'll be in that line when they come to Seattle.

Tyler Perry, Tiffany Haddish, Usher, Viola Davis, Spike Lee, Shaquille O'Neal, Lena Waithe, and Gabrielle Union, among other celebrities.[16,17] Building a restaurant empire has also brought Pinky personal wealth. "I made my first million when I was 29 years old,"[18] said Pinky in a 2024 interview while wearing earrings that retail for $29,000.[19] Pinky's income streams are bigger than the revenue from one restaurant.[20] She has multiple books, including *Eat Plants* and *B*tch: 91 Vegan Recipes That Will Blow Your Meat-Loving Mind*.[21]

Pinky Cole is killing it. She's in the room where decisions are made. She has a phenomenal personal and company brand. She's also been resilient across the years. She owns her story and talks widely about the bumps in the road and how she has experienced changes in her life with her successes. You can also be resilient across the years. Everyone is making pivots, and you need to be the storyteller who connects the dots for others. For Pinky, her work in TV in production at the Oprah Network spanned years. Her domain knowledge of operations and honing messaging for an audience can be a powerful skill set in many domains, such as a saucy restaurant brand and empire.

Own Your Story

It is powerful to own your story. It is powerful to share yourself with others. Do so with boundaries and thoughtfulness about what

---

[16] https://www.nytimes.com/2019/07/01/dining/slutty-vegan-burger-atlanta-restaurant.html
[17] https://vegnews.com/vegan-news/celebrities-slutty-vegan-fans
[18] https://www.instagram.com/reel/C5Bt1rrLtlL/?utm_source=ig_web_copy_link&igsh=MzRlODBiNWF1ZA==
[19] https://www.vancleefarpels.com/us/en/collections/jewelry/alhambra/vcarn9zr00---magic-alhambra-earrings.html
[20] https://www.cnbc.com/2022/02/18/slutty-vegans-owner-on-overcoming-failure-building-a-vegan-empire.html
[21] https://www.amazon.com/Eat-Plants-tch-Recipes-Meat-Loving/dp/1982178310/ref=pd_lpo_sccl_1/134-7321598-9718269?pd_rd_w=BcZwA&content-id=amzn1.sym.1ad2066f-97d2-4731-9356-36b3edf1ae04&pf_rd_p=1ad2066f-97d2-4731-9356-36b3edf1ae04&pf_rd_r=H30B25X8PM289K13QANT&pd_rd_wg=IHnbA&pd_rd_r=c067ace6-93ff-4076-b5ff-6a4f7a96d273&pd_rd_i=1982178310&psc=1

you are comfortable sharing. A key way to own your story is about sharing your strengths and how people can help you. When you are looking for something like an internship, a job, or a specific type of opportunity, it is better to be clear about what you want and need. People aren't mind readers! I have strategically used long-form posts to tell my story. Sometimes I'm scared to do so, but my friends keep telling me that leading with my strengths and reframing my story even to myself can be immensely potent and therapeutic. Thank you, friends!

Joan's Hot Take: People are NOT Mind Readers

News flash! People can't read your mind. Stop hinting. Own your story. Tell them your story.

With the huge number of layoffs that are happening regularly,[22] you've most likely seen a post where someone says, "I just got laid off from X company, looking for Y types of jobs in the Philadelphia area." These types of posts are helpful and clear, but they can fall flat. They might spark sadness when you read them. They aren't creative or telling much of a story.

Consider how you can incorporate yourself and your personal brand more into the post. When I was transitioning out of being the CEO at Women in Voice, I decided I'd write a post about it to request support from my network. Figure 6.1 shows the post.

This is a long-form LinkedIn post with a GIF of me kissing my dog. It performed well, garnering more than 14,000 impressions, 172 reactions, 27 comments, and 6 reposts. Instead of a few people for coffee, the message was shared with 14,000 eyeballs! The first few

---

[22] While I'm writing this, I saw yet another post of someone waking up to learn they'd been laid off from AWS. They were already locked out of their work email. Ouch! It can happen to anyone at any time. **https://www.linkedin.com/posts/john-smythe-595a1b4_another-round-of-layoffs-today-at-aws-and-activity-7181306782907031552-eBe0**

FIGURE 6.1   Joan's storytelling LinkedIn post[23]

characters of your post may be skimmed. Most people are just here to watch a GIF of me kiss my corgi. Here's the text of the post:[24]

---

[23] https://www.linkedin.com/posts/dr-jpb_dei-voice-conversationdesign-activity-6955205627614756864-h1S0
[24] A few clerical fixes have been made.

"It has been an Honor to serve as the CEO of Women in Voice for 4 years. And now I'm ready for the next role in my career trajectory. Can you help me find my next team?

> Know a team hiring? A person to meet? Send a DM 😊

On the job market, I'm talking to some amazing folks, but haven't yet signed with the right team. Job market right now is full of twists and turns- you've heard about these hiring freezes and startups not getting funding. It's not easy!

Job title? I'm open to lots (UX Researcher, TPM, Product Manager, Data Scientist, Linguist, Conversation Designer). I'd love to work in software on a collaborative team working on impactful products, ideally in conversational AI.

9 Years in Tech, Academia, Nonprofit, Agency, Enterprise, & Startups

After my PhD, I planned to be exclusively in R&D, but also felt called to champion DEI in my field. That's why I did technical work AND bootstrapped <u>Women in Voice</u>. Over the years, I've worked on many projects. Innovation moves fast! I'm curious, hardworking, and ambitious. Even if I don't tick all the boxes for a job, I continuously learn and grow 😊

🏔 *Location: Seattle, hybrid, or remote*

Software Highlights:

+ Voice & Conversational AI Linguist w AR/VR exp, ex-<u>Company</u>
+ Conversation Designer of IVRs & Multimodal Work: Intents, Flows, & Optimization
+ Mixed Methods Quantitative & Qualitative Researcher & Data Scientist: Created Actionable Insights N=200 Survey, Analytics, Interview, Usability, & Acoustic Data
+ Data-Driven Products: Found Bugs Fixed 17% of System in 2 Weeks
+ Mockup Designer: Created High-Fidelity Wireframes for Devs. & Clients
+ Cross-Functional: Work w C-Suite, Devs, PMs, UX, Design, Marketing
+ Client & Public-Facing: Copy Editor, Social Media Influencer, Polished Presenter
+ Verticals: Healthcare, IoT, EdTech, Language Learning, Contact Centers, Telehealth, Telecom

Hands-on Day-to-Day

+ *Operations: Scaled Agile, Documentation, Recruiting, & Lead Teams*
+ *Partnership & Biz Dev: Closed $500k+ in Sponsor Packages*
+ *Fiscal Modeling & Negotiator: Led cash flow, Reports, & Conducted ROI Analyses*
+ *Growth Hacker & Marketer: Grew Socials 150-400% YoY*
+ *Technical Advisor to Startup & Enterprise: Roadmapping & Strategy*
+ *Manager of 6-10: Constructive Feedback, Growth & Promotions*

Degrees & More

+ *Ph.D.: Field of Speech Language Tech, AI, ASR, TTS, NLP, HCI, UX*
+ *MA: Linguistics, Data Science, Experimental Design*
+ *Software: R, Python, PRAAT, Asana, Slack, Qualtrics, WordPress, Canva, Figma, Miro, Buffer*
+ *#4 Influencer in Voice AI*
+ *Speaker: Technical Evangelist, Speaker at CES, VentureBeat*
+ *Writer:* Harvard Business Review, *Cambridge University Press – Academic, UXmatters*
+ *Ethics & #DEI: Mission of Diversity, Equity, & Inclusion*

(GIF of Luna and me before stand-up paddling! Bonus! She'll join the team also 🐶 🤪*)*

#voice #conversationdesign #AI #nlp #data #job #career #work #research #hiring #tech #womenintech #datascience #ux #business #design #analytics #designer"

Narrative, face, and call to action are all key components of this post. The post gives some narrative at the top and displays my personal brand through emojis and by showing my face. The clear call to action is at the top: "Send a DM." It's short and has a question mark and even an arrow offsetting it ">." I list a version of my brag sheet and what types of roles I'm interested in. I list my skills, experience, and degrees. I tag companies and opportunities I'm affiliated with. It's like a short-form résumé in a post! No one needs to look at my full LinkedIn; they can simply look at this post.

In the comments, I tagged some of my friends who I know will help boost the post by reacting and commenting so it might also get seen by their network. Before I posted this, I alerted multiple friends asking them to support the post when it went live to share it as well as provide me emotional support if they could. Beyond the external analytics of how many people saw and reacted to the post, my DMs blew up. I got connected with roughly 30 companies from posting this, many new coffee intros, and multiple job offers. I tracked them all in a spreadsheet and followed up with the ones I was most eager to talk with. One CEO DM'd me that his CTO had seen the post. The CTO implored his CEO to get in touch with me ASAP. That's the kind of interest you can't get from just sending a CV into a folder.

If you are looking for a job, create your own version of this post and tag it to your featured section so it continues to stay at the top of your LinkedIn profile. Do you see how this post is more interesting and actionable than a bland post like, "I need a job in Philadelphia?" Just like any other social media platform, "engagement" is one of the key metrics. Do people stop scrolling and really read your post, click, comment, and share it? If so, typically the algorithm will also boost it to be seen by more folks. To date, the previous post has been seen by some 14,000 folks!

What stories could you tell on LinkedIn? If you were requested to post twice per week, ideally on Tuesday and Thursday mornings, what would you post? How do you talk about your current projects? What can you bring to the table that people are curious about? Whether it's about your lifeguarding summer job, your side hustle as a DJ at bar and bat mitzvahs, or examples of the best boss you've ever had, I'd write those up and schedule when to post them as you build the content out on your LinkedIn profile.

If you're pivoting, think about how you talk about your work as a masseuse, your training for that, and how you can share the overlapping skill set to being a project manager at a tech company. Consider showing a photo of you at the massage studio! How does being in touch with your customer's needs and environment translate well to managing multiple stakeholders and empathizing with difficult economic conditions. These examples are fake, but my advice is about connecting the dots. Show how you can connect the dots for readers. When I wanted to talk to new teams, I posted loudly, confidently, and clearly to my audience about what I was looking for in my next steps. It served me well. Pinky chose to start a restaurant company and frequently talks on stages about her career journey. Whichever path you choose, reflecting on where you've been and where you're going will serve you well. Crafting a story to share with tens, hundreds, thousands to millions of professionals can open up to opportunities and folks who you have yet to meet.

In this and the previous chapters, we've extensively covered the 80% People bucket of time: going to events online and in person, coffee chats, honing your personal brand, curating your LinkedIn profile and email signature, owning your story, and having STAR method stories ready to tell folks. Next, we're going to think about AI jobs if you want a job in AI.

Questions for Reflection

Questions for You

- [ ] What is your professional story? How do you talk about it?
- [ ] Do people know about a pivot or career journey you're embarking on? How can you make it clear to them?
- [ ] What support would be invaluable? People looking out for an internship in robotics for you in your town? Let people know.
- [ ] Do you post frequently? How do you share about your personal journey and build connections with people? How will new people know where you've come from and where you're headed?

CHAPTER 7

Chasing the AI Rocketship: Your Next Steps for a Fleeting Job Market

A common question I get in my DMs: "Joan, how do I get a job in AI?" I totally understand where they are coming from but wonder if they have a goal I don't recommend. This whole book is an answer to how to get a job and build a career. If the question behind the question is "How do I get job stability?" then we've already talked about how AI jobs aren't immune from layoffs. The AI sector doesn't always pay great salaries for all roles. If you're looking to build wealth, there are many options I recommend more (see Part 2 of this book!). Here's a short chapter to address the "Joan, how do I get a job in AI?" question directly.

I entitled this chapter "Chasing the AI Rocketship" since it's a sector with high volatility. If you want a job in AI, I get it. It's prestigious, and it can pay well. Some estimates say AI jobs pay 25% more than non-AI jobs at least.[1] Yet, that volatility makes it such a narrow sector that is hard to pin down practical advice. It is probable that by the time this book comes out, this section may already be out of date. It moves fast! My advice is to work on your personal brand, network,

---

[1] https://www.cnn.com/2024/05/21/business/ai-jobs-higher-wages-productivity/index.html

polish your storytelling, and get your financial house in order. But, if you really, really want that job in AI, let's talk about it.

Can I promise you'll land a job in AI? Of course not. But I did collect some data about current jobs available. You can check out LinkedIn, **Indeed.com**, **Monster.com**, and Glassdoor, among others. Any search on LinkedIn is going to be curated for you and tweaked based on all the algorithms they have on the backend. Feel free to do your own searches when you read this book and see how much or little has changed with the search term "AI" on job sites.

Through using filters on LinkedIn AI jobs worldwide, I reviewed which positions companies have job descriptions for that they posted online in April 2024. When I searched for "artificial intelligence (AI)" in the job search bar of LinkedIn with the location as "Worldwide,"[2] 204,650 results came up.[3] There are jobs in consulting, project management, ML model fine-tuning, and more. Tables 7.1 through 7.5 show the result of an April 2024 LinkedIn AI Job study, showing the percentage of jobs tagged by experience level, contract type, geographical location, work type, and most common job titles. While job descriptions are frequently tagged with the experience level, location, and more data about them, not all of them get these filtering tags. Of the jobs that were tagged for experience level, almost all were in the "Entry Level" and "Mid-Senior Level" range, 87%. A huge chunk of AI jobs were based in the United States, almost 50%. Of the 67% jobs tagged as "On-Site," 88% were labeled as "Full-Time" jobs.

TABLE 7.1 LinkedIn AI Job Study: Experience Level, April 2024

Experience Level Tag	171,077	
Entry Level	86,989	**50.8%**
Mid-Senior Level	62,242	**36.4%**
Internship	9,831	5.7%
Associate	6,947	4.1%
Director	3,888	2.3%
Executive	1,180	0.7%

[2] https://www.linkedin.com/jobs/artificial-intelligence-(ai)-jobs-worldwide/?currentJobId=3825525329
[3] https://www.linkedin.com/jobs/search/?currentJobId=3825525329&keywords=artificial%20intelligence%20(ai)&location=worldwide&origin=JOB_SEARCH_PAGE_JOB_FILTER&sortBy=R

TABLE 7.2 LinkedIn AI Job Study: Contract Type, April 2024

Contract Tagged	204,517	
Full-Time	180,395	**88.21%**
Part-time	10,978	5.37%
Contract	6,534	3.19%
Internship	4,847	2.37%
Temporary	1,051	0.51%
Other	476	0.23%
Volunteer	236	0.12%

TABLE 7.3 LinkedIn AI Job Study: Geographical Tag, Work Type, April 2024

Geographical Tag	180,196	
United States	85,796	**47.6%**
China	19,773	**11.0%**
Italy	19,683	**10.9%**
India	11,697	6.5%
Germany	10,981	6.1%
Japan	8,829	4.9%
United Kingdom	7,198	4.0%
France	6,413	3.6%
Canada	3,449	1.9%
Netherlands	2,565	1.4%
Brazil	2,287	1.3%
Mexico	1,004	0.6%
Argentina	521	0.3%

TABLE 7.4 LinkedIn AI Job Study: Work Type, April 2024

Work Type Tag	203,985	
On-Site	136,927	**67.1%**
Hybrid	40,619	19.9%
Remote	26,439	13.0%

TABLE 7.5	LinkedIn AI Job Study: Most Common Job Titles, April 2024		
Most Common Job Titles	**279,339**		
Electrical Engineer	74,115	**26.5%**	
Customer Service Representative	72,372	**25.9%**	
Software Engineer	31,070	**11.1%**	
Customer Service Specialist	29,736	**10.6%**	
Data Analyst	28,552	**10.2%**	
Data Scientist	15,256	5.5%	
Data Specialist	7,870	2.8%	
Algorithm Engineer	6,497	2.3%	
Machine Learning Engineer	6,451	2.3%	
Artificial Intelligence Researcher	1,432	0.5%	
Intern (AI)	1,362	0.5%	
Product Engineering Specialist	1,208	0.4%	
Artificial Intelligence Engineer	1,190	0.4%	
Product Manager (AI)	1,046	0.4%	
Director of Artificial Intelligence	629	0.2%	
Manager of Artificial Intelligence	553	0.2%	

As far as job titles, if we throw out the words "Artificial" and "Intelligence," the top typical job titles include the words "Engineer," "Specialist," and "Data." I discard the words "Artificial" and "Intelligence" because I'm looking for what the people would actually do in the job. It's fascinating to see how many customer service and data jobs are out there. If we were designing your career arc via this dataset, we might say that being in the United States and working on data and engineering would be the next steps. A job is one thing, but what about the salary?

AI Job Salaries

How much do these jobs pay? It's a complicated answer because this data is content employers typically want to keep a secret. A note about salary transparency and legislation. Here in the United States, it's more common that employers list a salary range of how much they will compensate the worker in a specific job. Pay transparency is legally required in California, Colorado, Connecticut, Maryland, Nevada, New York, Rhode Island, and Washington state.[4,5] This is becoming more and more common. This is especially important when we note that California and New York are the first and fourth most populous states in the United States, respectively, with Washington state at 13th.[6] I don't recommend you apply to jobs that don't have salary ranges listed. Any company that puts out a job description typically has already allocated a budget to pay the employee. Thus, they have already decided the number they plan to pay you. If they are not willing to post that range publicly, they are showing their hand that they want to low-ball you.

While I love their shows, Netflix is one of the top companies to list a role with a public salary range between $110,000–$440,000. It's outrageous, and so while they're technically sharing a range, it's clear they still want to keep the true number a mystery. Who does this hurt most? Women and BIPOC folks. My advice? Avoid these companies.

Let's look at this subset of AI jobs in the United States. Most are AI jobs based in the United States. They are tagged as Full-Time and either Entry-Level or Mid-Senior Level. Of the jobs that have a salary range tagged, LinkedIn's method is "$40,000+," meaning that the salary range for the given role is at least $40,000 per year in this example. I toggled between all the salary ranges listed and documented the corresponding number of jobs per each subset bucket, shown in Table 7.6. In the Entry-Level job bucket, of the 37,000 jobs listed there, only 11% had a salary tag. Not a great day for salary transparency! Of the 11% of companies that will share a salary range publicly, most say they'd pay more than $40,000/yr. That's hardly a well-paying job with high job security.

In the Mid-Level job bucket, of the 62,000 jobs listed there, 18% had a salary tag. It almost seems like the higher you rise, the more power you have to demand that you need to be paid better and know the employer's salary range. The number with salary tags got murkier for the Mid-Senior Level bucket since many of the salary ranges overlapped.

4 https://www.nerdwallet.com/article/finance/pay-transparency-laws
5 https://www.americanprogress.org/article/quick-facts-about-state-salary-range-transparency-laws
6 https://www.statista.com/statistics/183497/population-in-the-federal-states-of-the-us

---

TABLE 7.6 AI Job Salary Ranges, United States, Full-Time, Entry and Mid-Senior Level, April 2024

United States, Full-Time, Entry Level

Minimum Base Salary Pay Annualized	Number of AI Jobs	
Total Jobs	**37,486**	
Salary Range Transparent	4,232	11.29%
$40,000	656	**15.50%**
$60,000	604	**14.27%**
$80,000	563	13.30%
$100,000	510	12.05%
$120,000	446	10.54%
$140,000	415	9.81%
$160,000	387	9.14%
$180,000	349	8.25%
$200,000	302	7.14%

United States, Full-Time, Mid-Senior Level

Minimum Base Salary Pay Annualized	Number of AI Jobs	
Mid-Senior Level AI Jobs	62,242	
Total Jobs with Salary Data	**11,449**	18.39%
$40,000	3,222	28.14%
$60,000	3,214	28.07%
$80,000	3,178	27.76%
$100,000	3,130	27.34%
$120,000	3,054	26.67%
$140,000	2,958	25.84%
$160,000	2,802	24.47%
$180,000	2,398	20.95%
$200,000	2,173	18.98%

For the Mid-Senior jobs, the salary ranges were all over the place. The percentages don't add up to 100% because of the overlap in salary ranges. If you think this data isn't that clear or easy to read, that's by design. The companies and LinkedIn are fine making things less clear than they could because it is in their best interest. "Just keep applying!" they decree. Always negotiate your salary since you can tell these ranges are dramatic and there is definitely wiggle room for them to pay you more. Most employers want to pay you as little as possible. There are 3.3x more jobs in the Entry-Level section as there are jobs tagged as Mid-Senior Level. The idea that a person could be qualified for a Mid-Senior Level job and be paid between $40,000–60,000 is predatory for the value they bring to a company.

If you really do insist on going for a job in AI, this data would indicate that you bolster your skill sets in data and engineering and work your butt off networking. Will a specific skill set get you a $50,000 salary bump? What could take you to the next level? My gut reaction is getting to know the hiring manager via coffee chats. The landscape is shifting quickly. The only certainty is change. AI jobs researched in this section is that things will continue to grow and morph. I'd be surprised if the same jobs pay these same salaries by 2030.

Projecting from Jobs Today to the Future

From this AI job and salary data, current skill sets of interest are around data and engineering. "So let's get a data engineering certificate!" You might say. Not so fast. I *would* recommend you upskill in your knowledge of AI and data, but will a certificate really get you your job in AI? I'm skeptical. You need to build your network and focus back on that 80% People bucket. We'll talk more about certificates and degrees in the next chapter. I do not believe most professionals need to learn how to code. I code in Python and R. At a World Government Summit in Dubai in 2024, NVIDIA CEO Jensen Huang has publicly stated that people shouldn't learn coding. He says that coding is a skill of the past.[7] Headlines about his provocative statements include "NVIDIA CEO Jensen Huang says you shouldn't learn coding since AI will take your job anyway."[8] He suggests it would be wise for people to prepare for jobs in manufacturing, biology, and farming. I find it hard to take this advice too seriously though, because the current job requirements for jobs at NVIDIA almost all have significant software engineering and coding requirements.[9] This may be a case of "Do as I say, not as I do."

Another way to interpret this is that Jensen is saying most people won't be working at *his* company. That's something I'd believe. He wants NVIDIA to enable folks so that most humans do not *need* to learn how to code. I agree. Most people do not need to learn how to code in the coming next few decades. We will still need to have humans in the loop to debug, but far fewer folks. Are you delighted? Or perhaps you're getting a degree in computer science, and I've just burst your bubble. I've met more and more software engineers who thought their income and job prospects were safe. Now the rug has been ripped out from under their feet. If you're reading this book, though, I'm confident you can make your own roadmap.

Being able to code may help today, but it is NOT the golden ticket to future-proofing your career and income. My hunch is that jobs will be much more task, and project-oriented to pushing innovation forward in different industries. Again, I hope you see the forest through the trees, or the rainbow arc across the lily pads.

Questions for Reflection

Questions for You

- [ ] What are the jobs that excite you? Have you seen an AI job you're really jazzed about?
- [ ] Which companies are hiring for AI talent in your field? What expectations and requirements do they have about salary, location, or your being an on-site or remote employee?

[7] https://www.pcguide.com/news/nvidia-ceo-jensen-huang-says-you-shouldnt-learn-coding-since-ai-will-take-your-job-anyway
[8] https://www.pcguide.com/news/nvidia-ceo-jensen-huang-says-you-shouldnt-learn-coding-since-ai-will-take-your-job-anyway
[9] https://nvidia.wd5.myworkdayjobs.com/NVIDIAExternalCareerSite

- ☐ Do you know how to code? Are you a software engineer? Are you concerned about your job prospects long-term?

- ☐ Do you feel comfortable talking about data and how to use it? What projects and industries do you have experience with or would like to innovate in?

- ☐ Do you believe the AI jobs today will be the same ones as tomorrow? Why or why not?

CHAPTER 8

Actions Speak Louder Than Words: Degrees, Portfolios, and Getting Credit

A t the age of 22, Dorie Clark had the really rotten luck of being laid off on September 10, 2001. After her personal loss, the day she began her new job search was a day of US national tragedy, September 11, 2001. After graduate school, she worked in newspaper journalism, a dying industry. Media was shifting into a digital era. Clark didn't know it yet, but she would build wealth and a big career in the coming digital era.

In 2001, Clark could not find another full-time job in journalism. Clark found freelancing jobs, hustling to find work that paid $400–$800 per week. She then landed a job as a spokesperson in politics, but the candidate she worked for lost in the primary. "No job, I realized, is secure,"[1] she writes in her book *Entrepreneurial You*. Across time, she realized entrepreneurship with multiple revenue streams was a viable path, even if it wasn't her first choice. "I unwillingly became part of the Vanguard of entrepreneurs developing a portfolio career—piecing together freelance work and ultimately starting my own business with various revenue streams."[2]

---

[1] https://dorieclark.com/entrepreneurialyou, p. 8
[2] https://dorieclark.com/entrepreneurialyou, p. 9

Clark launched her business. She worked in marketing strategy consulting. She began by building a portfolio of "social proof." Social proof is external validation that recognizes the "well-established fact that others judge you by your affiliations."[3] She published her work in the *Huffington Post* and the *Harvard Business Review*. And she didn't stop there! She began consulting and speaking for clients such as Google, Microsoft, and World Bank.[4] She cultivated her personal brand and also made the decision to be an openly gay professional. She says it is an "incredible feeling of not hiding anything and being closer and more connected to your colleagues."[5] Her social media presence grew to new heights and so did her social proof.

From articles online to her six bestselling books,[6] Clark also began teaching at universities such as Duke and Columbia. She continued building her reputation and network and adding more and more revenue streams. She wrote in 2017, "Today, I actually earned my living in seven entirely different ways: 1. writing books, 2. speaking, 3. teaching business school, 4. consulting, 5. executive coaching, 6. online courses, and—since that aha moment from my friend John Corcoran—7. affiliate income through my email list. If one of those goes right, I have enough diversification that I don't have to worry. That's a far cry from my position at age 22 when I woke up the day after my layoff wondering how I pay my bills."[7]

Clark is incredibly resilient and so are her revenue streams. While she doesn't share her net worth publicly, Clark says that the years spent writing her book *Entrepreneurial You* has been her most lucrative one to date. She writes, "I grew my income by more than $200,000 that year."[8] She has become a director and investor.[9] Her email newsletter list has more than 71,000 subscribers. Beyond wealth, however, Clark writes that her freedom is one of the most powerful things about her business. Effectively monetizing your expertise is the "path to lasting influence, impact, and freedom."[10]

I find Clark's story a great parallel to that of the AI era. Gosh, her story sounds like mine! She was a journalist who eventually built a media empire via books with robust online revenue streams. All jobs

---

[3] https://dorieclark.com/entrepreneurialyou, p. 25

[4] https://dorieclark.com/about

[5] https://uptime.app/hack/succeeding-as-an-lgbt-professional-dorie-clark

[6] https://dorieclark.com/books

[7] Entrepreneurial You, p. 10

[8] Entrepreneurial You, xiii

[9] https://dorieclark.com/about

[10] Entrepreneurial You, p. 238

will need to grapple with the age of AI and transform in some way. In a book about AI and careers, we are truly seeing these industrial revolutions and media revolutions live out in our careers and the professionals around us. We'll talk more about my income, finances, and how you can grow your wealth in Part 2.

So how can you build your social proof? How can you translate your current skills into something meaningful and impactful that others understand? You need to build anecdotes and a portfolio of work to speak to, no matter where you're coming from.

Your Portfolio: Get Credit for the Work You've Already Done

In the last few chapters, we've talked about focusing on people and growing your network and strengthening your personal brand and storytelling. Pop quiz! What's my people-first career recipe again? "80% People, 15% Projects, and 5% Skills." Clark has a similar recipe! Dori recommends a three-step process: building your brand, monetizing your expertise, and extending your reach and impact online.[11] This section is all about project and skill building, directly informed by coffee chats and the networking you've been doing.

You don't need a polished website. Honing your LinkedIn profile is a great first step. With your precious time and energy, please invest in your LinkedIn profile and email game. In this chapter, we'll talk about projects and skills.

Projects are components of a portfolio of your professional experience. You need to be able to speak to them effectively. They are radiant marble orbs in your magical suitcase. When I asked VP of AI at Rev, Miguel Jetté, on my podcast *Your AI Roadmap* about career advice for listeners, he said, "If you have previous experience, then relevant experience on the projects is usually the first thing I look at. I don't necessarily look at the school you're from. I think that's maybe a secondary bonus thing where I look usually at the experience."

When you talk to people and have discussions back and forth, you can provide an example experience to share! You need to have

---

[11] Entrepreneurial You, p. 14

a strong personal story to share that could connect with people you meet. It's not helpful to come off as long-winded: "Um, I am a recent grad and I've been considering a bootcamp" or "I have been mulling over getting a master's degree." These are interesting directions, but when I ask them the "why" of these actions, many have half-hearted answers. "Isn't that what people want? I guess more experience...." You need to have more conviction in a multiyear direction. It's not the lack of confidence here that's unhelpful; it's the lack of data points and intentionality. It's not the best plan to just rack up degrees hoping that someone notices. Your network will be far more valuable to you.

Get credit for the work you've already done. I find that people give less weight to the projects they've already done. The degrees they already have. Start there! What have you learned? What lit you up inside? I had a friend who spent more than two years saying she hated her job and occasionally would polish a portfolio on a website and then get flustered that she thought it was never good enough. She trapped herself in a vicious cycle. To my knowledge, years later she still has the job she can't stand. Similarly, my friend dreams of working for a company that works on mentorships. But he keeps saying that his "golden handcuffs"[12] at his tech day job are holding him back. He has now worked a job he doesn't like for almost a decade. That's a long time to put your true dreams on hold. But I believe in you! You don't have to get stuck here.

Waiting for your "Cinderella moment" might have you working in rags for a long time. Do you remember the key to Cinderella getting her dreams? It was asking for help. As you and I have explored, the career game is not about collecting skills and hiding them away. It is about people and how you show your skills through projects. I don't want you to get stuck here.

Joan's Hot Take: Ask for Help

> Waiting for your "Cinderella moment" might have you working in rags for a long time. Ask for help.

---

[12] This is the phrase people use when they talk about their high salary and company perks. They feel like they can't leave their job. I don't buy into this mentality. You have agency of your own life. It also means typically they've played into lifestyle creep. Just because you have a high salary and a fancy job title does not mean that you are satisfied and have meaningful work that pays the bills. Beware of complacency. **https://www.merriam-webster.com/dictionary/golden%20handcuffs**

"I need a fancy website!" and "I need two more college degrees!" are common pieces of pushback Rachel Rodgers hears when people bluster before their next professional steps. Her response? "Eliminate all the fictitious obstacles."[13] I agree. Let's eliminate this clutter of fictitious obstacles and get you to living your goals and dreams. Let's get you some clarity and organization. We want you to be ready for these coffee meetings by saying, "Here's what I've done, where I'm headed, and the help I'd love from you, please."

Get Organized and Intentional

Who better to get advice about getting organized from than Marie Kondo? Marie is the famous creator of the KonMari method also called "Tidying Up."[14] Her three books on the topic have sold more than 11 million copies, and her Netflix show was so popular that it led to a 372% increase in Goodwill donations in certain parts of the United States.[15] While she might be a polarizing figure, there is a large amount of wisdom to her method. The KonMari method identifies what in your life brings you joy and focus on. The rest you thank and let go of. I was especially touched by an episode about a couple struggling with their lives and marriage while raising toddlers. On one horrifying occasion, Marie finds the couple's wedding photos from years that they had procrastinated on putting up. The wedding photos were literally found under a pile of household garbage.[16] Ooof, talk about a metaphor! By the end of the episode, the couple recentered their relationship emotionally and moved their wedding photos into a prominent place in the home. The solution was to take out the emotional and literal garbage. We also need to be more intentional and centered on what is important to us.

Many of us lack this rigor. I want you to find joy and meaning in your life. Ideally, both personally and professionally. When you share your

[13] *We Should All Be Millionaires*, p. 233–234
[14] https://konmari.com/about-marie-kondo
[15] https://www.washingtonpost.com/lifestyle/home/the-tidying-tide-marie-kondo-effect-hits-sock-drawers-and-consignment-stores/2019/01/10/234e0b62-1378-11e9-803c-4ef28312c8b9_story.html
[16] https://variety.com/2018/tv/reviews/tidying-up-with-marie-kondo-review-netflix-1203095107/#!

work with others, you need to get clear on what is powerful and impactful from your previous projects. Let go of your imposter syndrome of perfectionistic polishing. Share where you've been. To get to the clear goals you set in Chapter 14, I want you to be set up well to share your professional history with impact and gusto. I recommend the STAR method.

The STAR Method: Project Storytelling

What's a strong way to tell the story of work you did and its impact? When talking and writing about your work in professional settings, I recommend you leverage the STAR method.[17] "Make something, learn how to tell a story about that. Try to really bring to the fore what the impact of this thing is," says Daniel Robbins, principal designer at Adobe, on the *Your AI Roadmap* podcast.

In the next section, we talk about how you discuss your accolades and get credit for the work you've already done. The acronym stands for Situation, Task, Action, Result. Let's look at an example of the STAR method with Clark's story:

Situation: Clark needs to pay her bills after a layoff.

Task: Clark looks for a job but then decides to go into entrepreneurship.

Action: Clark builds a portfolio of social proof and monetizes them. She leverages her experience as a journalist and through freelance work. She starts her own company leveraging her marketing and branding skills. She began publishing in top-tier publications such as *Harvard Business Review*. She gets paid to speak and give keynotes. She writes six books. She consults and teaches. She launches an online course and email newsletter with affiliate commissions.

Result: Clark built significant social proof. She has seven diversified income streams. She makes $200,000+ per year. She has more independence and a future-proofed career and income.

What is crucial about the STAR method is the storytelling as well as the numbers measuring how the actions led to a result. The "Result" needs numbers and external validation. It is a storytelling arc like a corporate version of the hero's story!

---

[17] **https://builtin.com/articles/star-method**

While building my nonprofit Women in Voice, here's a STAR method version of my story:

Situation: At international conferences and prestigious tech laboratories, I experienced spaces where there were few women. Women were not well-respected or represented.

Task: I launched a Twitter handle in 2018 for @WomenInVoice.[18]

Action: I tweeted about asking people to sign up for leadership positions with a Google form link. See Figure 8.1. Twenty-seven people signed up for leadership positions. By 2020 there were more than 20 chapters internationally. I and my COO filed 501(c)(3) paperwork with the US government.

Result: Women in Voice became an approved 501(c)(3). Across three years, the Women in Voice team has raised $500,000 from sponsors such as Google and Amazon for collaborative projects such as a Summit and female founder pitch events. Internationally, more than 150 events in-person, hybrid, and online have been held by the 100+ Women in Voice ambassadors.

FIGURE 8.1   @WomenInVoice tweet calling for leadership on a Google form in 2018[19]

[18] This parallels Aliza Licht's Personal Brand story of the Twitter handle from Chapter 5! It was such an impactful platform to many of us as we invested in our brands and professional storytelling.
[19] https://x.com/WomenInVoice/status/1034104948894527488

You've now seen Clark's example and mine. What is your version? No matter how small a story, write one of your life stories in the following STAR method framework.

What kind of stories and tangible evidence could you provide as you tell your professional story? Pick one of your accomplishments you are most proud of. What was the situation of the story if you're telling it to someone new? What was the hurdle? What made it hard that you had to specifically do yourself? What action did you take? What was the result? How can you measure the result? Are there numbers or quotes you can use to demonstrate validation that could connect with someone else?

Try it:

Situation: _____

Task: _____

Action: _____

Result: _____

The STAR method is commonly used in interviews and also applies to your whole professional life.

Get Credit, Get Proof

As you consider how to chart out your career path, you'll need tangible evidence that demonstrates the actions and results of your work. As I mentioned in the networking advice list in Chapter 4, I strongly recommend you post on social media "before, during, and after" a networking event. The common phrase related to the imagery-first platform Instagram, "Pics or it didn't happen," applies here.[20] When you are building your credibility, make sure there are photos of your work, photos of you accepting an award, and posts documenting your work. You need a portfolio of work that shows that you're not just talking; you take action that leads places. This could be as simple as how you talk about

---

[20] https://www.theguardian.com/news/2015/feb/26/pics-or-it-didnt-happen-mantra-instagram-era-facebook-twitter

your work, it could be three LinkedIn posts that you tag to your featured section, and it could be a website showcasing work. Spend only as much time as is helpful and supported by the people you meet at coffee intros. If no one cares about looking at your website, don't give that time at this point. I often recommend to people I talk to about careers to have a "Brag Sheet" of their biggest accomplishments they can read to themselves. This is a list with the accomplishments clearly in the STAR method in bullet points.[21]

Take the Next (Small) Steps: Prototyping

I recommend taking small steps and prototyping as you build your portfolio. When you look at a cool job, you might have the urge to jump into the deep end saying, "Okay, I need to get that advanced certificate," "I'm going to pay for a $14,000 bootcamp to become a data engineer," or "Wow, I guess I need to get a PhD." Not necessarily! That's a big jump. That could take years and incur six figures of debt! How about we start with a smaller step?

Let's prototype. Let's validate your next steps down the path. Can we get some early indication that this path is for you? Is it worth years and massive student debt? "Prototyping is a great way of dipping your toe in the water and trying something out before diving in head first."[22] Prototyping is something between all and nothing. The word comes from making a draft, like a small architectural diagram instead of breaking ground on building the skyscraper. Similarly, instead of jumping into a robotics PhD or wishing you knew what to do and instead watching dog videos on TikTok, what about doing a small project on robotics and getting feedback from people in the field? How about we take some small action steps to confirm that this really is the path you want to spend money and years of time on? This is prototyping. You test out going

---

[21] This is a product we now sell: **YourAIRoadmap.com/Career**.
[22] **https://www.uxmatters.com/mt/archives/2020/02/designing-your-life-using-design-thinking.php**

down the path of one option. Prototyping takes the form of talking and listening or experiencing through hands-on work.[23]

Prototyping can look like any of these:

- **Coffee:** Go on 50 coffee meetings with people who have your "dream job."
- **Friendship:** Talk to your closest friends about what strength they see in you and whether the things you are pursuing match the goals you frequently talk about. Listen to their feedback about how you could improve and grow and what might be the things you let hold you back. If they are your true friends, they will want the best for you.
- **Hackathon:** Participate in a hackathon where people are building small projects in a domain.
- **Write:** Write a blog or LinkedIn post about exploring a field and sharing your insights.
- **Conference:** Go to a conference and set goals for yourself of who you'd like to meet and which sessions to attend.
- **Library:** Go to the local library and see what resources they have. Do they have free classes for people upskilling?
- **Podcast:** Listen to some podcasts from experts in the field.
- **Books:** Read books from experts in the field.
- **Consulting:** Get a consulting gig to do a small project for a company in that field.
- **Shadowing:** Request to shadow someone at work for a day to see if you find the work environment interesting.
- **Internship:** Apply or request an internship with the luminary you admire. Apply to an internship and write a compelling letter of what you bring to the table.
- **Attend:** Attend a lecture at the local university.
- **Learn:** Watch acclaimed documentaries and YouTube courses on the topic.

---

[23] https://www.creativelive.com/class/designing-your-life-how-to-build-a-well-lived-joyful-life-bill-burnett-dave-evans/lessons/intro-to-prototyping

- **Newsletters:** Sign up for newsletters from influencers in a certain domain.
- **Follow:** Follow companies online that you respect in the spaces you are interested in. Check out their LinkedIn, website, and other social media handles. Sign up for their newsletter if they have one. Begin commenting and reaching out to people who work there.
- **Market Research:** Research salaries in the domain you are considering going into.[24]

The ideal prototyping includes a smattering of several of these options. Prototyping needs to be cheap, quick, and relatively painless.[25] What is something between *all* and *nothing*?

Joan's Hot Take: Between All and Nothing

What is something between *all* and *nothing*? Tons! Ask yourself this often. I sure do!

What is something between throwing yourself into a path to get a PhD versus sitting at home playing with your cat? There is typically plenty of exploration and play that you can explore. It doesn't have to be overly expensive or arduous. If you are a student or low on cash, ask for a student discount or if there are volunteer opportunities to work for admission. It is frequently worth asking. I've gotten discounts when people needed more hands on deck.

Prototyping can significantly help you clarify your direction. You also need to listen carefully and hear the common threads in the resources. Does it map to one of your current skill sets? Could one of your hackathon projects be the key to unlocking deeper conversations at coffee intros? All of these will help you as you tell your story and that people know you're taking this whole career thing seriously.

---

[24] We'll talk more about money in Part 2 of this book.
[25] https://designingyour.life/insights/how-to-prototype-life-designs

The Stories We Tell: The STAR and WOOP Methods

We've been discussing the STAR method and prototyping; now we need to map it onto our broader goals. We want our professional stories (STAR method) to serve us on our way to our broader goals. You might also be thinking, "Wait a minute, which method? All the methods and recipes! My head is spinning!" Valid. Let's regroup. The WOOP method is your internal mindset, goals, hurdles, and motivations toward your goals. The STAR method is a curated story that you tell other people. The WOOP method is how you start, and the STAR method is how you talk about it after the work has been done. These things are connected, but they are not the same.

Let's look back at our draft WOOP about getting a job in AI from Chapter 2. Let's say your WOOP is "How do I get a job in AI?" Here's a WOOP internal version to achieve that goal. Let's expand and refine it based on the chapters in Part 2 of this book:

Wish: Get a job in AI.[26]

Outcome: Have a job title and project work in AI. Get paid to do this job.

Obstacles: When we review the obstacles, remember my People-First Career Building: The 80% People, 15% Projects, and 5% Skills Recipe. Let's unpack common obstacles.

- *Mindset about networking*: "I can't stand networking and have some fears" are feelings and mindset shifts you'll need to make. Pivot to "Networking is a powerful skill that can take me to incredible places in my career and is backed by a huge amount of data. I need to improve in this skill set and get support from others."

- *Personal brand*: I need to hone my brand and be intentional about how I show up online.

- *Network*: I need to grow my network in AI, since that's the real way to land the job and build a career I love. I am not yet known by people in the field who I admire and would love to work with.

---

[26] This is simply an example. This goal assumes you don't yet work in AI. You might already! I'm not a mind reader. Work with me here!

- *Projects*: I need to prototype and show my project work. I may need new skills that align.
- *Storytelling*: I need to own my story and professional brand.
- *Skills*: Learn if I need to hone skills I don't yet have, only spend 5% of time on this.

Plan:

- *Personal brand*: Build a personal brand. Take time to think seriously about how you show up online. Update your LinkedIn banner, headshot, and headline if necessary. I'd especially make sure to spend time on this *before* a big networking event

- *Prototype*: Start down a specific path and test the waters. Does it feel right to you? Instead of jumping in the deep end, what are smaller steps you could take to feel validated in this next direction?

- *Strengthen professional network*:
  - Set up a spreadsheet with 50–100 names of people to ask for informational interviews, and be fine with people saying now isn't a good time or not responding; they won't be your advocates anyway. Yes, I really do mean 50–100 people.
  - Go to 10 networking events in the next 8 months; find ones online, near you, and in the dream location where you'd like to live.

- *Follow up and feedback:*
  - Learn from the people you meet! Follow up with emails and LinkedIn messages to folks who were kind enough to give you their time.
  - Write down the resources they recommend and read them.
  - Follow up with introductions. If they said they were willing to connect you to someone else, provide a sample email copy for the connecting messages. Make it as easy as possible for them to connect you to the rando that could change your life.

- *Take feedback and educate yourself:*
  - If everyone is giving you the feedback that you need more experience with something, take the note.
  - Document the skills you don't have yet and see if they are worth your time to learn during this intense job hunting process.

- *Show, not tell:*
  - Take photos of your work and display them prominently on your LinkedIn profile. This is not a time to start projects from scratch.
  - Take credit for the work you've *already* done even if it's in a different field. What impressive work can you share that may need a cover to the work? An image from one of your graphs? An illustrative quote from one of your survey participants?
  - Organize projects that demonstrate valuable skill sets that you can share widely on social media and with your network; leverage the second-degree connections in your network to get the job.

After you've documented your obstacles and plan, know that this exercise is backed up by robust clinical research. You've got this! Okay, now let's imagine that you've already made it. Tell the story with the STAR method as though it's five years from now. I'll take some liberties to add some sparkles of details that may or may not fit your goals.

Situation: I had a goal to get a job in AI. Specifically, I wanted to go into AI for manufacturing because I took the advice of NVIDIA CEO Jensen Huang.

Task: I read *Your AI Roadmap* and did the exercises. I got data-driven advice on how to actually land the job in AI from someone who works in AI.

Action:

- *Personal brand*: I built a personal brand on LinkedIn and in my professional community and posted twice a week about innovations in the AI, data, and manufacturing space. I grew my network and found people I enjoyed spending time with who were also lit up by the opportunities in our field.
- *Build network*: I made connections in the manufacturing space by asking for introductions and going on coffee intros.
- *Prototype*: I validated that this was the right path for me by doing a project on nights and weekends. I got paid $8,000 to do a small consulting project to test an AI tool at a manufacturing company 15 minutes from my apartment.
- *AI job*: After I worked with the manufacturing company, they made me an offer to take a job there. I'd been sharing my story

of this consulting project with people at networking events and got another job offer at another firm. I considered both AI jobs I was jazzed about and negotiated with my favorite one for a 15% higher salary.

Result:

- o I learned by doing. I took a job in AI that I enjoy and get paid to do. I have built my network substantially and also validated my interest in the space.
- o I found opportunities by getting to know people and building projects that paid.
- o I continue to post on LinkedIn. I help others join the AI manufacturing field.
- o I give back and now support others who are prototyping by taking coffee meetings when my schedule allows.

Voilà! You've now seen how the STAR method and WOOP method connect. As you can see from this example, the whole process of goal setting, taking action, and telling your story to others is a flywheel. Once you complete a goal, you might realize you have new ones! You will keep learning and growing across your lifespan. You'll continue to hone, refine, own, and evolve your story and network. As you do this leaping around as the frog on the lily pads, I hope you see the rainbow arching overhead as the broader career path continues.

Your Personal Brand 101 Course

Before this book came out, my team created a course to help people upgrade their personal brands. You can follow all the steps outlined in this book and create your own roadmap for your path through the age of AI. In addition to the advice from this book, our course Your Personal Brand 101: From Invisible to Valued walks you step-by-step through many of the frameworks in this book. There are printable templates, fillable spreadsheet forms, sample copy for LinkedIn messages (redacted from messages I've sent!), and checklists for how to make an excellent LinkedIn profile. These tactics have worked for me and recent customers who said, "I revamped my profile and started seeing results in a few days" and "Great lessons, powerful messages, and excellent worksheets to hone how to personally show up." Learn more at **https://YourAIRoadmap.com/Courses**.

Okay, that was a huge amount of information. Let's review these data-driven steps to future-proof your career.

Recap of Future-Proofing Your Career Steps

In the last few chapters, we covered the following 10 steps of Your AI Roadmap to future-proofing your career:

- Resilience, Mindset, and Thought Work
- Goal Setting: WOOP Method
- Job vs. Career, Paycheck vs. Income
- 80% of Effort on Networking and People
- Professional Glow-Up and Personal Brand
- Own Your Story and Sharing It
- Mapping Your Work to AI Jobs (If You Want)
- Professional Stories and Getting Credit with the STAR Method
- Taking the Next Small Steps: Prototyping
- Get Ready to Talk about Money

That's your AI Roadmap for careers! Next, let's cover the finance side of your future-proofing journey.

Ready to Talk Money?

But wait! There's more to this book! Many books end here, but not this one. We're going to talk about money! As I've said from the jump, a job in any field is not secure these days. I want to make sure you have a plan for financial stability like Arlan Hamilton, now the millionaire investor who previously lived on food stamps.

We will talk about future-proofing your income. In this book, we'll talk transparently about finances, income streams, alternatives to the 9 to 5, confidence of having your own money in your own name, and how your income can expand far beyond a paycheck. Join me in Part 2, where we will discuss income and make sure that your income is future-proofed!

Questions for Reflection

Questions for You

- ☐ Do you resonate with Clark's story about getting laid off? When have you been challenged and it provided great insights?
- ☐ What things are you proud of? How do you talk about them professionally?
- ☐ Have you heard of the STAR method? How can you use external validation and numbers to bolster the strength of the story in professional settings?
- ☐ Have you heard of prototyping? What items in the prototyping example list resonated with you? Which are ones you haven't tried that might be fruitful?

Download resources from this book at **YourAIRoadmap.com/ Resources** or scan this QR code.

PART 2

Beyond the Day Job: Future-Proofing Your Income and Entrepreneurship

"Monetize Your Expertise, Create Multiple Income Streams, and Thrive"

—Dorie Clark, Entrepreneurial You, 2017

"Today, more than ever before, winning at wealth requires you to know when you're winning and how to position yourself to quit while you're ahead."

—Julien and Kiersten Saunders, Cashing Out: Win the Wealth Game by Walking Away, 2022

CHAPTER 9

B*tch Better Have My Money: Beyond the 9 to 5, Finances, and My 22 Income Streams

You will never be truly free, stable, and at peace until your financial house is in order. A pesky truth of the age of AI is that everyone's day job is at risk, but we all still need money. As the field of AI automates and eliminates many jobs in the next few years, jumping from job to job won't future-proof your income and provide stability. You need to have your own money, in your own name, in your own accounts. In the first section of the book, we talked about how to future-proof your career. In this section, we will talk about future-proofing your income by knowing, growing, and being in control of your wealth. This may be the longest chapter in the book, and my guess is that it might become one of your favorites. I'm darn transparent about my wealth! Here are two stories to illustrate how careers and income are interwoven but also separate.

Let me tell you about my friend Sharon. Confident, ambitious, and vibrant, Sharon has been climbing the corporate ladder for years. Working at glitzy companies you know the names of, she has closed $100+ million deals and now has a C-level title. Network and personal brand? Oh yes, Sharon's got them. Her LinkedIn profile is a work of art. She posts regularly about her amazing projects and conferences. She works hard, works fast, and has cultivated a huge network. She knows everyone in her industry and is well respected. I know and really adore my ambitious friend.

What about her finances? She has told me. Sharon's salary is $1.3 million per year. But here's the kicker. She makes $1.3 million and has been making this type of robust money for years, but she spends it. Her financial portfolio isn't secure. When she was telling me recently about really wanting to leave her current company, I asked her, "Instead of another job, could you retire at this point?" Her face went blank. "No, definitely not," she responded.

Between you and me, I do not know how she spends all that money yearly, but that's her personal choice. From her personal brand, you'd think that Sharon has it all. But the fact that she doesn't yet have her financial house in order prevents her from the full freedom and agency she craves in her career. Like Sharon, I wish you tons of career success and a robust income. We also need to talk about finances so you can have a future-proofed income. Now let me share a story about money and Trader Joe's cheese.

Groceries and Trader Joe's Cheese

As I started grad school in California, I was horrified to learn that my paycheck did not cover my rent and groceries. I did the math about how much money I got in my paycheck and how much money my rent was and calculated how much my groceries were be per month. If the overall cost of my groceries was too high at the checkout, I'd need to remove items and not purchase them. It was embarrassing at the Trader Joe's checkout to begin removing cheese and chocolate from my cart. Not the cheese! I felt hot waves of shame wash over my face as other patrons waited in the line behind me. I love Trader Joe's cheese.[1] After this happened, I knew something had to change.

What was my plan? I decided to increase my income. For context, I was a hardworking graduate student. I was investing heavily in myself, my education, my career, and my future. I taught at the university, took on a full-time slate of graduate coursework, conducted

---

[1] Try the Trader Joe's Unexpected Cheddar and thank me later.

individual research projects, and overall worked at least 60 hours per week. As an adult, I was off my parents' healthcare plan. I was financially dependent on my paycheck for all my bills. California is not a cheap place to live. Having three roommates and living frugally wasn't enough. Working hard wasn't enough. My paycheck didn't cover the basic costs of living. A single paycheck wasn't enough.

Income Expansion and Revenue Streams

So what did I do? I posted on Craigslist about being a French tutor.[2] I had a BA in French and had just moved back from a year working in France. I put out an offer, explained that I was a graduate student, that I had just been working in France, that I'd done tutoring before, and that I charged $40/hr. It was simple. It was effective. I got multiple inquiries. I then took on three students per week. One was a high schooler who needed homework support, another was a French-speaking family who wanted me to speak with their kids, and the last was a retiree preparing for a trip to France looking for a conversational partner. My students paid in cash or checks. That money went straight into groceries. In addition to tutoring, I let people know I was available for jobs. I walked dogs and did dog sitting. I was briefly an after-school nanny for a family. After that, I had money to buy my beloved cheeses and chocolate! Huzzah!

Soon enough, I found gigs that paid better and better. I found a gig at the Graduate Student Association on campus. It paid $500/month as the public relations officer to do marketing, host events, and write fancy emails to provosts. My friend referred me, I applied, and I got the gig. My grocery budget was now more secure for years! I then cut some of my least favorite tutoring students. Extra bonus! With more money, you can make different types of decisions for yourself and your life.

My Three-Part Financial Freedom Recipe

1. *Know* your finances.

2. *Grow* your income streams.

3. *Be in control* of your finances.

---

[2] See the text I used in this successful tutoring post at **YourAIRoadmap.com/CraiglistPost**.

Delicious. Scrumptious! While the recipe might seem daunting now, I'm confident that if you read the rest of this book, you'll be well on your way to having the financial freedom of your dreams. This is the step-by-step recipe I recommend for you to future-proof your income through the age of AI and beyond.

My example of putting out a simple offer and getting customers is the formula we talk more about as you boost your income and increase your number of revenue streams. I'd love your finances to not induce fear but instead enable the life you envision for yourself. When you have more money, you also have more choices about *who* you want to work with rather than living in desperation. I learned from these experiences that I could expand my income.

Looking for how to future-proof your income? My answer: income stream expansion and entrepreneurship. In the age of AI and a world of regular layoffs, we all need to future-proof our incomes. I've shared with you that I've been in AI layoffs. It hurts! It's becoming common as you saw from the data in the introduction. We need to be thinking outside the 9 to 5 job and a single paycheck. If I had stayed with only one paycheck and income stream back in grad school in California, I would have had to watch my grocery budget like a hawk. I would not have been able to eat what I wanted. Just one job and a single paycheck is risky. "The old model, the one that most of us grew up hearing about—'work hard, get a job, and you'll be rewarded'—has changed" writes Dorie Clark.[3] "Common wisdom tells us that we should diversify our investment portfolios because it's foolish to put all our money in one stock. But we're far less careful on the other end. Too many of us rely on one employer for our entire sustenance, just as I once did."[4]

Joan's Hot Take: Single-Paycheck Life Is Risky

Only one job and paycheck is risky. Being laid off in a day is possible. You need more options on how to make money. To future-proof your income, you need multiple income streams.

So, let's talk about income. In this section of this book, we explore *how* to future-proof your income. We talk about what

---

[3] **https://dorieclark.com/entrepreneurialyou**, p. 9
[4] **https://dorieclark.com/entrepreneurialyou**, p. 7

income is, how money can be strategically used for short- and long-term goals, and wealth expansion overall. You can hit your financial independence goals and ride out the volatility of the age of AI and beyond, regardless of layoffs and unstable day jobs. My goal for this section is to share a *broad* overview of personal finance and how you can grow your income to be resilient through the age of AI.[5] My guess is that if you're here reading this, you have a desire to learn more about wealth and recommendations. We cover how to future-proof your income by knowing, growing, and being in control of your wealth and income.

Topics out of scope for this section include how to raise venture capital funding, how to create a strong pitch deck, how to build a venture capital fund, and how to become an angel investor.[6] Additionally, it does not include how to do illegal things that could make you money but could also land you in jail, how to form or get involved in multilevel marketing schemes (MLMs), how to become a cult leader,[7] and other weird things I don't recommend. Are there other ways to make money than ways I recommend? Totally! These are my best, broad recommendations for you. A question I often get online or at conferences is "Joan, how do I use AI to make money?" As I mentioned in the FAQ section, AI doesn't make money in any legal ways I've found. You absolutely can use AI to help you make and monetize something. You can leverage an AI tool to make your sales more profitable. You can build AI tools and sell them. AI can enable and speed up routes to your goals. Ultimately, you will still need to monetize whatever it is you do. That's why I focus on income growth and monetization in the next few chapters. Overall, let's put these things aside for the moment and talk about money.

As someone who is rooting for you, I have your best interests at heart. A financial education is invaluable. The insights I share with you have changed my life for the better. For this chapter, I share with you my best financial advice as if you and I were besties. I hope this book and chapter can bring you clarity as you shape the future of your finances. Anyone can build wealth. Let's talk about money.

---

[5] Note that this is not intended to be a definitive resource guide. It is detailed. I wish I'd had this as a teenager.

[6] Want to learn more about investors, venture capitalists, angel investing, and pitch decks? Let me know. :)

[7] This list is meant to be jokes, clearly.

My 3-Part Financial Freedom Recipe: Know, Grow, and Be in Control

In this section, we go over my more detailed financial recommendations for you. This is how I set up my own finances and how I talk with my friends about money. While some of these items span more than one category, I've listed them in order of priority. Let's review my 3-Part Financial Freedom Recipe: 1. Know. 2. Grow, and 3: Be in Control of Your Full Financial Portfolio:

1. **Know**
   - **Overall Financial Picture**: Know your financial picture: Where is your money coming from and going? When does money hit your account? How is your cash flow (money in and out and when)?
   - **Emergency Fund**: You'll need 6–12 months of an emergency fund for living expenses parked in a high-yield savings account (HYSA). Know how much your basic living expenses are and be prepared to weather a storm—for example, layoff, pandemic, illness, etc. Some people recommend 3–6 months. With such a bad job market, I recommend having a larger number of reserves ready to go.

2. **Grow**
   - **Expand Your Money**: Instead of scrimping and squeezing, expand your income and number of income streams. There's only so small and scrappy your budget can go. You need food, rent, and medical insurance. If you're anything like me, money is a tool you're excited to use! You'll be more confident bringing bigger dollar signs in the door and knowing how to use them effectively.
   - **Retirement Goals and Financial Independence**: How much money do you need to retire? What's that number? What's your plan to get to that number? Based on my lifestyle here in Seattle, that number is around $2.5 million, and I track my steps to get there. While that may sound like a lot of money, the concept of retirement is to pay for the last third of your life. You may not be in good health and may need lots of support. This number needs to cover all your expenses. We'll talk more about financial independence and how to calculate your numbers later.

- **Risk Management**: Put 90–95% of your money in boring financial accounts like exchange-traded funds (ETFs), 401ks, IRAs, and diversified stocks and bonds. Put the other 5–10% in higher risk but higher return potential accounts such as individual stocks and startup investments. My portfolio is roughly 6% in high-risk startup investments. These are high risk and potentially high reward! Many of the startups in my portfolio are doing great! I could lose the investment in them, but they could get me huge returns such as 300%–1,000% in 5–20 years.

3. Be in Control

- **Money Review**: I review my money for my business daily and my personal finances twice per month. I set aside time on my calendar to make sure all things are going smoothly and check if I'm on track with my goals. Sometimes I find I'm ahead of my goals, and sometimes I find a glitch that needs to be fixed. Instead of letting anxiety boil up, I check my money regularly and am in control of it.[8]

- **Life Insurance and Wills**: If others depend on you and your income, it's time to look into life insurance in case you pass unexpectedly. Today, there are modern online tools to get life insurance quotes. I got my will done online for $300 in an hour. You need these documents up-to-date and to cover you and your family in case of an unexpected early death. Your money could be in limbo for 12–18 months and not fully go to your family if you don't have a will properly set up. This is especially important if you have a mortgage and are a parent or caregiver.

- **Password Manager**: Boring but important, my family and I use a password manager. Instead of sharing passwords to accounts via DM and screenshots, we can access important files for each other. All my online financial accounts are easy to access, shared with the right folks, and have secure long passwords that are better protected from phishing and cyberattacks.

---

[8] For any *Schitt's Creek* fans out there, this is what the family didn't do! While the family became billionaires, they did not check on their finances regularly. Only too late, they realize that one of their employees was embezzling their funds! Don't lose your wealth like this! Make your money and still check on it. https://collider.com/schitts-creek-underrated-comedy, https://web.archive.org/web/20200416231620, https://o.canada.com/entertainment/cbc-schitts-creek

Which tools and companies do I use? They can all be found at **https://YourAIRoadmap.com/Money-Tools**. Many recommendations from my list may look familiar to you. Some may be new. Do you agree with my recommendations? Just like mine, your personal finances are personal. In this book's introduction, I shared with you about privilege. Everyone is different and starts at a different financial place and knowledge background.

In this chapter, we'll work on the "know" part of my recommendations. Coming up, I share my 22 income streams (Wow, there were more than even I thought!), address the "taboo" of talking about money and who it serves (spoiler, probably not you!), U.S. census data about huge pay inequities, dreams about wealth and future-proofed incomes, and the concept of universal basic income.

Let's talk about those income streams. *Income stream* is a fancy way of saying how money is coming to you. A stream of income. Imagine several water sources all going into a huge rain barrel. In Chapter 8, we learned that Dorie Clark has seven income streams. I share my income streams in the next section. I hope this book expands your mind and your own plans for your income streams.

Please remember, I am not a certified wealth planner. There is a financial legal disclaimer at the beginning of this book for a reason. Do your homework. There is roughly a 99.99% chance I will get trolls on social media for speaking about money. I've fretted about sharing my numbers so publicly because many influencers I follow are careful not to publicly share these things.

However, I am writing this book for you, my dear reader. I believe in my heart that you have wild and fabulous ambition. I believe that having someone in your corner who is transparent, clear, and data-driven about finances and wealth building could be immensely helpful. It certainly has been life changing for me! Men and women have shared their financial advice with me, and when I asked how they learned it, they said they read a lot of boring materials and got advice from senior men around them. This matches my experience also. To be clear: I'm not satisfied to know about ways to become wealthy myself. Everyone deserves a financial education and to know that through the age of AI they can take care of themselves. Living into my values, if I don't share the knowledge with you and am complicit in gatekeeping, I'm not living into my values, and I'm repeating gatekeeping cycles all over again.

Let's talk more about financial advice and income streams! Of course, also do your homework. If you have other fabulous legal and ethical recommendations not listed here, feel free to share them with me![9] Okay, here are my income streams.

My 22 Income Streams

These are my 22 income streams across the last few years that I also plan to expand:[10]

1. **W-2 Income**: W-2 contracts are typically for full-time jobs. This is also called a "base salary."

2. **Equity**: Working for companies as an advisor or employee, I have gotten equity in the private company. I've signed equity terms between 0.2%–2.5%. This equity vests across a period of time, typically vesting 25% every year across four years, i.e., 0.625% every four years up to 2.5%. *Vest* means that I get that chunk of equity in that time frame. Typically, companies want to keep me around. They could grant me stock when we sign a contract, but what if I leave in a few months? Vesting schedules can be a mutually beneficial way to keep me working on projects across time. If I have 2.5% stock in a company that sells for $150 million, my payout would be around $3.75 million before taxes.

3. **Signing Bonus**: A signing bonus is an amount of money companies give you as an incentive and celebration for signing a contract. I've seen plenty of signing bonuses $3,000–50,000+. For bigger companies, signing bonuses can be in the millions.

4. **Company Bonuses**: If the company is doing well and there are annual bonuses, they can be paid out to you on a quarterly, project-based, or annual basis. This might be 2% to 30% of your base salary.

5. **Advisory Fees**: If I sign paperwork with a startup and help them along their journey, I can get advisory fees. Typically, this is in the form of cash or equity. Payouts in cash can be $400, $3,000, or $600,000 depending on the stage of the company and the escalatory nature of support. I have also negotiated equity as an advisor to pair with the advisory fees of 0.1% to 2.5%.

---

[9] The email for my team is **hello@hireclarity.ai**.
[10] You might notice I don't give exact numbers for each category. I'm sharing with you what I feel comfortable sharing. As I grow my wealth, the numbers change. The concept is you see that you could grow your income streams. *Voilà!*

6. **1099 Income**: 1099 contracts are for shorter and part-time work such as consulting, advising, and project work. I've been paid as little as $100 and as much as $17,000/month on 1099 contracts.

7. **Business Ownership**: As the sole owner of my business, the profits of the company are mine. The bulk of my wealth today comes from items 1–7 on this income stream list.

8. **Severance**: When my employment has been cut, I've been given a small amount of money.

9. **Book Deal**: I signed a book deal and got an advance for this book. I also get a negotiated percentage of revenue from book sales.

10. **Public Speaking**: I have been paid to speak at events, for example from $100 to $33,000.

11. **Influencer Sponsored Post**: I have been paid to post to my followers. I posted the content. I included a disclaimer that it was a sponsored post. The company paid me a few hundred dollars.

12. **Digital Products**: People pay me for digital products such as PDFs.

13. **Courses and Workshops**: I teach paid courses, workshops, and bootcamps, i.e., Your AI Bootcamp.

14. **Affiliate Commissions**: Some of my social media posts and website links provide me affiliate commissions when people buy using the link. It's a way for them to pay me back for vouching for their good product.

15. **Buy and Sell Small Items**: As a thrifty person, I buy and sell items on sites like Craigslist and OfferUp for an average price of $20. I can sell clippings of my plants and that old lamp I don't use. This doesn't rake in serious cash, but it's enough to cover sushi and pizza once in a while!

16. **Intergenerational Wealth**: As mentioned before, my parents and grandparents have supported me financially in various ways. This includes my parents paying my undergrad tuition and living expenses, paying for vacations, letting me live in the basement during transition moments, and my grandparents and parents giving me gifts such as on birthdays, holidays, and other milestones. From talking to my parents and relatives, it appears that this type of support has been consistent across the last four generations on both sides of my family.

17. **HYSA Interest**: High yield savings accounts (HYSAs) are modern savings accounts that regularly pay you large interest to keep your

liquid cash (aka easy to access money). My account currently pays me 4.6% APY.[11] I have seen rates as high as 5% APY at different companies. I can get paid $600 monthly from an emergency fund sitting in an HYSA.

18. **Real Estate**: I own real estate. It is growing in value, at an estimated 5% to 13% year over year appreciation (increasing in value), which outpaces my mortgage interest rate of 3%. I list it as an income stream because it already has increased hundreds of thousands of dollars in value and I may one day rent it.

19. **Stock Portfolio**: I have money in stocks, index funds, and ETFs.[12] Examples of stocks are E.L.F. Beauty (ELF) and NVIDIA (NVDA) for individual stocks and Vanguard S&P 500 ETF (VOO) for ETFs. My money in certain portfolios has increased 35% in one year. Be sure to watch out for expense ratios of what sliver of a percentage they are taking of your money. Is it 0.04%? 0.43? It is important to compare the fine print. Overall, be sure to invest!

20. **Bond Portfolio**: I have money in bonds that align with my values and balance out my overall stock and bond portfolio. Historically, bonds are less risky but currently are performing terribly. I currently have a 90% stock to 10% bond ratio. This ratio depends on your risk tolerance as historically stocks have higher risk and higher reward. Traditional advice recommends having a higher ratio of bonds as you get closer to retirement.

21. **IRAs: Traditional, Roth, and SEP IRAs**:[13] Individual Retirement Accounts (IRAs)[14] are specific tax-advantaged accounts for money designed for retirement. There are significant tax advantages from the U.S. government to prepare money for retirement so you won't be on their dime in your retirement years. I have more than six figures in my IRAs, which I've been contributing to since I was a teenager. Depending on your income level and other factors, the maximum contribution limit for a Roth IRA in 2023 was $7,000 for the year.[15] They keep changing these limits and all the rules around

---

[11] APY means "annual percentage yield." Most people know this number as it relates to credit card debt and how much the credit card company will charge you annually. In this case, it's how much my HYSA pays me! It pays to know these small percentages here and there that can translate into hundreds and thousands of dollars. **https://www.nerdwallet.com/article/banking/what-is-apy**

[12] **https://www.investopedia.com/terms/e/etf.asp**

[13] **https://www.irs.gov/retirement-plans/individual-retirement-arrangements-iras**

[14] **https://www.irs.gov/retirement-plans/individual-retirement-arrangements-iras**

[15] **https://www.nerdwallet.com/article/investing/roth-ira-contribution-limits**

them. Yet another reason to have a competent CPA supporting you! Consider also looking into solo 401ks if applicable to you.

Simplified Employee Pension (SEP) IRAs[16] allow self-employed people to put aside up to 25 percent of each employee's pay into a retirement account. SEP IRAs are magical for entrepreneurs who pay themselves. In 2024, the maximum contribution was $69,000 for SEP IRA yearly contributions. This can be 10x the amount you can put in your Roth IRA for the year. Now imagine putting money in *both* a Roth IRA and SEP IRA to work on hitting your goal retirement numbers![17] Wow, that could add up fast.

22. **Investments in 12 Startups**: You can invest in startups even without immense wealth at smaller price points via crowdfunding sites such as Wefunder and Republic. I now have shares in these companies I've traded for money. Startups are an inherently risky asset class. You have to know that you could lose all the money you invest in assets this risky.

These are my 22 income streams. You'll see that some of them are common ones you've heard of, and others might be new! Some are small income streams, and some are very large.

Many of these types of income streams I learned about because of male friends who shared their knowledge. Thank you truly to Abhishek, Amir, and Josh[18] in particular! Their advice has led me to many of my 22 revenue streams, at least $80,000 more money in my accounts today, and millions in equity and vesting if things go well with certain companies tomorrow. When I asked these friends *how* they learned about it, they cited senior male mentors. I've joked with friends that the true title of this book could have been "Money Tips Dudes Share with Each Other on Golf Courses." Now that I have this knowledge, I want to share it with you!

Back to specifics, early readers commented they were surprised not to see a 401k. For whatever reason startups and other companies either haven't offered 401k retirement accounts or had a long intro vesting period before I could contribute. If you are offered 401k retirement

---

[16] https://www.irs.gov/retirement-plans/plan-sponsor/simplified-employee-pension-plan-sep
[17] I hadn't heard about SEP IRAs until I heard a wealth influencer talk about how they dramatically helped her hit her financial goals faster. I can't thank her enough for mentioning it.
[18] The only name in this list that isn't a pseudonym.

accounts, max them out and get the maximum possible matching from your employer. It's free money! Some of my income streams are small, and some are robust. I invest in ETFs and IRAs because they grow my wealth and provide tax-advantaged benefits over my lifetime. In a later chapter, we'll dive more into investing.

A Note on Net Worth

When I add up all the money from these buckets and after I pay my taxes, my net worth as of the writing is $1,547,605.14 USD (Figure 9.1).[19] In this context, "net" means sum of assets and liabilities. A net worth is calculated by the sum of all the assets you have in different accounts minus all the debt you have. For example, in this context, I add all my stocks, index funds, ETFs, cash savings, real estate value, value of car, and all other assets, and then subtract any liabilities like debt. Debt includes all categories such as credit card, medical, student, and car debt, back taxes (if you owe the IRS money),[20] depreciating mortgages, and more.

FIGURE 9.1   Net worth

---

[19] Net worth means the addition of all my assets across accounts. This fluctuates most with the value of my real estate moving around with the market. **https://www.investopedia.com/terms/n/networth.asp**
[20] **https://www.investopedia.com/terms/b/back-taxes.asp**

While I'm not going to give each detail for all my accounts, I will say that from allocating money yearly into retirement, I now have more than $150,000 in my IRA accounts. I ask you to respect that I'm comfortable sharing a *lot* with you, but not every tiny detail of my finances. My financial institution and I consider my mortgage an asset because my interest rate is 3% and my real estate is appreciating (increasing in value 5%–15% yearly). Thus, it is an asset that it is growing in value. In the finance community, there are debates about mortgages as "good debt" and an asset, whereas other types of debt are "bad debt." I'm not here to debate that. Whole books could be written about why women are often shamed for spending a dime on pedicures and lattes, while men are encouraged to spend money on golf clubs and memberships. Personal finance is *personal*. Your choices have to work for you and your family. Which financial institutions do I use? The banks and investment portfolios I use change with new policies and practices of the banks. To view a list of my favorite companies to bank and invest with, check out **https://YourAIRoadmap.com/Money-Tools**.

As someone who wants to know, grow, and be in control of my finances, I've hired a certified public accountant (CPA). As my taxes have gotten more complicated with more than 20 pieces of paperwork, she finds clerical errors and makes sure I'm in compliance with my taxes.

Do I have a financial planner? Nope. Today, I manage my finances myself so that my financial portfolio matches my goals and values. That may one day change. You also want to make sure that your financial planner is a fiduciary, meaning that by law, they are required to act in your best interests. Sadly, many financial planners are not fiduciary and thus may be actively working on your portfolio and managing it for *their* best fiscal returns. Do you have a financial planner? Are they a fiduciary? If not, end your contract. Run for the hills!

As you learn more about money, I'm so excited to be on this journey with you talking about money transparently. Growing up, I felt like the topics of money, savings, and investing had some kind of strange cloak over them. Secrets that one day might be revealed. I was told things like "max out your Roth IRA every year" and "make more money than you spend," but nothing about stocks and curating a financial portfolio. I went to public schools and private schools for decades of my life. I never attended one class about personal finances. If the class was ever offered, I didn't know it existed. Growing up, it was taboo in my household to talk about money and still is. Is this the case for you? Does your family of origin and friends speak openly about money? Well, you're here now! So let's talk about an elephant in the room.

The "Taboo" of Talking About Money and Who It Serves

Hey, you and I are going to be talking about money, finances, and income in depth. Maybe you already openly talk about money, and maybe not. You may have some strong positive and negative reactions. Breathe deeply, take a walk, and drink some herbal tea.

While writing this book, my Aunt Bonnie and my friend Kassel discussed our discomfort when talking about money.[21] Feelings of being lost, missing out on money, and trauma came up. Resentments about being underpaid and treated poorly came up. Perfectionism and worrying about making mistakes also came up. Does that feel familiar to you? How comfortable might you feel? Overall, though, when we talked and shared our knowledge, we were better able to share tips, goals, and support. I want everyone to speak about money in data-driven, inclusive, and optimistic ways. Let's keep learning together!

Who does it serve when we don't talk openly about money? The people who currently already have the money and power. White men who run companies benefit from other people not being paid well. White men pay themselves well, to your detriment. Fortune 500 CEOs pay themselves 400% more than the typical employee.[22] While the average worker is making $62,000, the CEO is making roughly $17 million per year.[23] Sound ridiculous? Yep, I agree. Let's look at some examples. The CEO of Google Sundar Pichai made $225 million in 2023. Google job listings on Glassdoor give ranges of $81,000–$119,000 for some roles. Apple CEO Tim Cook made $99 million the same year.[24] Researching this book, I found an Apple job listing for entry-level folks that paid $63,000 per year.

This is white capitalist patriarchy in action. The typical worker would need to work five lifetimes to make the same income as a Fortune 500 CEO makes in one year.[25] Please read that sentence twice. It's crystal clear: He's making money from exploiting the average worker. If you're the average worker, he's making bank from exploiting *you*. He's not going to be helping you build wealth. Why do I say "he"? In 2023, 92% of CEOs

---

[21] Not pseudonyms, used with permission.
[22] https://www.epi.org/publication/ceo-pay-in-2021
[23] https://fortune.com/2023/08/04/ceo-worker-pay-gap-ratio-afl-cio-report-highest-paid-ceo-america-tim-cook-sundar-pichai-apple-live-nation
[24] https://www.visualcapitalist.com/the-highest-paid-ceos
[25] https://www.cnn.com/2023/08/03/business/nightcap-ceo-pay/index.html

were men.[26] In 2018, there were more CEOs named "John" than women CEOs.[27] Similarly, in 2024, there were twice as many board members named Richard, Rick, and Dick as Hispanic women on the 4,429 companies traded on the NYSE and Nasdaq.[28] The average corporate board in the United States is more than blatantly discriminatory, it hurts the bottom line. Diverse teams perform better than homogeneous teams on financial returns.[29] Just think of a school project when someone else who doesn't look like you mentions a key factor that could take your work up a level. That diversity of thought and voices translates into real money in corporate environments. While it might not be fun to talk about, I have noticed over and over again that capitalism is prized more highly than racism and sexism. If this is the only thing that helps them move the needle, then let's use the carrot of money to move the needle!

Are you ready to work five lifetimes to make the income a CEO makes in one year? Or you could build your own wealth outside of an average-paying 9-to-5 job. Hint, hint, that's what we cover together in this book!

Additionally, most of the CEOs are white. The U.S. Census Bureau reported in 2020 that "75% of managers are white. The senior manager level is 83% and the executive level is 85% white."[30,31] In a study published by NPR, it is estimated that only 2% of executives are Black and 3% are Latino.[32] Executives and managers get to decide who gets paid what at companies. These executives and managers decide company policies and who gets hired and fired. Every time I've been laid off, it was by a white man giving me the news. Across all layoffs, women are laid off more often.[33] When I've been in layoffs and women and BIPOC folks are cut, it was my white male coworkers who kept their jobs.

---

[26] https://www.axios.com/2023/04/27/women-men-ceo-sp500
[27] https://www.nytimes.com/interactive/2018/04/24/upshot/women-and-men-named-john.html
[28] An old-timey nickname and not related to genitals in this context. Article citation: https://www.inc.com/christine-lagorio/elf-cosmetics-calls-out-lack-of-us-board-diversity-with-dicks-campaign.html
[29] https://www.forbes.com/sites/forbescoachescouncil/2023/11/22/boost-the-power-of-diverse-teams-seven-tips-for-stronger-connections
[30] https://www.cnbc.com/2020/06/11/companies-are-making-bold-promises-about-greater-diversity-theres-a-long-way-to-go.html
[31] https://bonusly.com/post/diversity-inclusion-statistics
[32] https://www.npr.org/2020/09/10/911464100/how-to-survive-in-a-mostly-white-workplace-tips-for-marginalized-employees
[33] https://www.axios.com/2023/07/06/tech-layoffs-2023-female-workers

U.S. Census Salary Data by Race, Gender, and Sexuality

You might also not know how much your manager makes. Horizontally and vertically, the executives know what people are being paid. Who else knows? The government. The United States collects census data. The data shows that white and Asian men are paid the best. U.S. Census Bureau and PEW Research Center data demonstrates that paychecks are correlated with race, gender, sexuality, and disability status. Let's look at Table 9.1, standardized to a $100,000 salary based on compensation data from 2021–2023.

White and Asian men are paid better. A coincidence? Definitely not. We live in a white patriarchy and capitalistic society. Table 9.1

TABLE 9.1	Wage Gap as Compared to a Cis Straight White Man Making $100,000 USD[34,35,36,37,38,39]
Demographic Group	**Annual Salary**
Asian Straight Man	$114,000
White Gay Man	$110,000
White Straight Man	$100,000
Asian Straight Woman	$93,000
White Lesbian Woman	$75,000
Person with Disability	$70,000
White Transgender Man	$70,000
White Straight Woman	$83,700
Black Straight Man	$73,000

(Continued)

[34] https://19thnews.org/2021/08/its-black-womens-equal-pay-day
[35] https://www.investopedia.com/wage-gaps-by-race-5073258
[36] https://www.pewresearch.org/short-reads/2016/07/01/racial-gender-wage-gaps-persist-in-u-s-despite-some-progress
[37] https://www.gao.gov/products/gao-23-106041
[38] https://www.pewresearch.org/social-trends/2023/03/01/the-enduring-grip-of-the-gender-pay-gap
[39] https://www.hrc.org/resources/the-wage-gap-among-lgbtq-workers-in-the-united-states

TABLE 9.1 *(Continued)*

Demographic Group	Annual Salary
Latino Straight Man	$69,000
White Bisexual Man	$65,000
Latina Straight Woman	$65,000
Black Straight Woman	$63,000
White Bisexual Woman	$60,000
White Transgender Woman	$60,000

also doesn't adequately consider intersectional identities. What about a Latina who is straight and with disabilities? There isn't enough data collected about all these intersections. As a white woman, it's clear to me that sometimes I'm paid better than the BIPOC folks around me. I also have learned that white men are paid better than me in workplaces I've been at. I was paid $115,000 a year, and my friend Nolan was paid $130,000 for the same job with the same title. I had a higher degree than him, and he was a few years older than me. Have you learned that someone at work gets paid more or less than you? How does that feel? Can you imagine how you might feel if you learned you weren't being paid fairly? Can you empathize with others around you? How could you advocate for those around you? Please reflect on these questions. I hope you can empathize and advocate for others.

If you are not being fairly as compared to your peers, imagine what you could do with that money if you were being paid *equitably*? Imagine what you could do with an extra $40,000–$98,000 per year![40] It's also not just about one year. It's about a lifetime of earnings across decades. I could go on and on about these inequities, but I hope you're getting the point that race, gender, sexuality, disabilities, and other demographics do not need to be connected in any way with how much income someone is bringing in. The two are related today but do not need to be tomorrow.

Is your blood boiling right now with frustration, or is that just me? This world isn't fair. Not new news, right? But still painful to talk about. Wow, that was not a comfortable section to write! I hope you get the point that in this country, not everyone is paid equitably. It's clear that some folks are making 40% to 400% more than other folks per year. Yikes!

---

[40] Please keep this number in your head for later. We'll talk about just how impactful $40,000 could be.

So now we've talked about the "taboo" of talking about money and who it serves. Making it seem "taboo" to talk about money serves the people who are in power and already have wealth. I have to tell you, men on golf courses talk about money and do business deals. My male friends at tech events share stock tips with each other. When I have been given honorarium at speaking events, I have sent messages to people also speaking there. I shared how much I was offered to be paid to make sure they were paid comparably. As a white woman, I want to make sure I am paid equitably to my white male peers, and I want the women to be paid equitably to me and the white men as well. It's just basic math here, not rocket science!

When we learn more about money, when we share how much we're making, when we share our financial tips and acumen, we can help others. That's a goal of this book! When we brave through discomfort we might have, we are changing society. Throughout this book, I share conversations I have had with family and friends about income, contracts, retirement, and how we can better take care of ourselves and our finances. Big emotions might come up, but when we get more comfortable, we can have more agency and knowledge in our lives. The same freedom to say we're done working for $62,000 while the CEO is making $17 million.

Are you ready? Let's talk about money more! When we grow, know, and are in control of our money, we have so many more opportunities and ways to expand our lives and the world. The "taboo" of talking about money doesn't serve most of us. But it doesn't mean it might be easy to put away shame and anxiety about talking about it. This is a safe space.

Joan's Hot Take: The "Taboo" of Talking About Money

The "taboo" of talking about money serves multimillionaire white men. It keeps the majority of women and BIPOC folks from knowing more about money and how to build financial independence outside of patriarchal corporate structures. Let's talk more about money! Break the taboo! Make your own wealth!

I want you to have economic freedom. I want you to be equipped to chart your own path. To do that, we need to put aside shameful narratives from white patriarchy and talk honestly and openly about money.

Regardless of who you are, you deserve the right to a life of dignity. You deserve to be able to make the money you need to live a good life.[41] You deserve to have an income to support yourself.

Wealth and the City: 4 Fabulous Pals

Do you talk to people in your life about death, sex, and money? "Women will talk about sex, death, and religion more than they do about money," says Tori Dunlap of Financial Feminist.[42,43] I find this to be true with my friends! So maybe we need a new TV show instead of *Sex and the City*; it's called *Wealth and the City*, about four fabulous pals who build wealth. They come from different backgrounds and talk openly about their path to wealth. In my version, the protagonists are fully in charge of their finances, careers, and destinies. They spend $40,000 on fabulously expensive shoes if they want to,[44] but in my modern twist, some of them work in AI, and *all of them* have future-proofed their incomes. They have the confidence to pursue their heart's desires professionally. In this book, I'm going to give you the resources to do exactly this.

A Note for My Beloved Older Readers

One of my octogenarian advanced readers of this book has built tremendous wealth in his lifetime. He recommended I add a note for my beloved older readers.[45] He said he agreed with all my financial recommendations for you in this chapter. Across his lifetime, he has made money mistakes, but for the most part investing has been crucial for maximizing his wealth for the life he lives.

---

[41] I really hope you're not an ax murderer.
[42] https://www.marketwatch.com/story/women-will-talk-about-sex-death-and-religion-more-than-they-do-about-money-tori-dunlap-wants-women-to-command-the-same-financial-respect-that-men-get-11661243980
[43] https://herfirst100k.com/financial-feminist-book
[44] https://www.bustle.com/entertainment/carrie-bradshaw-net-worth-and-just-like-that-spending-finances-explained
[45] You rock, my beloved older readers and fabulous octogenarians!

For older readers who are retired and have IRAs and 401ks and want to protect them as best as possible, consider tax opportunities such as minimum required distributions (MRDs) and qualified lifetime annuity contracts (QLACs). MRDs tax the sheltered pre-tax funds (like IRAs). QLACs offer an "escape" from MRDs for the longest living individuals. There is legislation in the works to repeal this type of tax loophole by 2029,[46] but they could still be helpful to know about before then. Who knows if they'll get repealed.

If you're going to use tax loopholes in general, I'd ask you to also make donations to charity and community projects around you that you believe in. In general, I find that many wealthy men around me know about and use loopholes in their lives, while women in my circles rarely talk about money and have never heard of these wealth tips and tricks. For example, when my friend and I recently talked about her mom navigating money in retirement, I shared these options, and my friend and her mom hadn't yet heard about them. If this is applicable for you or a loved one, consider learning more.

Hail Mary: Universal Basic Income

One of the things people in tech talk about sometimes is the hope of a Hail Mary from the government. If AI is taking all our jobs, perhaps the government will help. The term is called "Universal Basic Income."[47] The idea is that the government would give everyone a basic income to live on. I appreciate what the government does for us, but I am incredibly doubtful that Uncle Sam will pay for all of us to cover our groceries and rent. Think of the support people got during the pandemic with relief checks! It was helpful but didn't cover my rent for even a month. I don't believe anyone is coming to save us, but ourselves. Let's build wealth for ourselves today. As an adult, it's time to get your financial house in order. You can do it, and I'd love to talk through my recommendations of how you're going to do it and grow your income dramatically. In the next chapter, we'll talk about money, income, and living expenses.

---

[46] https://www.investopedia.com/threat-to-mega-backdoor-roth-conversions-5211038
[47] https://basicincome.stanford.edu/about/what-is-ubi

Questions for Reflection

Questions for Reflection

- ☐ How comfortable are you talking about money? Do you discuss money with your family and friends? Why or why not?

- ☐ What emotions came up for you when you read this chapter? Where do you think those come from?

- ☐ What of these financial recommendations have you heard before? Which are new?

- ☐ Which income streams from the list had you already heard about? Which ones were new to you? Which might be really interesting for you to pursue?

- ☐ What type of income streams list do you want someday? What type of big financial picture do you dream of?

Want to download the resources from this book and see my money tool recommendations?

Go to **YourAIRoadmap.com/Money-Tools** or scan this QR code:

CHAPTER 10

You Want to Be a Millionaire: Money in and Money Out

Think I speak too bluntly about money? Wait until you meet Rachel Rodgers! Rodgers writes that "Every woman needs to see at least seven zeros in her bank account, at the bottom of her own balance sheet, and in her cumulative net worth. Every woman needs to know what it feels like to wield economic power. That's how we make change. That's how we serve our children. That's how we serve the world."[1]

Even if you're not a woman, I'm confident you can see how all people could benefit from economic power and agency in their lives. Rodgers is a Black woman, wife, mother of four, and multimillionaire.[2] She is the owner of Hello Seven and We Should All Be Millionaires: The Club. She is the author of *We Should All Be Millionaires*,[3] a book that has profoundly changed my life. I've listened to every word of that audiobook four times. In this chapter, we're going to talk about earning more, why to shoot for seven figures, and why to watch the cost of living expenses, debt, and lifestyle creep.

---

[1] https://rachelrodgers.com, p. xi
[2] https://helloseven.co/podcast/2020-review
[3] https://rachelrodgers.com

Shoot for Seven Figures

Why is Rodgers' goal seven figures, not six figures? "Even in the most affordable metro areas in the United States, $100,000 households are left with 2% disposable income. (That's only $2,000 per year.) After paying their basic expenses."[4] Therefore, for many U.S. folks, "You are likely only one emergency away from financial distress."[5] This is especially exacerbated for women who make less per paycheck. Rachel writes that the real reason women are not yet millionaires is because they "give away key resources, forfeiting our independence, our time, our power, and ultimately our success." She writes, "Deep down, a lot of us believe that we are somehow at fault for not getting what we deserve, whether that's equal pay or a spouse who does their share of the chores."[6] When we have little to no income and are in an emergency from financial distress, we do not own our success. We cannot future-proof our income or be in control of our finances and lives. That stinks! Let's shoot for millionaire status.

I've learned a lot from Rodgers. One of my favorite ideas of hers is about focusing on vastly increasing my income to enable the life I want. Don't focus on making myself tinier. Make yourself stronger! There's only so much smaller we can make our budget! Stop eating? Have nowhere to live? Definitely not what I want for you.

Let's think expansively. This may be a big change from your current way of thinking. Or maybe you already think like this! If you've been working on being scrappy and not about boosting your income, this is the sign you've been waiting for! Huge potential awaits you, my friend! Let's talk more about money in and money out. In the previous chapter, we talked about income streams and how much money you can bring in. In this chapter, we'll focus on talking about money in, money out, and left-over money for saving and investing. Later, we'll talk about dramatically boosting your wealth!

---

[4] **https://helloseven.co/the-book**, p. xvii
[5] **https://helloseven.co/the-book**, p. xvii
[6] **https://helloseven.co/the-book**, p. xvii

You Can Only Save as Much as You Earn, So Let's Earn More

As you consider how to grow your wealth, you know more about your money coming in, going out, and what you do with what's left over. The concept "you can only save as much as you earn," was a revelation to wealth influencer Vivian Tu when she learned it. It is a mantra she often says.[7] Vivan worked on Wall Street as an analyst before transitioning to sales at Buzzfeed and later a content creation empire on TikTok. When you think about how much you can save, it's simple math: (Money in) – (Money Out) = (Money for Saving and Investing). It may seem obvious but is profound. We *cannot* save more than we earn, so let's boost that earning! Table 10.1 shows a quick example of this equation of money in, money out, and money that is left over.

TABLE 10.1 **Money In and Out Subtraction Equation for a Year**

Money In: Income	$30,000
Money Out: Total Living Expenses	$28,075
Money in - Money Out = Savings & Investing	$30,000 – $28,075 =
"Left Over" Money for Savings & Investing	$1,440

That table is a simplified version of looking at a financial picture of income, living expenses, and money left over across a year. Let's see how much a person might have left over at three different income levels, which I show in Figure 10.1. I use the average U.S. salary of around $60,000/yr,[8] and I'll also put in a similar salary to my graduate student days and an increased income from scaling a side hustle.

---

[7] https://fortune.com/2022/12/06/asking-for-raise-key-to-building-wealth
[8] https://wallethacks.com/average-median-income-in-america

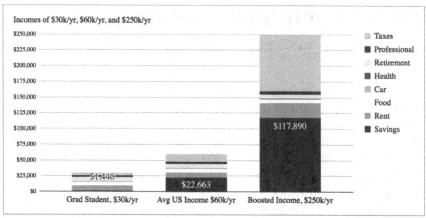

FIGURE 10.1 Savings examples from grad student, average U.S. income, and boosted income

This stacked bar graph shows just what a huge difference a larger income can have to your overall financial picture. In the span of just one year, you have more money to play with. More fun decisions to make. For me, when I made more money via tutoring, I could more easily buy groceries. I put money into my retirement portfolio and maxed my Roth IRA out every year. In addition to the money, I had more freedom and choice. When I began my fancy gig doing marketing and sending emails to Provosts, I increased my income even more and let go of the least pleasant French tutoring students.

Now that you've seen the graph version, let's look closer at the details. In Table 10.2, we see what a total income of $30,000/yr, $60,000/yr, and $250,000/yr would look like after we factor in living expenses such as rent, groceries, car costs, taxes, health insurance, retirement, and professional expenses. The taxes are estimates from SmartAsset's calculator and are assuming you live in Davis, California.[9]

Just like Rodgers mentioned, if you are really living in a scrappy place, like being a graduate student, the leftover money isn't even $2,000 for the whole year. By contrast, if we wildly boost that salary, which means we do pay significantly more taxes, but we still have more than $100,000 leftover to use for savings and investing. This is a dramatic example. There are many assumptions and choices I've made while making the table. The data in the table assumes that you still

---

[9] Use the tool here: **https://smartasset.com/taxes/income-taxes**.

TABLE 10.2	Yearly Money Examples: Grad Student $30k/yr, Average U.S. Income $60k/yr, Boosted Income $250k/yr		
	Grad Student $30k/yr	**Avg US Income $60k/yr**	**Boosted Income, $250k/yr**
Living Expenses			
Rent: Grad =$650/mo, Boosted = $1,900/mo	$7,800	$7,800	$22,800
Groceries and Eating Out: $500/mo	$6,000	$6,000	$6,000
Car: Insurance, Gas, Maintenance	$1,200	$1,200	$1,200
Health Insurance	$600	$600	$600
Retirement: IRAs, etc.	$6,500	$6,500	$6,500
Professional Expenses: Conferences, Travel	$2,000	$3,000	$5,000
Taxes: State and Federal in California	$4,460	$12,237	$90,010
Income: Money In	$30,000	$60,000	$250,000
Total Living Expenses	$28,560	$37,337	$132,110
Income - Living Expenses = Savings	$30,000 - $28,560 =	$60,000 - $37,337 =	$250,000 - $132,110 =
"Left Over" Money for Paying Down Debts, Savings, and Investing	$1,440	$22,663	$117,890

drive that beat-up car from college for a while (yearly expenses $1,200) but that your rent goes up (from $650 per month to $1,900 per month). By boosting my income and not spending all of it, this was the exact way I saved my first $100,000 and then my next $200,000. I wanted to use that money toward big goals!

Does my story about Trader Joe's cheese and increasing my income via tutoring from Chapter 9 also make more sense in context? A few hundred dollars in the $30,000/yr budget are highly impactful to a grocery budget. When I made more money, I also felt emotionally more stable and fretted less about my grocery bill and covering my rent. I focused more on my research instead. All of this changed when I began working in tech and being paid a whole lot more. I saved my first $200,000 from my tech salaries and contracts and living frugally. I lived in decent apartments with low rent so I could save up. I then invested that money and saved for a down payment for a house. The money left over is your money to decide what to do with. It's all about knowing your numbers and having agency over them. Does that make sense? Your money, your choice.

I'm guessing a huge amount of emotions might be bubbling up for you. The first time I did this type of exercise was terrifying! OMG, where is my money going? Am I making huge mistakes? Could I make more money? How are other people doing this? Why did I not learn this in school? I went to public school for so many years!

These are all great questions. Take a breath. I believe in you. We're leading with curiosity here. We want to know more. We're not here to blame or catastrophize. We're here to get clarity. We're here to explore what's currently going on. We can design the future next. We need to meet ourselves where we're currently at. Again, let's repeat together the current concept we're talking about: "You can only save as much as you earn." Now, let's talk more about money and pitfalls so we can know more about our financial picture and grow our portfolios. Taxes, debt, and lifestyle creep are pitfalls as you build your financial portfolio. Are they fun? Nope. As you construct your roadmap, let's face these pitfalls to know better about them and how we can avoid and conquer them.

A Note on Taxes

Pay your taxes. It's as simple as that. Pay your state and federal taxes. I'd rather have plenty of money and a country with good infrastructure than worrying that the IRS is going to come nab me in the night. Pay your taxes. If you bring in more and more income via alternate methods, you may need to begin paying amounts to the government quarterly. You might be able to deduct expenses for your home office. Learn more on the IRS page about this: **https://www.irs.gov/businesses/small-businesses-self-employed/self-employed-individuals-tax-center.**

Like I said, taxes can get complicated. This is why I hired a CPA. She ensures I'm compliant. I sleep great at night. A note for international entrepreneurs: much of my advice for businesses and entrepreneurship assumes you're a U.S. citizen. If you're not, check out Unshackled for resources about talent visas and legal support: **https://www.unshackled.club**. There's a new startup called Alma to support U.S. immigration cases that seems promising with personalized, data-driven results: **https://www.tryalma.ai**.

Joan's Hot Take: Taxes

> Pay your taxes. End of story.

Debt: Credit Card, Medical, Student, and Auto Loans

Most Americans have some form of debt. Mortgages are a loan with a bank, but ideally they create wealth for you because house, condo, and apartment values increase. Credit card, medical, student, and auto loan debt are some of the most common types of debt in the United States.[10,11] In this section, we'll discuss each type, the average numbers, and how inequities play a big factor:

- **Credit Card Debt:** Credit card debt averages $5,733 for the average U.S. adult in 2023.[12] To me, that doesn't look like Ferrari money; that looks like living expenses kind of money. Whether that money was spent on groceries or golf clubs, I don't know. What I can say is that if you made more money, you could pay it all off.

- **Medical Debt:** Medical debt is most typically $1,000–$10,000 and affects 14 million people in the United States.[13] Your debt could be

---

[10] https://abc17news.com/stacker-money/2022/08/24/5-most-common-kinds-of-debt-in-the-us
[11] https://www.businessinsider.com/personal-finance/average-american-debt?op=1
[12] https://fortune.com/recommends/credit-cards/average-credit-card-debt
[13] https://www.kff.org/health-costs/issue-brief/the-burden-of-medical-debt-in-the-united-states

a lot higher or lower than that. Medical debt hits Black and Latino households harder than it does wealthy white people. Black and Latino households hold far more than twice as much medical debt as white and Asian households.[14] Medical debt in my mind simply means our country doesn't have the sufficient infrastructure to keep folks who live here healthy. When I worked in Europe for a time, I saw the doctor for the flu once. The copay was only 20€ (around $22 in the United States).

- **Student Debt**: Student debt is $37,000 for the average federal student loan, but that can vary widely. Personally, I believe it is predatory to have 19-year-olds signing up for six-figures of student debt loans. My friend has more than $300,000 in student debt. White and Asian men have the lowest debt.[15] Black women carry the highest student debt.[16] My friends with advanced degrees often carry six figures of debt. My white friends have less debt than my friends of color. It's as simple as that. Emotionally though, it's not that simple. Debt is hard. The stigma and shame you might feel are real. This system is entirely American. My friends in Europe got stipends for living expenses while earning their degrees. Good for them!

- **Auto Loan Debt**: Auto loans average $24,000 for the average American. Many people have to drive to get to work. If the average auto loan is $24,000, then truly this isn't a fancy car, but most likely a practical one. New Porsches can cost $68,000–$243,000.[17] Based on how our societies are shaped, many cities and towns are not walkable, and cars are a basic regular cost and necessity.

But what if you were paid equitably? If you were paid fairly, see inequitable pay in the tables in Chapter 9, you would be not paid equitably by $40,000. If you were paid fairly, you could wipe out $40,000 of debt in one year. Please read that sentence again. That is the power of pay equity regardless of race, gender, and LGBTIA+ status. The hard thing about these forms of debt is they can also grow. With interest rates, the debt can initially be $14,000, but over time can scale to far higher numbers. I don't want to linger here because this can be deflating to talk about.

---

[14] https://www.lendingtree.com/personal/medical-debt-statistics
[15] https://www.bestcolleges.com/research/how-many-people-have-student-loans
[16] https://19thnews.org/2023/07/student-loan-debt-pay-gap-black-women
[17] https://www.porsche.com/usa/models

If you have debt, that's okay. So do other folks. We can acknowledge the debt as part of a financial picture today and something to work on. So let's earn more, wipe out that debt, and move on to our wealth building and future-proofed income. We're going to talk in depth about income expansion. Before we talk about that, we've got to talk about the pitfalls of lifestyle creep.

Lifestyle Creep: When Living Expenses Balloon

There are many reasons you can have debt, including medical and student debt. If you have credit card debt from spending beyond your means right now, you might be experiencing lifestyle creep. Do you feel societal pressure to upgrade your car? Buy the face masks you keep seeing on TikTok? Upgrade your sweater game to match your friends? It's common but can be dangerous. Have you ever heard the expression "keeping up with the Joneses?" It became even more solidified with the 2016 movie about a new family in the neighborhood, *Keeping Up with the Joneses*.[18] The concept is that you might always be trying to keep up with people around you. However, this phenomenon can make your expenses go up while not actually building real wealth for yourself. Sweaters and cars are both typically depreciating assets, which means that they only continue to go down in value over time. My recommendation is that you acknowledge that sweaters and cars are what people around you are buying, but you have fabulous goals for your money.

I like to keep my expenses low and earnings high, so I have more options of what to do with my money. I was invited on a last-minute $6,000 vacation. It sounded cool, but it didn't match my goals. I already had another international trip scheduled a few months later. I had retirement goals to hit in the next few months to max out my retirement accounts for the year. While people were annoyed I declined, I was happy to make a choice that worked for me and my own plans and goals. I have robust lifestyle and retirement goals. Beyond vacations, I find cars can be a common place money goes in the United States.

---

[18] **https://www.imdb.com/title/tt2387499**

My Beat-Up Car

I currently drive a beat-up hybrid car, "Little Luce." Little Luce gets 47 mpg, which is pretty darn good for an old car. The car is ugly, it's got a few bumps and bruises, but it runs just fine! Fixing the cosmetics of the car (I got an estimate of $10,000 to fix it) is more expensive than the car is worth ($3,000). That math doesn't make sense! It's just a few scratches! People make fun of me when they see my car in the parking lot of posh tech events. I'm an investor and I drive this car? So what? I'd rather put my money into other parts of my portfolio. Little Luce has been chugging along for many years longer than I expected! One day Little Luce will die, and I'll make another plan. Laugh all you want! I'll grow my wealth and not make the car repair folks rich!

The goal of this chapter is to talk about money in, money out, and how you want to use that money left over. Build wealth and the life you want! There's a reason we call it cash *flow*. You are the mighty Poseidon with water flowing all around you![19] The cash is flowing everywhere. You can monetize every electrical charge you make with every big wave! Okay, okay, Joan, simmer down. You don't need to be a Greek god to get my point. The point is that there is power to being in control of your money and know what's going on with it.[20]

Now that you've seen some example financial pictures, how about you fill out your own financial picture? This is the stage of getting to know our finances better. Of course, we hope that your money is increasing more than you're spending. If not, let's work on it! Meet me in the next chapter where we can talk about your money making money via the magic of investing.

Your Yearly Finances: Fill Out Your Current Financial Picture for One Year

Know your financial picture today: Fill out your money in and out like the examples from the chapter.

---

[19] **https://www.worldhistory.org/poseidon**
[20] If you have someone controlling your money and your money is not in your own accounts, this is something you need to deal with immediately. Read *Financial Feminist* by Tori Dunlap. Make sure your money is in your own accounts in your own name with you being able to access them.

Write down your total income for the year, and add up all your living expenses. If you pay rent monthly, then take your rent and multiply it times 12 for the annual number. How much do you spend on groceries monthly? Multiply it by 12.

Yes, this may take time. I still recommend you take the hours to really understand your current financial picture. Make sure to daydream expansively about how you could expand your income in the next few years.

I keep a big spreadsheet where I track my finances per month. I also use financial tools online. To view a list of my favorite financial tools, banks, and investment accounts, check out **http://YourAIRoadmap .com/Money-Tools**.

Use Table 10.3 for your income and living expenses for a year:

TABLE 10.3 Track your own income and living expenses

Annual Expenses and Income	Total Income:
Living Expenses	$_____
Rent/Mortgage	$_____
Groceries and Eating Out	$_____
Car/Bike/Bus/Transportation	$_____
Taxes: State and Federal	$_____
Health Insurance	$_____
Retirement: IRAs, etc.	$_____
Gifts and Donations	$_____
Paying Down Debt	$_____
Other Expenses	$_____
Total Income: Money In (Total Annual, we're trying to simplify thing here)	$_____
See total living expenses total here	$_____
Total Income – Living Expenses = Savings	$_____ – $_____ =
"Left-Over" Money for Paying Down Debts, Savings, and Investing	$_____

Questions for Reflection

Questions for Reflection

- ☐ How do you feel about the idea of shooting for seven figures in your portfolio?

- ☐ What emotions came up for you when you read this chapter? Where do you think those come from?

- ☐ How do you feel about your income? How do you feel about your spending?

- ☐ Do you have debt? Where did the debt come from? How do you want to make a plan to pay off that debt? Would making more money help?

- ☐ Have you experienced lifestyle creep? Have you seen people spending more and more as they make more? What goals do you have about money?

- ☐ Did you learn anything in this chapter? What ideas might you want to apply to your own life?

CHAPTER 11

Your Money's Making Money: Saving vs. Investing

Now that you know more about your money in a one-year time span, let's talk about your money over a longer time span. Let's talk about saving and investing. Great news! The phrase "your money's making money" is real. While writing this book over a few months, my investments made thousands without me having to lift a finger! Does that sound interesting to you? In this chapter, we'll look at savings, investing, and my advice to have a diversified financial portfolio.

When I was a kid, I heard advice like "Make sure to save money from that paycheck" and "Be sure to save" and "Don't spend it all." While the people who said these words might have meant well, they are pretty abstract. What does "Don't spend it all" actually mean? What do you do with the money? Therefore, this book is far more concrete with tons of specifics! When I got an early reader in her 20s to review this book, she told me she skipped this chapter since her dad taught her about stocks when she was 13 years old. Lucky her! If you're more like me and didn't get this type of education before, or simply want to see some cool money data, then let's dive into the chapter.

Investing Is Better Than Saving

Let's clarify these terms. Saving money means storing it, typically with a low chance of losing it. Investing money comes with higher risk, but also higher reward.[1] If you are risk averse, you might think "Oh no, I would never want to invest my money—that is so dangerous!" But what is truly dangerous in my mind is not knowing the options you have, while other people make 40% returns on the money they invest. I simply want you to have options and know what is available to you. Saving is great. Investing is fantastic. We can also minimize your risk when you invest by making sure your investments are diversified. I promise I'll explain!

As mentioned in the broad recommendations in Chapter 9, I recommend keeping 6–12 months of your annual living expenses and keeping them in a high-yield savings account (HYSA). That's a lot of money typically! But it's worth it for the calm it can bring to your life. An HYSA is a new-aged savings account that pays you money to have it sit there. My HYSA[2] pays me 4.6% annually, which means they give me a few hundred dollars per month to put my emergency fund in their accounts. For example, "Emergency! My car Little Luce dies!" In this scenario, I want to have money set aside for purchasing a car if I need one. For your income to be future-proofed, you need to have money on hand for emergencies *and* also be investing. Putting your money in an HYSA (rates I've seen are 3%–5% APY) won't get you as high of yields as investing in a diversified stock portfolio (historical rates are 7% average across time) but a solid emergency fund can help you sleep better at night. When you've set aside your emergency fund, it's time to invest! As you increase your income, I recommend you put the rest of your money beyond your emergency fund into investments, but I have a sense you may still want to be as conservative as possible, so let's consider these two scenarios across 10 years.

Let's imagine you are working hard to grow your income and know your financial picture. In both versions, you start with $1 in the account.[3] You also commit to putting away $833 every month ($10,000 every year) for 10 years. You put aside $833[4] every month based on your income and expenses of the month. During the 10 years, there are no stock market crashes, and the stock market gets an average of 7% yields. Do the same math for yourself with NerdWallet's tool.[5]

---

[1] https://www.investopedia.com/articles/investing/022516/saving-vs-investing-understanding-key-differences.asp

[2] To view a list of my favorite companies to bank and invest with, check out **YourAIRoadmap .com/Money-Tools.**

[3] I chose this because of the online calculator tools.

[4] $10k/12 months=$833.33 repeating, so for simplicity's sake we're saying $833.

[5] https://www.nerdwallet.com/calculator/compound-interest-calculator

Scenario A: Savings: You are conservative. You put your $833 monthly into a 0% APY savings account.[6] Every month for 10 years, you put in $833. At the end of 10 years, you have roughly $100,000. Impressive! Well, it's less than it sounds because of inflation; 10 years from now bananas are more expensive! But imagine if you had invested that exact same money.

Scenario B: Investing: Each month, you put $833 into a diversified stock portfolio. Every month, the money is compounding, growing! Even by the end of the first year, you have $10,324.10. Next year, you continue to make your $833 monthly contribution, but you start with the higher number! This happens year over year. After 10 years, you have $144,181.65. That's $44,000 more! It's also 44% more than if you had left it in the 0% APY savings account. Imagine what you might want to do with an extra $44,000! I'm going on a worldwide trip with all that money! This is an oversimplified example, but my hope is you see that compounding interest can work really positively for you if you can make positive returns in a healthy portfolio. Want to see these scenarios graphed? Check out Figure 11.1 for what this looks like visually represented.

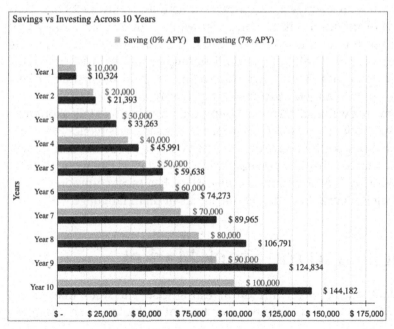

FIGURE 11.1 Savings versus investing across 10 years

....

[6] At least use it as an HYSA! Don't break my heart letting companies make money on you! Sadly, I learned a friend parks her money like this in a debit, or 0% savings, account.

If you're thinking the way I do, you'd wonder what might happen if you invested even beyond that $833 per month! The power of investing means there is a whole lot more money in your portfolio because it wasn't sitting around; it was making you more money!

A Note on Inflation

One of my neighbors bought her house for $10,000. In Seattle? *How* is that possible? It's possible because she bought it 50 years ago. What happened between then and now? The value of the house went up and so did inflation. Inflation is a fancy word to say that things get more expensive over the years. Typically, inflation is related to production costs, the demand for products, and fiscal policies.[7] Inflation is a key factor to our portfolio.

A factor that isn't accounted for in the bar graph about saving versus investing is that inflation can eat away gains made. For example, the U.S. Federal Reserve estimates 2% inflation over time.[8] If you just leave your money in savings at 0% growth, it actually is losing 2% per year because of inflation. Yikes! Thus, you want to invest your money so it makes more than the rate of inflation. If your investment is making 10% per year and inflation goes a little higher, say 3%, then the value of your investment still grows 7%. Again, I know I must sound like a broken record, but *you must invest*, my dear reader!

Now that we've talked about saving and investing, let's talk about how much money we might want to have easily as reserve emergency funds and the rest of our portfolio in diverse investments. In my overall recommendations, I talked about an emergency fund. What is an emergency fund?

There are lots of options for investing. The most common form of investing is stocks. Let's talk about stocks in plain language.

Stocks and the Stock Market

The stock market is a common investing tool. The stock market is a place where shares of companies are bought and sold as a central place

---

[7] https://www.investopedia.com/ask/answers/111314/what-causes-inflation-and-does-anyone-gain-it.asp
[8] https://www.federalreserve.gov/faqs/economy_14400.htm

of exchange.[9] A stock is a percentage of a company, typically a tiny, tiny sliver of a company. The value of your stock increases or decreases as the value of the company changes. Let's look at an example.

Let's say I want to buy some Apple stock. Apple is a publicly traded company with the stock ticker symbol (AAPL). I pull up my stock portfolio app.[10] During trading hours, typically 9am to 5pm EST, I take $5 to buy 0.00599 shares in AAPL. So tiny, right? But the returns can be big. Across the last year, AAPL stock has increased 8.8%. Across the last five years, the historical returns for AAPL stock has been 308.61%. Wowza! That's your money making money for sure! All I had to do was make the money, transfer it to these accounts, and wait. Basically, I pressed some buttons on my phone. Did that blow your mind?

Are you shaking your head like, "Gosh, this is so unfair, why did no one teach me this?" "Is this gambling or perhaps illegal?" "Is this really possible for me?" You can invest with as little as $1. If this is new to you, welcome! This is the power of investing. You might be skeptical, thinking, "It is not this simple. Investing is risky." That's partially true and partially false. Investing over the long term is extremely safe. Investing in only one stock is risky. Let's look at some examples.

Only One Stock Is Risky

Here's an example where I invested in only one stock and lost money. In my stock and investing adventures, I bought 0.0025 shares of Zoom stock (ZM) for $58.89. Since then, the stock has mostly gone down, 13.24% across last year. Oh no! Also, I've been unimpressed with Zoom's leadership and what they're saying in the news. If I don't believe in the company and the stock isn't performing well, for me that's a time to sell the stock. I sold my shares and ended up making $0.13. For me, the goal here was learning and trying things out. It was roughly $60 I was willing to lose. What was my mistake here? My mistake was that all that $60 was going into only one company. That is not diversifying your investment! What if the company's CEO is discovered to be sexually harassing employees and is sent to jail? The value of the company tanks and investors lose their money. This is possible. But if you own

---

[9] **https://www.investopedia.com/terms/s/stockmarket.asp**
[10] I do not use Robinhood. My favorite money apps, tools, and companies I recommend are here: **YourAIRoadmap.com/Money-Tools.**

stock in several companies, you know that some might go under and some might exponentially grow! You need balance.

Diversification: Complex Word, Easy Concept

You need a diverse portfolio. The fancy term is *diversification*.[11] You want your investment portfolio to have lots of different stocks from different companies. If you were growing a garden, you may plant lots of different types of plants. One of the plants may flourish and produce tons of mint! Another plant might get eaten by all the neighborhood bunnies and not make it. By having lots of different plants, your chances of having some flourishing plants is high! Similarly, it's good to have a diverse portfolio with lots of different stocks.

Joan's Hot Take: Investing Is Powerful. Just Do It.

> Invest. Invest in lots of different ETFs. Keep investing.

Diversification has been made even easier because people have decided to make bundles of stocks called *index funds* and *exchange-traded funds* (ETFs). People know it is a good idea to diversify, so they made it easier. Instead of buying by hand small slivers of 507 companies, you can buy shares in Vanguard S&P 500 ETF (VOO).[12] Imagine the headache of buying tiny amounts of 500 stocks! A lot of manual clicking around. Instead, VOO has 507 companies inside it. For example, of those 507 companies, VOO has 6.8% Microsoft shares, 3.78% Amazon shares, 1.2% Tesla shares, and 0.79% Home Depot shares inside it as of June 2024, as shown in Figure 11.2.

Thus, you can simplify your investing and buy VOO shares that are already significantly diversified. ETF simply means a fund that is

---

[11] **https://www.investopedia.com/investing/importance-diversification**. Why do people use such weird jargon? Short story: gatekeeping. If everyone could understand it and invest, the people on top today wouldn't make 400% more than others.

[12] **https://stockanalysis.com/etf/voo/holdings**

Vanguard S&P 500 ETF (VOO)
NYSEARCA: VOO · IEX Real-Time Price · USD

506.81 +2.28 (0.45%)
Jul 3, 2024, 1:00 PM EDT - Market closed

| Overview | **Holdings** | Dividends | Chart |

VOO Holdings List As of May 31, 2024   Filter...   Exp... ⌄

No.	Symbol	Name	% Weight	Shares
1	MSFT	Microsoft Corporation	6.96%	190,708,070
2	AAPL	Apple Inc	6.30%	372,548,193
3	NVDA	NVIDIA Corporation	6.11%	63,394,476
4	AMZN	Amazon.com, Inc.	3.64%	234,607,952
5	META	Meta Platforms, Inc.	2.32%	56,465,895
6	GOOGL	Alphabet Inc.	2.29%	151,245,266
7	GOOG	Alphabet Inc.	1.94%	126,632,033
8	BRK.B	Berkshire Hathaway Inc.	1.70%	46,697,324
9	LLY	Eli Lilly and Company	1.48%	20,466,349
10	JPM	JPMorgan Chase & Co.	1.32%	74,199,808

FIGURE 11.2   VOO Top 10 holdings from June 2024[13]

actually a pool of multiple underlying stocks.[14] VOO is meant to be an overview of the top 500 companies in the United States. Index funds are similar to ETFs where they match or track parts of the financial market. Other types of diversification can include U.S. stocks versus international stocks and small cap (smaller market share) versus large cap (big market share companies). I'm only sharing this to expand your mind, I hope without overwhelming you!

I myself have purchased shares in more than 10 different ETFs. This means I have hundreds of little slivers of companies in several sectors. I feel more confident that my investments are diversified by spreading my money across many sectors. Overall, my retirement portfolios have made 22% over time, and my ETFs and stocks have grown 45% as of the time of this writing.

....

[13] **https://stockanalysis.com/etf/voo/holdings**
[14] **https://www.investopedia.com/terms/e/etf.asp**

To get even more concrete and practical, let's jump into another example. Let's say I put $28,904.84 into several different stocks. Across a year, I got great yields of 28.5%. I let the money grow across time and made $8,265.37, shown in Figure 11.3. Imagine how many hours of tutoring I'd have to do for the same amount—207 hours at $40/hour! Wow, that's a whole lot of work.

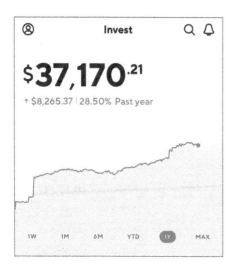

FIGURE 11.3   Stock portfolio example, 28.5% increase in past year

This example is in a strong market. This is a really short and optimistic example. You can't always expect to get these types of returns. However, if you keep investing, you can make substantial money. Your money is making money! Do I sound a little repetitive? Indeed! I want the idea to sink in.

Historical Stock Market Performance of 150 Years

How has the stock market performed historically? In Figure 11.4, you can see that starting in 1870, there are times when the stock market went up and went down. Over the long run, even through world wars and the Great Depression, the stock market has been at its lowest lows and highest highs. If you were to draw a line across time, from 1870 to 2020, it would be a line with a positive trajectory.

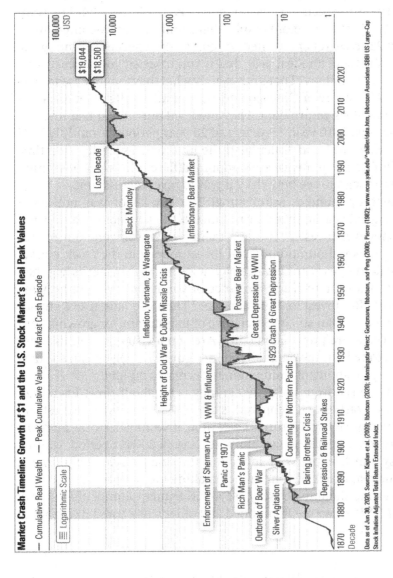

FIGURE 11.4 Stock market across 150 Years, 1870 to 2020[15]

[15] https://www.morningstar.com/features/what-prior-market-crashes-can-teach-us-in-2020/chart-growth-of-1-dollar-headline-3x-106e17d32465fecbc901f2eba32e5cf3.png

Honestly, I was pretty surprised when I saw this graph at just how resilient the stock market is over time. People are ambitious and work really hard to grow companies, and many succeed across time, over time. Perhaps the section feels too much like math class, but I do want to show you just a few more graphs that I find extremely compelling.

In 2023, researchers wanted to look at the concept of timing the market. Was there an ideal year that if you invested you'd clearly lose money or make money? That's not exactly what they found. Researchers from the University of Chicago and Dartmouth College[16] published a study about stock return data. They modeled out "if you had invested for all possible 1–10 year, 15-year, and 20-year periods" from July 1926 to September 2023 and "calculated the total returns during that time period."[17] The researchers were sampling different time periods within this 97-year span to see how risky it was to invest across time.

What they found is astonishing! The key factor was not about which magical year to invest or not invest; the key factor was *for how long* money was invested. It didn't matter when someone put money in, but the overall duration. If you invest money in the stock market for more than 8 years, the chance of you losing your money is less than 5%. That means there is a 95% chance of you maintaining or growing that money. But invest for only one year? Then you have a 25% chance of losing money. But still a 75% chance of maintaining or growing your money! Those are pretty good odds! Are you a visual person like me? Great! I plotted out the data for you in Figure 11.5 so you can see how much the probability of losing money decreases rapidly.

What we see from these two graphs is all about time. Even after the biggest crashes and depressions since 1870, the stock market can provide you great fiscal returns. Over time, investing in stock can make you more money, and the risk plummets over a 20-year period. Waiting isn't easy, but keeping your money in the market for a long time is where the real magic of your money making money happens.

"Investing shouldn't be sexy," says Tori Dunlap, author of *Financial Feminist*.[18] When we see Robinhood and other stock apps talking about

[16] https://papers.ssrn.com/sol3/papers.cfm?abstract_id=4629613
[17] https://www.wealthfront.com/blog/risk-and-time-horizon
[18] https://www.markettradingessentials.com/2021/11/investing-shouldnt-be-sexy-heres-where-millennial-influencer-tori-dunlap-is-putting-her-money

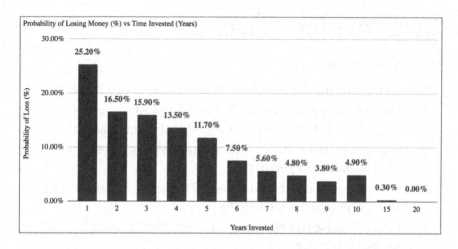

FIGURE 11.5 Probability of losing money (%) versus years invested based on 97 years of data

wild ups and downs of getting rich, these schemes can also leave you losing a huge amount of money. It would be more strategic to invest in more than 500 slivers of stocks, like in an ETF, and know that across 20 years, there's almost a guaranteed likelihood you'll be making money.

When it comes to types of investments (you may have heard about stocks, bonds, mutual funds, index funds, target-date funds, and more!), I focus on ETFs. I have found these to be simple and also diversified by design. I personally have the largest chunks of my portfolio in ETFs, real estate, and my own company. I'm not going to go into detail about bonds and other types of investing. Many, many, many other books have been written about bonds and portfolio construction. Be sure to check out Chapter 5 of Tori's book, *Financial Feminist.*

In this chapter, we discussed a summary of my best, broad recommendations on stocks and ETFs so this can match your goals. While this might feel scary right now, you being in charge of your finances and knowing your numbers is incredibly valuable for you. You are well on your way! Knowing your numbers will serve you today and for the rest of your life as you build the life you want. Overall, your money could be making money for you. Investing is powerful. I recommend you get yourself into making more money and getting that money to make money for you. In the next chapter, let's discuss short-, medium-, and long-term goal planning so you can make moves toward financial freedom.

Questions for Reflection

Questions for You

☐ What have you previously heard about investing and stocks?

☐ How did you think about saving versus investing before you read the chapter? What did you learn in this chapter, if anything?

☐ What are things you've heard about investing? Does the idea of losing money hold you back?

☐ Had you previously heard about ETFs and diversification? Does the concept make sense to you?

☐ Does it surprise you that since 1870, the stock market has such an impressive track record?

☐ What are your takeaways from the study about trying to time the market versus time *in* the market? Did that surprise you?

☐ How do you feel about stocks overall? What did you learn in this chapter?

CHAPTER 12

How Much Money Do You Want? Goals, Retirement, and Financial Independence

I was recently on the phone talking to a close childhood friend about money. "I'm so excited about the next steps in my career," she said, "and I'd really love your help negotiating my salary when I get the offer," she added.

"I'd be happy to!" I said. She's one of my best friends in the world. "Those base salary numbers we negotiate will be awesome so you can work on 401k matching and can max out your IRA," I mused.

"IRA? What are those?" she responded. "Do you contribute to your Roth IRA every year?" I asked. The phone line went silent. "Joan, what are you talking about?" she said. "People always told me to 'save for retirement' and I thought that meant after I'd landed a big adult job," she continued.

"Oh gosh, okay," I stammered. I was stunned. "Um, I have six figures in my IRAs right now. I've been maxing them out every year." She didn't miss a beat, "Dang, good for you!" she replied and then paused. "Okay, how can I catch up?" So, for the rest of our phone call, we talked about her plans for retirement and her broader financial goals. She is currently getting a degree where she has incredibly high salary potential. I'm confident she will retire well, but it'll take time.

As a kid, I was told "Max out your Roth IRA every year you can." Was there a lot of explanation about this advice? Nope. But I took the advice and diligently put money into my IRAs since I had a summer job at the age of 15. What luck and privilege. The handwavy advice given to my friend had been vague, and she waited. Over a decade later, our Roth IRAs were different by $150,000.

In this chapter, we are going to talk about goal setting, retirement, and financial independence. *Knowing* your numbers is crucial to future-proofing your income. Some people have called these numbers "f*ck you numbers," because when you have this amount of net worth, you can walk away from just about anything that you don't want to do, contracts that don't serve you, the threat of layoffs, and much, much more. To future proof your income, you need to know, grow, and be in control. This chapter is all about knowing and getting prepared to grow to these multimillionaire net worth numbers and beyond.

When people talk about long-term financial goals, retirement is typically the big one. As you've probably been taught, retirement is the idea that at the end of your life there's money saved up that you can use to take care of yourself when you can no longer work. The U.S. federal government begins retirement benefits for people in their 60s.[1] This is still in a system that assumes you'll have a 9-to-5 job for 30 years of your life. That model is wildly out of date. Retirement thought has been shifting to say that people no longer need to work full-time jobs. If $10 million hit your bank accounts tomorrow, would you keep your 9-to-5 job? I certainly would rethink how to spend my time! So, let's talk about your financial goals, retirement, and more about the financial independence movement.

Goal Setting and Financial Timelines

My financial portfolio and income streams are set up to match my short-, medium-, and long-term goals. Where you put your money and how easily you can take it out of certain accounts needs to match those goals.

---

[1] https://smartasset.com/retirement/retirement-definition

When you think about what money to bring in and what kind of accounts you want to set up, consider the time frame. Ask yourself the questions in Table 12.1.

TABLE 12.1 Financial Goals by Time Frame Example

Time Frame	Question	Example Costs	Bigger Examples
Short Term	What do you want in the next few months or year? For example, fun trip, pay off student debt, money to take care of a dog and subsequent medical bills.	$5,000	$30,000
Medium Term	What goals do you have in the next 2–5 years? For example, wedding, buy an electric car, start a side business.	$10,000	$75,000
Long Term	How about in the next 5–10 years such as big financial milestones? Ex: save for a house downpayment, have the finances to raise a baby and childcare, retire, etc.	$300,000	$2.5 million

These are financial goals and time frames many people shoot for. If you want these things, you'll need to save up for them to be able to pay for them. What goals do you have? On what time frame? Fill out Table 12.2 for yourself.

TABLE 12.2 Your Financial Goals by Time Frame

Time Frame	Question	Example Costs
Short Term	What do you want in the next few months or year?	Your answer and costs: _____ _____ _____
Medium Term	What goals do you have in the next 2-5 years?	Your answer and costs: _____ _____ _____
Long Term	How about in the next 5-10 years such as big financial milestones?	Your answer and costs: _____ _____ _____

When you know more about your goals and what time frame they are on, you can begin to better plan for them. Be gentle with yourself. Everyone is at a different stage in their financial journey. Some people never want to buy a car, have kids, or own a big house. All good! Your goals are your own.

I want to remind you that your goals can be big even if you're starting off with small ones today. I'll remind you that there were times when I had trouble covering my grocery bills. Today, I'm an investor. Your circumstances can change over time. Back in my early graduate student days, I really had only one income stream, my paycheck from working at the university as related to my graduate studies. Now I have 22 income streams that have ramped up over time. My income has changed and so have my goals over time.

Retirement, Care, and Aging

Retirement is one of the most expensive milestones of our lives. As we have the privilege of getting older, the last third of our lives if we live into our 70s to 100s might be the *most expensive years of our lives.* Maybe you have parents, grandparents, aunts, uncles, cousins, and friends who have gotten older and suffered tremendous illnesses. It also might be everyday practicalities. When she could no longer drive a car, my grand-mommy needed a ride to get to her beloved hair salon and to spend time with her friends. On the other side of my family, my grandma was very ill in the last eight years of her life and needed lots of special care. People with disabilities also sometimes need care from others in their daily lives. Caregiving costs money. Medical support costs money.

Whichever vantage point you see it from, if we are lucky enough to age, it can be expensive. Costs for nursing homes can be \$8,000/month (\$96,000/yr),[2] senior living facilities and assisted living can be \$5,700/month (\$67,000/yr),[3] and senior medical bills can easily be five- to six-figure costs. So how much money do we need to take care of ourselves in old age? We can make estimates based on where we live and the standards of living we want the older versions of ourselves to have.

---

[2] https://www.theseniorlist.com/nursing-homes/costs
[3] https://www.theseniorlist.com/assisted-living/costs

How much money will we need in retirement? How about financial independence? Let's calculate these numbers together.

What Is Financial Independence? How Much Money Do I Need to Retire?

The traditional idea of retirement is that at the end of a 30-year career you can retire. However, I think about retirement as what needs to be hit in total financial assets rather than what age a person needs to reach. By law, if you are 65 or older, the government gives you Social Security checks of $1,501–$1,905 per month as of 2024.[4] I got to tell you that here in Seattle this amount of money isn't even going to cover a cheap apartment to rent. Studios in nice neighborhoods are going for $2,300 per month. I was taught not to rely on Social Security, but that it could help to supplement money I had saved in retirement. Based on a large number of people retiring and fewer workers paying into Social Security, the odds of there being robust money for you in your golden years from the government is slim.[5] I wouldn't bet on it.

Contrary to waiting until your 60s, the financial independence, retire early (FIRE) movement is the idea that you can choose not to work when your assets have hit your financial independence (FI) number. The FIRE movement has grown in popularity as people are disillusioned from 9-to-5 work. While the movement was notoriously popularized by young white men working in tech with high salaries who cut their expenses down to the bare bones, I'm excited to share with you that plenty of other women and BIPOC folks have realized that financial independence may be their ticket out of corporate structures and parts of society that don't serve them.

You don't necessarily need to bike to work and eat discounted cans of beans and cheap bananas with brown speckles to hit your FI number.[6] People figure out their financial independence number, the net worth they need to live the rest of their life without working, and

---

[4] https://www.ssa.gov/news/press/factsheets/basicfact-alt.pdf
[5] https://www.ssa.gov/policy/docs/ssb/v70n3/v70n3p111.html
[6] https://www.washingtonpost.com/business/2018/12/03/myths-about-this-early-retirement-movement

then they cut their living expenses, maximize their earnings, and strive to hit that number. There is a lot of privilege in this type of plan. What if you're a caretaker? What if you have a child with special needs? What if you have a medical condition and need expensive medication for life? Everyone's financial picture is different. The good news about future-proofing your income is that I believe anyone can do it.

Joan's Hot Take: Financial Independence Is Freeing and Data-Driven

> Knowing how much money you want and need is freeing. Having data-driven goals instead of an age is rational and helpful for goal-setting. Calculate your number!

I am less keen on the "retire early" part of the FIRE movement and very interested in the "financial independence" part. I want to decide what my day and life looks like. How much or little I want to work. How I live into my values and my Ikigai, the meaning of my life.

How do you calculate your FI number? Even if the concept of retiring early isn't of interest, I do recommend learning what your financial independence picture would look like. Expand your mind and consider lots of options. Let's do it together.

What Is Your Financial Independence Number?

Broadly, your FI number would be a high dollar amount that you could invest and live off the returns of that investment. The concept of "living off" returns is that your overall portfolio stays large and you can feel secure in spending money within a threshold. This threshold is typically known as the 4% rule. A diversified stock portfolio historically has around 7% returns. If you spend less than your returns and make sure to adjust for inflation and other changes around the corner, experts believe you can have a 93% chance of not running out of money across a 30-year period.[7] This idea of a "4% rule" or drawdown number helps us do the calculation. I've seen people also advise drawdown percentages between 3.3% and 4.95%.[8] I'll stick with 4% for the examples here.

Some popular blogs recommend advice like "Let's say you think you'll need $50,000 per year to cover your post-retirement expenses. Your FI number would be $50,000/0.04, or $1.25 million."[9] As you see in the calculation, this blog recommends dividing by 0.04, which is 4%. My FI number is around $2.5 million based on my higher cost of living in Seattle and my desire to travel post-retirement. This means that across my whole net worth, I'll need to reach $2.5 million in assets to have reached financial independence. Some people are so excited about this type of financial freedom they are willing to live below their means to get out of traditional jobs even earlier.

This calculation is broad, but I hope it's simple enough to be useful as a thought experiment. There are several important factors to talk about as we look at these numbers. Let's do the calculation (Table 12.3) and then discuss those factors.

TABLE 12.3   Broad Financial Independence Calculation

Example from the Blog: Yearly Amount Needed Post-Retirement	$50,000	4% draw-down	$50,000/0.04 = $1,250,000
Example: Joan Estimated Want Post-Retirement in a City	$100,000	4% draw-down	$100,000/0.04 = $2,500,000
Your Version: How Much You'll **Need** Annually Post-Retirement	Your annual cost here: _____	4% draw-down	$_____/0.04= $_____
Bigger Version: How Much You **Want** Annually Post-Retirement with More Vacations, Delicious Food, More Support	Your annual cost here: _____	4% draw-down	$_____/0.04= $_____

[7] *Cashing Out*, p. 275
[8] https://www.cnn.com/cnn-underscored/money/four-percent-rule-retirement
[9] https://pearler.com/explore/learn/blog/how-can-i-calculate-my-financial-independence-number

Let's look at several pieces of this calculation. First, here in Seattle where I live, living on $50,000 a year would be really lean. Dividing that by 12 for the amount per month, $4,167 per month might barely cover rent let alone groceries, medical bills, and a vacation. Your FI number will differ greatly based on where you live. Retirement in Florida versus New York City are two completely different numbers. Now you understand more of why retirees often go to sunny states where it's cheap to live!

You can return to your financial picture calculations in Chapter 10 to see how much you currently spend in a year. Make sure to add a buffer of medical expenses and senior care you might need in the last years of your life. I'd recommend asking a grandparent or friend how much they spend monthly in retirement if they are willing to talk with you about it. A big factor will also be whether people have a house and have paid off their mortgage. If they have paid off their house, then their rent and mortgage payments are not a factor, and instead they just need to calculate property taxes and home maintenance average costs.

So as we look at these numbers, you might be shocked! OMG, I need $2 million to retire? That's outrageous! How will I ever have that much money in my portfolio?!!? It's a big number most likely! True! And in the next few chapters, we'll be walking through how to dramatically boost your income. In the past, people thought about this number as the one that you saved across 30 years or more of work. The cost of living has risen dramatically over the years. I wish we talked more often about retirement and how much money we need. This goes back to that "taboo" of talking about money and how it isn't serving most of us.

If you would like to one day retire and have more than $1,500 per month to live on from Social Security when you're in your 60s, then we need to grow our financial portfolio to hit our short-, medium-, and long-term goals. There are helpful financial tracking software tools out there. Figure 12.1 shows an example of one I use where you can model out different numbers and the probability that your portfolio has this value across time.

Figure 12.1 shows potential spending power and the percentage chance of that being in a portfolio across time. For this current version of the model, it shows that there's a likely outcome of the portfolio being $2.58 million by January 2040. If you'd like to check out which money tools I recommend based on my recommendations today, head to **https://YourAIRoadmap.com/Money-Tools**. As you process

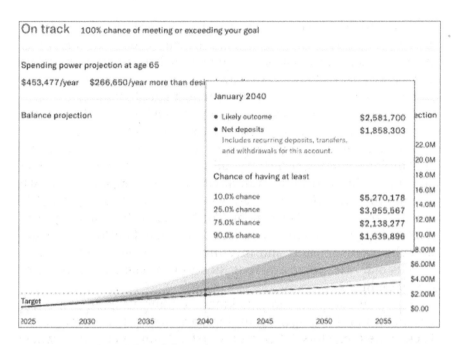

On track   100% chance of meeting or exceeding your goal

Spending power projection at age 65

$453,477/year $266,650/year more than desi

Balance projection

January 2040	
• Likely outcome	$2,581,700
• Net deposits	$1,858,303
Includes recurring deposits, transfers, and withdrawals for this account.	
Chance of having at least	
10.0% chance	$5,270,178
25.0% chance	$3,955,567
75.0% chance	$2,138,277
90.0% chance	$1,639,896

22.0M
20.0M
18.0M
16.0M
14.0M
12.0M
10.0M
8.00M
$6.00M
$4.00M
$2.00M
$0.00

Target

2025   2030   2035   2040   2045   2050   2055

FIGURE 12.1   Financial portfolio tracker

more about financial independence, I'd love to share with you some stories about all kinds of people who have achieved high financial independence numbers and what that journey has been for them.

Imagine you had $100 million in assets by the time you're 31. That was the story of entrepreneur Alex Hormozi who had a nine-figure net worth at 31.[10] His companies made $85 million in revenue yearly, and he was passively making millions annually. He had plenty of money to live on. Alex went into "pseudo-retirement" for nine months, but instead of being free and happy, he ended up depressed.[11] He decided to come out of retirement and work on his books, businesses, and other projects. This was his choice. He had the financial means to make this choice.

Female millennial wealth influencers Tori Dunlap and Vivian Tu both publicly have said they have hit their "FI" numbers. Dunlap's book *Financial Feminist: Overcome the Patriarchy's Bullsh*t to Master Your Money and Build a Life You Love*,[12] explores how women can get out of

---

[10] https://www.acquisition.com/bio-alex
[11] https://www.youtube.com/watch?v=ahslH-8qoFY
[12] https://herfirst100k.com/financial-feminist-book

societal mind traps created by white patriarchy and be in charge of their finances and lives. As a white woman, she talks openly about privilege and the privilege of a financial education from her parents. Her website uses the slogan "Fight the Patriarchy, Get Rich."[13] Dunlap reports that her business has a lifetime revenue of more than $13 million.[14]

First-generation Chinese immigrant Vivian Tu[15] rose through the ranks at JP Morgan Chase on Wall Street before monetizing her viral social media handles. In her book *Rich AF: The Winning Money Mindset That Will Change Your Life*, Tu talks about her shock realizing that the people who worked on Wall Street were terrible with their own personal finances. Her coworkers wildly overspending compared to their incomes. She began making TikTok videos that blew up. Her frank and playful content shows clear math about how to grow wealth through income streams and investing. Tu became a millionaire at 27 years old.[16] Her company, Your Rich BFF, brought in a revenue of $3 million in 2022.[17]

Black families also are working on trailblazing in the FIRE movement and changing the game for Black Americans. Atlanta-based Black content creators Julien and Kiersten Saunders are the owners of rich & REGULAR.[18] Their book, *Cashing Out*, discusses how they didn't trust the corporate companies where they worked. "It's time to stop being a cog in the machine that leaves you under-appreciated and underpaid."[19] In workplaces full of white men who got to make the decisions, they wanted to build wealth for their family and "win the wealth game by walking away." Both of them walked away from their corporate jobs before turning 40.[20] This is both impressive and completely counterculture to much of the wealth discussions I've seen in online spaces that are predominantly white, male, and tech-centered. The Saunderses paid off their mortgage and debt and now have financial independence with revenue coming in from their financial portfolio and revenue streams of their book, podcast, and online courses.

---

[13] https://herfirst100k.com
[14] https://herfirst100k.com/grow-instagram
[15] https://www.cbsnews.com/boston/news/vivian-tu-author-podcast-personal-finance-young-people-wealth-changemakers
[16] https://techiegamers.com/your-rich-bff-net-worth
[17] https://www.theleap.co/blog/vivian-tu-your-rich-bff-interview
[18] https://richandregular.com
[19] https://www.amazon.com/Cashing-Out-Wealth-Game-Walking/dp/0593329554
[20] https://www.amazon.com/Cashing-Out-Wealth-Game-Walking/dp/0593329554

Across the pond, Ken and Mary Okoroafor are Black content creators in the United Kingdom (UK) who also reached financial independence. They wrote a book called *Financial Joy* that gives their recommendations and tells their story.[21] Ken and Mary are both first-generation immigrants to the UK. Ken built his career over 14 years. Ken worked as the CFO of a venture capital firm. After working grueling 15-hour days and commuting for 2 hours home, Ken got home after midnight and saw little of his family. But all that changed. After a horrible blood-strewn accident of hitting his head on the bathroom sink in the middle of the night, he landed in the hospital wondering what his life had become. He also realized he never saw people over the age of 50 at work. Especially as a Black man, he felt like his days were numbered in the corporate world. He and Mary reevaluated their lives. They made a plan to get him out of the corporate job and become content creators. They launched their business in a dedicated way in 2020.They hit their financial independence numbers at age 34 with two children.[22] They both choose to operate the Humble Penny but have plenty of money without it. Their work now reaches more than 3 million people world-wide.[23] Now, they sell products such as courses, PDFs, coaching, membership, and more. Their website, The Humble Penny, even includes screenshots of their recommendations of which stocks are part of their portfolio.[24] They take off the whole month of August every summer. They travel extensively with their children to more than 50 global destinations.[25] Similar to the title of the book, *Financial Joy*, Mary asks people to "Imagine a life where your financial situation no longer causes stress, anxiety, or sleepless nights. A life where money becomes a tool for empowerment enabling you to pursue your dreams, support your loved ones, and make a positive impact in the world. This is the essence of financial joy."[26]

I am in awe of these people. They are going against core aspects of our society. Beyond just leaving a 9 to 5, they think about their wealth and meaning of life in different ways. Here in Seattle, I'm surrounded

[21] https://geni.us/financialjoy
[22] https://thehumblepenny.com
[23] https://thehumblepenny.com
[24] https://thehumblepenny.com/best-vanguard-funds-etfs-and-index-funds-for-financial-independence
[25] https://thehumblepenny.com/super-simple-investing
[26] https://www.cnbc.com/2024/03/01/93percent-of-women-are-stressed-about-money-a-cash-reserve-can-help.html

by many folks climbing corporate ladders in software tech companies. The social environment can be intense and toxic. The lives of Homozi, Dunlap, Tu, the Saunders, and the Okoroafors are very different. Yet, these entrepreneurs and influencers openly discuss their finances and life choices with passion and frankness. They know their numbers; they know how much they pay for their living expenses; they know how much money they *need* to maintain a certain lifestyle. They know what they *want* as they grow their businesses and portfolios. They can choose to stop at an FI number they pick or keep on building their wealth.

Despite their varied backgrounds, it's notable that owning a company and being content creators is a common path for these modern wealth-builders. Being entrepreneurs was key to many of their journeys in deciding how much money their company's revenue would bring in and how much they would pay themselves. For example, my family friend knew her FI number. When a company approached her saying they wanted to acquire her company, she said yes when the company would pay her enough to cover her FI number. Smart!

While you may not believe me now, I hope that as you read this book you begin seeing how much money you could bring in. Instead of thinking of the smallest FI number you might want to shoot for, you could think about what flourishing and thriving mean to you. How do you want to structure your life? What is the meaning of your life and how could financial independence help enable that?

Wants vs. Needs

In much of this chapter, we've talked about how much you *need* to pay for annual expenses across time. I would also like you to consider how much you *want*. Instead of thinking lean and scrimpy, what would a big, strong, fabulous life look like for you if you also included how many vacations, what delicious food you want to be eating, what lifestyle you might want for you and your family, and how you give back to your community.

Later, we'll talk more about money and meaning. You can want far more than the bare minimum. This seems obvious, but I wanted to say it. I was always taught to be frugal. While that served me in one part of my life, there's also so much beyond pinching every penny.

There is a big, rich life awaiting us as we build our wealth and look at a world where many people can be financially independent to have more power and agency over their own lives. In the next chapter, we'll talk about wealth expansion and a plethora of ideas of how to build your wealth! Exciting.

Questions for Reflection

Questions for You

- [ ] What narratives were you told about money when you were growing up? Did your family talk about IRAs? Do you talk to your friends about retirement?
- [ ] What short-, medium-, and longer-term goals do you have about your financial portfolio?
- [ ] Have you heard about the FIRE movement? Do people around you talk about their FI numbers?
- [ ] What is your FI number?
- [ ] What emotions came up when calculating your FI number?
- [ ] Have you seen elders around you have enough money in their later years? Through illnesses? How do you want to live your life today? What about as you grow older?
- [ ] Do you use a financial tracking system to know your current net worth and financial portfolio? Would graphs help you see that modeled out?
- [ ] Have you heard stories of people who have hit their FI numbers? What do you think of these?
- [ ] How much do you *need* versus how much do you *want* if you increased what your financial picture might be in the future? Do you think in scrappy versus expansive terms?

CHAPTER 13

Are You Ready for It? Wealth Expansion, 41 Ideas to Grow Your Income Streams

In the last few chapters, we've explored getting to know our financial picture better. Here comes more of the fun stuff, growing your money! When I moved to Arizona for my PhD program, I transitioned my side income from French tutoring to tech consulting. When I arrived on campus, I had tons of intro meetings with professors and staff around campus. I learned that several professors had connections with start-ups and companies. They were eager to hire relatively cheap and highly technical PhD student interns and consultants. Companies saw a direct line between my graduate research in linguistics and technology to the products they were developing. This is the strength of weak ties! I began to be known as "the PhD student who does speech tech stuff," and even people who didn't know me well referred me to opportunities. My personal brand worked in my favor. Quite literally, it was helping pay my bills.

Usually it went something like this for warm intros: professors sent email introductions. I'd take a meeting with the company, and then we'd talk about potential partnerships and work. If it was mutually beneficial, we'd start a project. Especially for warm, friendly introductions, companies often already had a specific project in mind they wanted side help with. Maybe they didn't want to hire a whole research and development team. But they did want an outside opinion. So I'd say phrases like, "If you'd like an external evaluation of your dashboard product from a PhD candidate linguist, I charge X for a dashboard report." If they wanted the report, they signed a short statement of work (SOW) and paid me when I sent the invoice.

More and more, I would cold email (an email to someone I did not know and had no connections to) to companies with products in my field that matched my research. I explained who I was and said, "hire me!" Most stakeholders at companies opened the email (I put email opening trackers on them), and most did not respond. But some responded! I'd say roughly 15% responded. I struck gold! One of them had me do a free trial project with them. When we built a working relationship and saw the value of my research, they donated $10,000 worth of software to my PhD research. They also got research in-kind from me and iterated their product to make it better. I was so proud that my research and work actually mattered. Thousands of people use that product internationally! A win-win-win!

For my consulting work, payment terms changed also. For tutoring, people paid me via cash or check monthly or after each lesson. When it came to consulting, payments were less frequent, but they often were larger payouts, a few hundred to a few thousand dollars. Companies paid 30 days after getting an invoice from me (NET 30) or even 60 days from the date of invoice (NET 60). During this time, I shifted my pricing from hourly to project-based. I work quickly. My expertise and work is more valuable to companies than micromanaging me for 15 hours. They just want the report! As long as it's lucrative for you, I recommend you make the shift to project-based and milestone-based pricing as soon as you can. In the next chapters, we'll talk about how you can craft your own offers and products to grow your revenue streams.

Consulting doesn't sound that exciting to you? No sweat, that is just one of the 49 side income options we'll review. I want to get your creative juices flowing about what options might be of interest to you! When I was in my PhD program, I paid my own bills and invested heavily in my education. As you set your own goals, remember that we discussed in Chapter 10 how six figures aren't enough. We're going to shoot for seven figures, being a millionaire and multimillionaire, in fact!

In this chapter, we'll cover:

- 5 Common Paths to Becoming a Millionaire
- 5 Simple Steps to Make a Side Income

- 16 Fancy Obstacles to Avoid
- Pineconing: Label and Address Fears
- 41 Income Stream Ideas, Easy to Medium Difficulty
- 10 Ways to Make Quick Cash
- Revenue, Profit, and Margins

Goodness, that's a lot of lists! I really love all the options, and my early readers did also. We will then talk about the dirty secret of revenue versus profit. I'll share how to avoid this common pitfall by getting organized! Okay, let's dive into common paths to becoming a millionaire.

5 Common Paths to Becoming a Millionaire

How do most people generate their wealth? How do you become a millionaire? In a study of 233 high-net-worth individuals, four main paths emerged about how to build wealth.[1] All of these are probably common to you. Titles for each come from me and the research study. I've also added the last path, legacy wealth and being born into money. Most people who become millionaires fit into these main five paths:[2]

1. **Saver-Investor:** This person saves a huge amount of their income. They are always thinking about how to grow their wealth through saving and investing.
   - Tori Dunlap saved $100,000 by the age of 25. She didn't work a job that paid more than $80,000.[3]
   - Julien and Kiersten Saunders paid off their mortgage and car debt of $200,000 in five years.[4] Talk about saving and using that money!

---

[1] https://www.cnbc.com/2019/11/19/fastest-way-to-become-a-millionaire-is-the-hardest-says-money-expert.html

[2] These could be the identities of people on my "Wealth and the City" TV show! Netflix, still waiting on my phone call!

[3] https://www.msn.com/en-us/money/personalfinance/i-saved-100k-by-age-25-now-i-have-a-fortune-of-millions-before-30/ar-BB1ljZcS

[4] https://www.thecut.com/article/we-paid-off-200k-in-debt.html

2. **Corporate Climber:** These folks work at large companies with high salaries and devote significant time and energy to get senior executive positions that pay well.

   - My friend Rebekah Bastian worked at Zillow for almost 15 years. She rose the ranks from program manager to VP with a base salary of $275,000.[5] She also gave me permission to tell you that as an early employee at Zillow her stock options and grants, in addition to her base salary, were the way she made her millions.

   - My friend Sharon makes $1.3 million per year with a C-title job at a large company you know the name of.

3. **Highly Paid Professional:** Doctors, lawyers, and investment bankers are jobs that currently pay more than $200,000+/year. Most require advanced degrees that could land you in $100,000+ of student debt.

   - My uncle is a retired anesthesiologist who had a multidecade career. In a study of 635 salaries, the median was $339,000 base salary, not including bonuses, profit sharing, and commissions. Total pay can be $156,000-$503,000 per year or more.[6] Now imagine that salary across decades.

   - My friend is a senior lawyer. She bills her time at $400 per hour to customers

4. **Big Earner:** Entrepreneurs, professional athletes, successful actors, musicians, and best-selling authors can make high earnings from big successes.

   - Serena Williams has made more than $95 million from her tennis career prize money.[7]

   - Sara Blakely founded Spanx. She has a net worth of $1 billion dollars from her empire.[8]

5. **Born into Wealth:** Your family is wealthy. You are a millionaire with a trust full of money.

   - Stuart Lucas is the son of the family who owns Carnation, makers of Friskies cat food, Coffee-Mate creamers, and Contadina

---

[5] https://www.businessinsider.com/quit-job-zillow-become-startup-founder-right-decision-2022-5?op=1

[6] https://www.payscale.com/research/US/Job=Anesthesiologist/Salary

[7] https://www.sportingnews.com/uk/tennis/news/serena-williams-net-worth-career-earnings-prize-money/bul7qaoj3ftsmlnhg0ljaex8

[8] https://finance.yahoo.com/news/spanx-founder-sara-blakely-makes-024614487.html

tomato paste, among other brands. As a kid, he got stock for holiday gifts. The company was bought by Nestlé. When he was 24, he realized that in his accounts was "a pile of cash."[9] He has put $10 million in various trusts in his 40s.

- Julia Louis-Dreyfus is the television star of *Seinfeld* and *Veep*, and the hit podcast *Wiser than Me*.[10] Her father had a net worth of $4 billion.[11] This does not diminish her work but demonstrates that she had a different safety net and bank account than most of us.

Looking at these five common types of wealth building, I'm a hybrid of the Saver-Investor, Highly Paid Professional, and Earner paths. I have saved my money and put it into retirement accounts since I was a teenager. With my PhD, I have been able to negotiate higher compensation. I also am a dreamer and entrepreneur. I also have dreams of being a best-selling author![12]

In the age of AI, there is a lot of disruption on the corporate ladder. As we've discussed, most managers and CEOs are white men. For the rest of us, I want to consider ways to future-proof your career that doesn't get you stuck worrying daily about layoffs. I'd love to explore with you ways to increase your income. This is iterating on the Earner path, but in far more practical and data-driven methods! If future-proofing your income is a part of your life path, I recommend you maximize your earnings and save as much as you can. More money in, thoughtful spending out. If you dramatically increase your income, own your own business, and have freedom to choose your own path, your income will be future-proofed. Your income won't depend on only one revenue stream as you get more money into your accounts and diversify where that money goes. Does that sound lofty? Ambitious? For sure! It's entirely possible for you. Ever been in a bad work environment and had bigger dreams for yourself? Liz sure did.

After earning her master's degree, Liz quit a job in a bro-filled finance company that wanted her to clean the office and answer phones instead of upskilling and rising the ranks. She quit and co-created a

---

[9] https://www.nytimes.com/2013/03/26/your-money/trust-fund-children-need-an-education-about-money.html

[10] https://lemonadamedia.com/show/wiser-than-me-with-julia-louis-dreyfus

[11] https://www.nickiswift.com/1300035/julia-louis-dreyfus-wealthy-family

[12] Let's hope you like this book! Please share it with a friend and on social media. It would mean the world to me.

company that grew to a $1.4 billion valuation. She got bought out from the company for $400 million in 2018.[13]

In her book, *Dream Big and Win*, Liz writes that "Entrepreneurship is not only the great equalizer, but it's the key to changing the world."[14] She built the company through a simple offer, resilience, and scaling the company to tremendous profitability. "I am where I am today because of entrepreneurship,"[15] writes Liz. Ownership of a company is tremendously powerful. You have agency and ownership over the company, its choices, and its monetary values. So let's go step-by-step through how you could start simple, build an offer, and make substantial income.

Start Simple

Whether you have no experience or tons of experience, let's walk through simple steps to scale an income stream to make yourself a millionaire. To start making money outside a day job, here is the five-step basic start list.[16]

5 Simple Steps to Make a Side Income

1. **Offer:** You need an offer or product. This needs to be a transformation from point A to point B for your customer. For example:
   - Mowed lawn. (A. Mangy lawn to B. Beautifully trimmed)
   - Graduation photos (A. No photos to B. Professional photos of graduation for a lifetime)
   - Online course on personal branding.[17] (A. Want to learn more about personal branding to B. Well-versed in personal branding with tons more knowledge and checklists to update LinkedIn profiles)

---

[13] **https://www.amazon.com/Dream-Big-Win-Translating-Creating/dp/1119904366**, p. 228
[14] **https://www.amazon.com/Dream-Big-Win-Translating-Creating/dp/1119904366**, p. 236
[15] **https://www.amazon.com/Dream-Big-Win-Translating-Creating/dp/1119904366**, p. 236
[16] This section is inspired greatly by the work of Rachel Rodgers and Alex Hormozi.
[17] This one is real; check out **YourAIRoadmap.com/Courses**.

2. **Simple Marketing Content:** Start really simple. When you know your offer, tell people about it! You can prepare an email, text, and/ or social media post. Have your two- to five-minute elevator pitch ready. This is not the moment to create a fancy, multipaged website! Look back at the STAR method framework for storytelling structure, Chapter 8. For example, prepare content about how to share your graduation photo services with family and friends, offer graduation photos to families with graduating students, write a post showing examples of awesome graduation photos you've taken with reviews from customers (if you have them!).

3. **Price:** You need to set a price. Start with one product and one price. If people want more than one or a variation on the offer, then you can make changes if you'd like.

     Sample message: "Hi Alicia, it's graduation season! I'm offering professional graduation photos to seniors who want something more than a selfie this year. Are you interested in professional graduation photos for Morgan? Here is an example photo and a testimonial from a recent customer! 'Tony is usually shy in front of the camera, but Joan was really warm and supportive. Joan communicated well and got genuine smiles out of Tony. In the end, we love the photos and will definitely book a time with her when Tania graduates in a few years! 10/10 would recommend.' We schedule a 1-hour photo shoot, then you'd get 10 edited photos for $500 within 2 weeks. If you're interested in scheduling a photo shoot or know someone else who would be, email me at [your email]. Thanks!"

4. **Payment:** Set up a way to take money when you get paid. Make sure to enable your Venmo to your bank account. Examples: Cash, Venmo, Zelle, CashApp, Stripe online, credit card.

5. **Simple Sales Methods:** Now that you have an offer and marketing material people can read, how will you get the offer in front of them? Most people I know love preparing, but the whole sharing part of the offer is scary! In her book *We Should All Be Millionaires*, Rachel Rodgers recommends sharing with at least 50 people in bunches of five at a time. Alex Hormozi recommends 100 reach outs per day.[18] It can be scary to get your offer out, but I promise you if you don't share about it, no one will know about it, and no one will buy. Sharing is caring!

---

[18] https://podcasts.apple.com/us/podcast/the-game-w-alex-hormozi/ id1254720112?i=1000624977839

For example, you post your tutoring offer on Craigslist, you print out flyers with contact info and put them around the park where your target buyers with dogs walk their dogs daily, you write up an email and send it to friends, asking them to share it with their church group, etc. You may need to send this offer out to 100 people to make the money you're looking for.

In summary, the steps are Offer, Simple Marketing, Price, Payment, and Simple Sales Method. It's really that simple. If you have done a side gig in the past, you may have already done these steps previously! The number-one mistake I see when people work on an offer is they don't get it in front of enough people. You need to share and socialize your offer. Get feedback and get it in front of your target customers. Use word of mouth, emails, the Internet, social media, flyers, and whatever methods are legal and ethical!

Joan's Hot Take: Start Simple, Make Money

Just get started. Making money and starting with these simple steps can help make your wildest wealth dreams happen. Get going!

Thought Work Revisited

In fact, if it feels easier to say some AI influencer convinced you to start a side hustle or business, feel free to blame me! Example text might read: "I read this book *Your AI Roadmap* and was convinced I need to move forward with my dream of launching a dance studio. Sign up here for a six-week dance cardio series!" You are welcome to tag @ JoanBajorek and @YourAIRoadmap on your first offer post on socials. Putting yourself out there isn't always easy, but it is crucial to be seen and known by your future customers.

As you get more customers, you can then scale the business. Before we get too grand, though, I recommend starting small and simple. Ever heard the phrase "Keep it Simple, Silly" (KISS)? I absolutely agree with it. No need to overcomplicate and stall getting all knotted up in the weeds. I see many people get stuck overcomplicating and overpolishing these things. Obstacles beware! I sometimes overpolish myself! Usually with my team, we define what the main goal is and make sure to hit it and not go beyond that for the defined time frame. If you have tried something and gotten stuck, here are common obstacles I see people frequently butting up against. Let's address them.

16 Fancy Obstacles to Avoid: List of Things You do NOT Need to Start:

1. ~~Tons of Social Media Followers~~
2. ~~Huge Email Newsletter~~
3. ~~Your Mom's Approval~~
4. ~~Fancy Degree or Certificate from an Ivy League~~
5. ~~All the Confidence in the World~~
6. ~~Perfect Product~~
7. ~~Rich White Dude's Thumbs Up~~
8. ~~Feeling Good Enough~~
9. ~~Stunning Website~~
10. ~~Business Cards~~
11. ~~Business Name~~
12. ~~Memorable Website URL~~
13. ~~Have Everything Figured Out~~
14. ~~Gorgeous Business Plan~~
15. ~~Slick Logo~~
16. ~~Impressive x-FAANG Employees~~

Do any items on this list resonate with you? Have you come across unnecessary obstacles at the start? I sure have. Some of these things are really nice. Are they needed to start a side hustle? Nope. If you find yourself spending hours and hours polishing a website but haven't even sent your offer to any potential customers, please go back to "Five Simple Steps to Make a Side Income." Do these basics. Mindset and being able to overcome fear of failing publicly are what often comes up for me here. If you have trouble launching, I'm right there with you. Sometimes, I recommend instead of questions of fear you might be having ("What if things go wrong? What if it flops?") that you do thought work and reframe to asking yourself, "What if things go well? How impactful and *fabulous* could this be?" Labeling and addressing fears are important skills.

Pineconing: Label and Address Fears

Do you sometimes fastidiously work or freak out about something, but when you come up for air realize your anxiety is about something else you can't control? Like spending hours publishing a website when what you really need to have is a frank conversation with a friend? Yep, I've been there. I have come up with the term *pineconing* to label when this happened. Pineconing means you are fixated on one thing that actually doesn't matter much because there is something else that is important you feel anguish about.

If I get overwhelmingly consumed by something relatively unimportant, the "pinecone" project, I try to realize it and step back. I work to pause myself from that one task, step back, and reflect on why I am doing that one task and what I am avoiding. For me, it can look like avoiding situations that are uncomfortable, where I might experience rejection or generally have anxiety around a topic.[19] It's that pesky desire for external validation again and getting out of my comfort zone!

When I step back and see the forest through the trees, often I realize that while focusing on this one task might be vaguely important, I am merely distracting myself from intense emotions going on in other parts of my life. If you find yourself pineconing and using a task as an excuse for busywork procrastination, I recommend you get support from other people and talk through what is going on. Getting outside perspectives that are supportive can be invaluable. Obstacles are inevitable. The perspectives of others can help you see the forest through the trees. In fact, if all of this were easy, everyone would have already done it! You're charting an amazing course. By addressing these concerns and pinecones, you can get more support, navigate the journey more effectively, and have a higher likelihood of hitting your goals! Okay, now that we've talked about fears, let's get back to talking about making that offer and money.

---

[19] My therapist helps me with this!

41 Income Stream Ideas, Easy to Medium Difficulty

Let's say you aren't sure what your side hustle is going to be. Mowing lawns, taking graduation photos, and online courses don't inspire you. Not to fear! Joan, the income fairy godmother is here! Let's look through a huge list of 41 awesome side income opportunities I've compiled just for you in Table 13.1! They are alphabetized and not in any order of my preferences.

TABLE 13.1 41 Income Streams to Set Up, Easy to Medium Difficulty[20]

#	Income Stream	Description
1	Affiliate marketing	Earn commissions by selling other people's products through affiliate marketing.
2	Blog	Launch a blog on a topic you are passionate about. Monetize with products, ads, and brand partnerships.
3	Bookkeeping	Learn QuickBooks and other software. Offer bookkeeping services for businesses that need to keep their fiscals organized.
4	Build and sell AI products	Learn about a pain point customers have, i.e., automations, data management, etc. Sell them products to solve these problems.
5	Chimney cleaning	Become a chimney cleaner and scale a business cleaning chimneys.
6	Cleaning	Offer cleaning services in your area; get many customers that pay monthly or quarterly on retainer.
7	Coaching	Offer personal coaching or training services, potentially through online platforms like Zoom.
8	Commercial drone services	Provide drone video services for industries like real estate, roof inspection, and events.
9	Craft sales	Create and sell handmade goods on platforms like Etsy.
10	Creating an app	Develop a mobile application and generate income through sales, ads, or subscriptions.

....

[20] If you'd like to download this list, go to **YourAIRoadmap.com/Resources**.

TABLE 13.1 (*Continued*)

#	Income Stream	Description
11	Dog daycare and walking	Walk and provide daycare services for dogs for neighbors and people in your area.
12	E-commerce	Sell products online through various platforms.
13	eBook	Create an eBook online and monetize it.
14	Fitness classes, yoga, Zumba, Hip-hop	Conduct fitness classes online or in person.
15	Food truck	Start a food truck or catering business.
16	Freelance writing	Write articles, posts, and content for websites and publications.
17	Gardening and landscaping	Provide garden services and landscaping.
18	Graphic design services	Offer design services for businesses needing logos, marketing materials, and other visuals.
19	Host events	Organize local or larger scale events that can be ticketed or sponsored for revenue.
20	Influencer	Launch an online presence around a topic. Build a following and monetize the following via products, paid advertising, brand deals etc. Warning this works for less than 10% of content creators.
21	Make and sell videos	Create a video studio. Make your own videos to sell your products or offer video services for others like influencers, course creators, real estate companies, golf courses, restaurants, etc.
22	Mastermind group	Facilitate a group where members meet regularly and pay for membership.
23	Membership group	Start a membership service, like for a gym or a golf course, where members pay recurring fees.
24	Newsletter	Launch a newsletter that give important information in a niche; monetize via ads or paid subscriptions.
25	Notary	Become a travel notary who offers signing services around your city.
26	Online courses	Develop and sell online courses, leveraging expertise to reach a broad audience.
27	Painting services	Offer painting services for repainting walls, houses, projects.
28	Photography	Offer professional photography services, such as wedding photography or graduation headshots.

(*Continued*)

TABLE 13.1 (*Continued*)

#	Income Stream	Description
29	Plant business	Sell products from hobbies, e.g., selling clippings of my plants.
30	Podcast	Launch a podcast and monetize it as you grow it.
31	Pressure washing	Help people take care of their houses by offering pressure washing services.
32	Project-based consulting	Do consulting projects for companies.
33	Resell furniture	Buy broken down furniture, restore it, sell it for way more money.
34	Sell digital products	Create and sell digital products, potentially using AI and machine learning tools.
35	Subscription boxes	Start a subscription box service in a niche market where customers get products monthly.
36	Create a music studio, i.e., piano	Create a piano studio and teach music lessons.
37	Teaching and tutoring	Teach and tutor in subject matter you know or could learn.
38	Translation services	Provide translation services if you are fluent in multiple languages.
39	Vending machines	Own and operate vending machines in high-traffic areas.
40	Virtual assistant services	Offer administrative services remotely to businesses; get several customers.
41	YouTube channel	Create a YouTube channel and monetize it.

Source: Adapted from [20]

What do you think of the list? Are there any that you'd like to consider? Some you've already tried or you have a friend who has tried these? While some of them might not be of interest, I hope this list opens your mind up to ideas that could be super lucrative for you. Got ideas I haven't listed? Great! This is meant to be a starting point to get your creative juices flowing.

Operational Costs

As you scale your side income into a flourishing business, you'll need to consider a few key things. Just like your personal finances, you'll need to figure out how to bring money in, where money goes, and how to use the money left over. This is called *cash flow*. You'll need to make sure to watch these operational expenses including when payments to your company come and when you'll need to pay expenses.

Other factors you'll need to figure out might include filing for a business license, choosing a company name, launching a website, tracking revenue and operational costs, filing taxes, getting industry-specific certificates, setting up a business bank account, expanding and honing your sales approaches, updating your marketing, hiring others, giving team members feedback, firing others, organizing company finances, expanding your product services, saying no to bad contracts by reading them carefully, and avoiding multilevel marketing schemes (MLMs), and unethical business models. (MLMs prey on women and minorities,[21] and 99% of folks end up losing money. Do not join an MLM.[22]) All entrepreneurs who are successful in scaling their businesses have to figure these out. These take time, and you'll get to these hurdles when you get there. You do not need to do it alone. By the time you get to one of these things, ask for help! I have a CPA and lawyer on speed dial!

I believe in you! Anything is figure-out-able. Recently, I told my mom I was scared about how big a deal I was about to close, and she said, "You know you can always change your mind!," and I said, "I've been working on this deal for 10 months. Just because I'm scared doesn't mean I can't figure it out!" This is the same advice I give to you.

Quick Cash

Do you need to make quick cash? What if one of these 41 items totally excites you, but you need some cash to launch your vending machine empire? The initial cost of a vending machine with flip flops in it at a party venue costs $800. Table 13.2 shows a list of income streams that don't scale well but could make you some quick cash to enable your dreams. I've included sample revenue and operating costs for each way to make quick cash. There are other more risqué ways of making

[21] https://www.law.georgetown.edu/gender-journal/in-print/volume-xxiv-issue-1-fall-2022/multilevel-marketing-an-unwinnable-lottery-how-mlms-illegally-target-women-and-minorities-using-deceptive-and-predatory-recruitment-practices-and-the-need-for-specific-and-expanded-legal-protections

[22] https://www.huffpost.com/entry/mlm-pyramid-scheme-target-women-financial-freedom_1_5d0bfd60e4b07ae90d9a6a9e

TABLE 13.2 10 Ways to Make Quick Cash

No.	Income Stream	Revenue	Operational Cost	Description	Example Websites
1	Part-time jobs	$200	$0	Find part-time work through job postings.	Craigslist, OfferUp, Fiverr, Upwork
2	Online surveys	$50	$0	Earn extra income by completing online surveys. It is $1–$50 here and there if you need quick cash.	NewtonX, Swagbucks, InboxDollars, Survey Junkie, Branded Surveys, Toluna
3	Fellowships and awards	$200	$0	Apply for fellowships, awards, scholarships, and competitions relevant to your field to win monetary prizes.	**Scholarships.com, FastWeb .com, Niche.com, StudentScholarships.org, Unigo.com,** InboxDollars
4	Ride-sharing driving	$300	$75	If you have access to a car, work for ride-share companies for quick cash.	Lyft, Uber
5	Sell home items (clothes, lamp, etc.)	$150	$0	Sell items you no longer need or use. That coat you haven't worn in three years. Outfit to friend's wedding you'll only wear once.	Craigslist, OfferUp, Facebook Marketplace, Poshmark

TABLE 13.2 (Continued)

No.	Income Stream	Revenue	Operational Cost	Description	Example Websites
6	Delivery apps	$300	$40	If you have access to transportation like a car or scooter, you can deliver groceries, take out, and items.	Instacart, Doordash, Uber Eats
7	Babysitter, after-school care, nanny	$300	$0	Take care of kids and caretaking duties.	Craigslist, **Care.com**
8	Elderly care, driving to errands	$300	$0	Take care of elderly people, drive them to errands, etc.	Craigslist, **Care.com**
9	House cleaning	$500	$0	Clean houses in your neighborhood.	Craigslist, **Care.com**
10	Pet care	$600	$100	Take care of dogs, cats, and birds around you.	Craigslist, **Care.com**, **Rover.com**

money, but I'm only including ones I recommend that I'd be willing to do myself. Your mileage may vary. Your preferences and comfort levels are your own.

It's possible to scale these into a multimillion-dollar revenue opportunity, but typically, I see people using these routes to make cash to enable their other dreams. Notice in this table I've included potential revenue you'll get in and potential operational costs. I didn't include this in the other table, because it got too big for the size of the book! We'll talk more about operational costs in a minute.

Another option for these methods for quick cash is that you really love one of these options and want to scale a large-scale business that offers these services. You want to set up the premier elderly care errands company in your city. Fabulous! I love that creativity. These are ideas on the page. Overall, if you need to make some cash to enable the next steps in your business, instead of going into debt, I recommend you do one of the quick cash methods.

Revenue Is NOT Profit: Important Pitfalls to Avoid

A really important thing that many entrepreneurs do not track carefully enough is profit versus revenue. Let's say you are scaling your photography business. At first you take photographs for 3 families, then 5 families, then 30 families, then 100 families. You have websites, ads online, and a booming business. You hire other photographers to do some of the photo shoots. You hire someone to build a gorgeous custom website. Eventually, your photography business has $600,000 in revenue from all that work. However, you also need to pay the other photographers ($150,000), you need to pay website costs and ad spend ($300), and you have taxes to pay ($200,000). All of these operational costs could add up quickly ($350,300) if you're not tracking them. Profit is the amount of money left over after you pay *all* your operational costs. So in this case Revenue − Operational Costs, $600,000 − $350,300 = $249,700. When we divide profit by revenue $249,700 by $600,000, we get the margins for the business: 42%.

Have you ever heard the phrase "that company has healthy margins"? If so, this is what they are talking about. Some software companies run such lean operations that they have 70% margins! Why do you want larger margins? Margins show the health of a business. It's good to pay your staff equitably and make investments into sales and marketing. However, if you have no money left at the end of the day, you have almost no safety net. In the event of a key team member dying unexpectedly, a catastrophic event happens (like a pandemic!), or there is a big change in your industry, having little reserves in the bank leaves you with less opportunity to make pivots and save the business. In the previous example, if you spend all the revenue money on operations and have $100 left in the bank account after one year, your company might struggle in hard times. If you have $200,000 left in the bank, there's a higher chance you could be resilient across the years.

Revenue and profit are something I learned about later in my journey than I'd wished. There are several mistakes I could have avoided! Oh well! Most people are excited by how much money is coming in the door, but few have a lot of interest in tracking how much money they are spending to get those sales! So the next time you hear "We sold $3 million worth of energy bars!" or "We have more than 5,000 customers!" or " We just closed a deal with Walgreens!" consider what those operational costs might be at the company. What are those hidden numbers behind the curtain?

How to avoid pitfalls? Simple: you must have a system to track your "money out." I check my company bank account daily for any discrepancies. Are payments from customers coming in on time? Was there an unexpected fee or charge to dispute? You may want to review yours twice a month. If financial accounting is not your strong suit, that's totally fine! You don't need to have an accounting degree to be successful in this arena. You can hire a bookkeeper who sends you monthly reports and flags issues to you if they come up. There's much you can learn along your journey. You also do not need to do it all alone. Anyone who tells you that you have to do it alone is plain wrong. There's no honor in suffering alone. Get the support you need! Ask for help! I swear to you, the right people in your life are going to be so excited to help you realize your dreams!

By this point, I hope you are getting excited but potentially are also feeling lots of nervousness bubble up. Let's add more structure and give a concrete example of how you might start on your path to making millions based on your offer, starting with eight weeks of dedicated planning.

Questions for Reflection

Questions for You

- ☐ Do you have side income streams today? What are they, or what could they be?

- ☐ What emotions came up for you while reading this chapter? Are there doubts that bubble up? You are good enough, and you can figure it out FYI!

- ☐ Have you ever gotten stuck overpolishing? Focusing on a fancy obstacle rather than the actual offer and getting the email or post out the door? How can you work to overcome this?

- ☐ Were there any topics in this section that were new to you?

- ☐ Do you have money set aside for projects? How could you make quick cash?

- ☐ Have you heard about revenue, profit, and margins before? What surprised you about this section? What did you learn that you might apply to your own side hustle scaling?

CHAPTER 14

You Better Werk: Get Organized, Find Time, and Make Money

Before we talk about jumping into your multimillion-dollar adventure, I'd love to share with you how I've started to create organizations that started small and grew things bigger and bigger. I hope that through these stories you can see opportunities for yourself to start your ventures and grow. You and I might be starting in different places, but I bet there are parts of your journey that might map on to some of mine.

When I went off to college for undergrad, I was a young woman with colorful clothing and a passion for languages. I couldn't wait to meet other people from around the world who spoke different languages—especially French! The University of Washington (UW) boasts a beautiful campus in Seattle with humanities, social science, STEM, and business schools alike. When I arrived, however, there was no French Club. There were running clubs, pre-med clubs, and badminton clubs, but no French. Never fear! I went to an event about how to set up a club and formed the UW French Club.

Founding UW French Club

As the president of the French Club, I hosted events. We met weekly at Suzzallo Café, the beautiful cafe at the Cambridge-esque library at the heart of the campus on Red Square. Created by yours truly, our main slogan was "Come for the Food, Stay for the French."[1] We published our events on Facebook (now Meta), and I created friendly posters that we disseminated around campus.

I let French professors and the language departments know about the UW French Club to encourage their students to attend. As someone who loved to bake, I would bake cookies and cakes weekly. Little by little the club grew! People became friends who looked forward to seeing each other and attended every week and every quarter. I would arrive before the weekly meetings to move around chairs and tables as our numbers grew to 30–50 people weekly. We ate sweets, spoke French, and sometimes played games in French. I loved the community and served as the president for three years. Community and good food are some of the best parts of life. Don't you agree?

My passion fueled my desire to create the organization. UW French Club certainly didn't make me any money, but the experience helped me learn how to:

- **Setup:** Set up an organization
- **Name:** Name the organization (my name was obvious and clear, if not a tad boring)
- **Certification:** Get a club certified by the university so we could post on official boards around campus
- **Marketing:** Create marketing materials (graphic designs printed out and on social media)
- **Team:** Get support from members who wanted to help organize events and lead the club
- **Product:** Get experience with event planning, hosting events, and rallying people
- **Feedback:** Listen to feedback from people about what they liked and didn't like about the event
- **Improvement:** Iterate the types of events, games, and time of events

---

[1] Gracious! I didn't realize how long I've been moonlighting as a slogan writer. This whole time!

The stakes of the club weren't high, but it gave me experience for several other projects. The first one I closed $500,000 for was Women in Voice.

Founding Women in Voice

To date, I am most famous for being the founder of Women in Voice. Today, Women in Voice is a certified 501(c)(3) nonprofit with 20+ chapters on 6 continents with 100+ ambassadors. We have hosted hundreds of events internationally.

But it started small. In 2018, I was finishing my PhD and working on how to optimize datasets and voice AI projects for my research and for products of companies I worked for. I kept realizing how obviously bad our datasets were. For example, common ones had only 30% female voices in the speech dataset. I also noticed more and more as I worked in tech and began interviewing at tech companies that it was almost always rooms full of men. There were very few women and very few Black and Brown folks in any of these rooms.

It was the same story at tech conferences I spoke at, and it was the same story in buildings where the products were being created. When I went to interview at a company, I did not see another woman in the whole building during my time there. I was scared for my life! I got the job offer but didn't take it. The problem I wanted to fix in the performance of the AI we were building was the same problem in society. Now, I have never heard a man I've worked with say "I want to build a bad product that is racist and sexist," but sadly this happens every single day.

It dawned on me that if I was working in this field, I had only two options: be complicit in normalizing this world of men building projects that have no oversight and are racist and sexist or do something. I was tormented by this. I was so passionate about this field and these projects! I woke in the night as though a demon possessed me. I told people I wanted to start a nonprofit. My family was skeptical. My uncle said, "Joan, you're finishing your PhD and interviewing for a job; this really isn't a good idea to start a nonprofit. You think you have time for that?" I'm glad I did not take his advice.

I launched Women in Voice in 2018, as I mentioned in Chapter 8. I created a dinky logo, created a name, and created the account "@WomenInVoice." I created some posts and posted a form to ask people to express interest in "leadership positions." There was a flood of interest!

A few months later, I signed my first job that paid more than $100,000 per year. I scaled the community with events, got support from other women and men, and continued to post and attend conferences. We hosted events in Seattle, Madrid, the Netherlands, London, Mexico, and Japan! People of all genders attended our events, fueled by the love of voice AI, innovation, and inclusion. We created stages for women's work to be showcased and celebrated. We became one of the biggest brands in our field.

From the beginning I was the one paying the costs. Need to get a website up? Sure, I can pitch in $30. Need some food for that event? Okay, Here's $50. But eventually things got grander. In fact, we became so popular that Google and Amazon were banging down our doors to partner with us. We had always known we didn't want to profit off of women, so we decided to formalize as a 501(c)(3) nonprofit.[2] When we did that, I closed our first $100,000 sponsorship check with Google. In the next few years, my team and I closed $500,000 in sponsorships and membership dues, hired a team, and hosted Summits and Founder pitch events. Our board members work at Google, Amazon, and AI ethics institutions. I'm proud of what my team has accomplished.

If you look at these experiences, founding UW French Club and Women in Voice were on a tremendously different scale, but they had a lot of similarities. There was a name for the organization. There was a mission. I was exceptionally passionate about a topic and mission. I rallied people around an area of interest. There were events. Events and product offerings started small and got bigger over time. I didn't know how to create an event marketing poster until I did it for the French Club! I didn't know how to file for nonprofit status or set up a nonprofit bank account until I asked around and found a lawyer to help us. Was it easy? No. Was it all possible? Yes, yes, indeed.

Joan's Hot Take: Entrepreneurship Recipe: Build, Monetize, Scale, *Voilà!*

Entrepreneurship might be long, fancy work. But truly it's about selling a product. That's it! Oh, all the silly fancy jargon. Enough with fancy, let's just make some money.

---

[2] This is not the only path! You can have impactful organizations that are for profit. I prefer B corps. Do your homework! Know that I do not recommend creating a nonprofit these days based on the bad power dynamics with fundraising.

From my story to yours, what would you like to build? What is your point of departure to start or expand what you are building? As I'm writing this book for you, I'm realizing how easy it could be to read this book and then close it. To do nothing with all this rich information! I've been dreaming about how to make this book as practical and actionable for you as possible. How can I make this the most practical and actionable book for you? More structure. Templates! Next, I outline step-by-step how to get organized, set aside time, and make money.

Often, I dive in and then figure out the details of my venture. If you are currently at the edge of the diving board searching for courage and direction, let me provide more structure and frameworks. You can jump into the pool or take the stairs. Just make sure you're well on your way to making more money on your path to financial freedom! This next section is especially for you if you have no clue what you want to do next. The recommendations I have assume we're starting from ground zero. If you already have something underway, I recommend walking through the steps to make sure you have all your bases covered. This section is a "one-path-fits-many" path. I will work to be as clear and direct as possible.

Just Start: Online Businesses

As I mentioned in the introduction, lucrative opportunities are available to anyone with a computer, Wi-Fi, and time enough to take action. Multimillionaires and media moguls Arlan Hamilton, Dorie Clark, Amy Porterfield, Rachel Rodgers, Alex Hormozi, and Tina Tower all have content about their recommendations to build wealth via online businesses. The perks of an online business include no physical space, often low operating costs (i.e., rental space), and a heightened ability to scale to a lot of people (a few thousand to a million people might live in your city; billions of potential customers are online).

Businesses online are often less complicated, sometimes *because* they are digital. There is no restaurant with greasy vegan burgers, candle wax, or dog hair from the grooming salon to worry about. If easy to start sounds good, let's start here with online businesses. In this next section, I synthesize recommendations of these multimillionaires, especially investor Arlan Hamilton.[3]

---

[3] The "5 Steps to Making Your First Million in 24 Months!" episode of her podcast was super helpful: **https://open.spotify.com/episode/08aPYNXc6XVcRrjijZoVcU.**

Scaling to $1 Million in Revenue: The 3 Step PSS Framework

"A journey of a thousand miles starts with the first step," wrote sixth-century Chinese philosopher Lao Tzu.[4] So too can your journey to $1 million in revenue start with a first step. The PSS Framework has three steps: Product, Sales, and Stay the Course (PSS). Overall, this PSS Framework requires you to:

1. **Product:** Pick a product.
2. **Sales:** Sell the product by crafting an offer and marketing the product.
3. **Stay the course:** Continue to sell the product for at least two years.

With this overview, let's break it down into the first eight weeks. Like I said, I'm giving you a clear structure. I'll also walk you through how I could scale Your AI Bootcamp training into a $1 million revenue stream or more as an example using these methods. Table 14.1 shows an overview of the 24 months for the PSS Framework that starts with an intensive eight weeks.

TABLE 14.1	PSS Framework Overview to $1 Million in Revenue in 24 Months	
PSS Framework: Overview		
Week 1	Product	Choose a product (see the 41 ideas in Chapter 13!). Research marketing strategies.
Week 2	Sales	Choose three marketing strategies.
Week 3	Sales	Craft offer and transformation statement. Set up signups. How to pay.
Week 4	Sales	Launch offer. Tell the world.

....

[4] https://www.britannica.com/biography/Laozi, https://www.socratic-method.com/quote-meanings/lao-tzu-the-journey-of-a-thousand-miles-begins-with-one-step

TABLE 14.1 *(Continued)*

PSS Framework: Overview		
Week 5	Sales	Build the company.
		Rev up marketing.
		Batch content creation.
Week 6	Sales	Grow your leads and sales.
		Learn, grow, and iterate.
Week 7	Sales	Bolster your knowledge of sales.
		Maximize conversion.
Week 8	Stay the course	Stay consistent.
		Keep going for at least 22 months.

Week 1: In week 1, choose a product. Stop dilly-dallying around. Pick something! Can you change it later? For sure! The point is to get started and pick something. I recommend choosing a product that fits your expertise and interest. Choose a product, whether you've made it yourself or you're going to be selling for an affiliate or commission route. Remember that you can find a list of 41 income streams with product options in Chapter 13.

In the example here, I'll pick the bootcamp my team and I created to help people grow their networks and personal brands. It's called Your AI Bootcamp and is a training online and also offered asynchronous as a course by the name AI Brand Builder. If you're still feeling lost about which product to sell, there is a list of 8 to choose from in Table 14.2. These are accessible and can also scale to millions in revenue.

TABLE 14.2 **8 Digital Product Recommendations**

Easy and Scalable Products	
1	Online course
2	Online membership
3	Affiliate marketing
4	Consulting one-on-one and group
5	Agency
6	Trainings in person or virtual
7	SaaS subscription
8	eCommerce

Week 2: Once you've chosen a product, let's dive into research. In week 2 of the first eight weeks, you need to research marketing strategies. How will you connect with potential buyers? Who buys this type of product? Where are they? In Table 14.3, you'll see five easy digital marketing strategies to consider. I recommend you pick three of these. For Your AI Bootcamp, I promote it on the Your AI Roadmap podcast, via social media on LinkedIn, and via webinars and masterclasses.

TABLE 14.3   Marketing Strategies for Flywheel

Marketing Strategies	
1	Podcast
2	YouTube
3	Social content (Instagram, LinkedIn, TikTok, etc.)
4	Webinars
5	Workshop

Why do I recommend choosing three marketing strategies as you scale to $1 million in revenue? You want to be able to create a marketing and sales flywheel, like the example in Figure 14.1. Flywheels are very powerful. Here's an example of how you could sell bootcamp spots. Traditionally, many salespeople and marketers used funnels where a visitor enters the top of the funnel and then buys. Potential customers might download a free handbook PDF (a lead magnet) and then get sent into an email marketing until they buy a product. A flywheel is designed to adapt to customers who may want to get to know the brand and have multiple touchpoints.

People may want to see my social media posts, attend a webinar, hear me on my podcast, and begin knowing my public content for months or even years before buying. The flywheel allows me to update my content and approach based on what is working. If all my content about personal brands performs best (people comment more, react more, and are more engaged with this content), then I can make sure to focus on this type of content and build more products of this type. You can make add-ons and improve your core product offering.

Marketing Flywheel

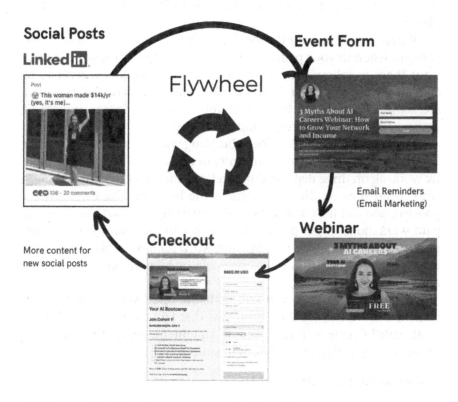

FIGURE 14.1   Marketing flywheel example for Your AI Bootcamp

Recently, I sold some Your AI Bootcamp spots by posting on social media about the bootcamp through storytelling.[5] The post had a link to an upcoming webinar. This took people to the event form. If people signed up, there were email reminders via email marketing. These folks then attended a webinar I hosted. The webinar had content about AI careers and then promoted Your AI Bootcamp. People then could purchase the bootcamp. All of the material in the bootcamp and webinar are content for more social media posts! This is the power of a flywheel. People give me feedback about the social media content and

---

[5] See the post for yourself at **https://tinyurl.com/4hj74ryj**.

the bootcamp. We watch our analytics in email marketing to see which content gets people to open the emails and buy. For my marketing and sales software recommendations, go to **YourAIRoadmap.com/ Flywheel.**

When you set up your flywheel, people might see your social media content, listen to your podcast, and then sign up for a workshop. You want them to follow the links and go from a passive observer to an actively paying customer. Social media content and YouTube content are some of the easiest because if you have a computer and Wi-Fi, anyone can set up an account and post things.

Ideally, you have already been building your personal brand online and have an audience and community in the areas of interest you have. By working on three dedicated marketing lanes, you can attract people who spend time on different parts of the Internet. You can launch a podcast, you can host webinars relatively easily, you can offer free and paid workshops to get people to engage with you, and you can also publish your work. Pick options that work for you. Make sure all the links are set up before you post on social media. Be open to feedback and iteration!

Week 3: In week 3, you will craft the offer. What would people want to buy? What are their problems that you can provide solutions to at scale? Create a transformation statement. When they buy your product, they will go from state A to state B:

Transformation statement:

A. Want to learn more about personal branding?

B. Be well-versed in personal branding with tangible knowledge and checklists to update LinkedIn profiles.

What will you teach them? How will you help them with a problem they have? How can they learn from you?

Week 4: In week 4, you'll launch your offer. This could be emailing or texting friends. This could be posting on social media. This could be creating a video on YouTube talking about it. You also need to set up a way for people to pay you for the product. In Table 14.4, you'll see five easy ways to set up signups and payment. Many people call this "conversion." You want people to give you their email and pay for the item. You can also ask them to sign up for the waitlist and demonstrate interest. Don't overpolish this. Get it ready to go out the door!

TABLE 14.4 Payment Options Ideas

Payment: Set Up How to Get Signups and Money (Choose at least one; don't overpolish)	
1	Email
2	Google Form
3	Website with Buttons
4	Course Hosting Site
5	Calendar Form

Week 5: In week 5, you'll build more content for your marketing lanes to increase exposure and sales.

Week 6: In week 6, you'll grow your leads and learn more about how to do sales for your product and marketing channels. Are quizzes the best idea? Do you need a free PDF as a lead magnet to encourage people to join your email newsletter? Research, iterate, and deploy.

Week 7: In week 7, you'll look at your sales conversion numbers. You'll iterate and get feedback from your community. Notice how weeks 5–7 build on each other. You need to spend significant time ramping up and iterating sales and marketing work.

Week 8 and Beyond: In week 8 and beyond, you'll stay the course to consistently make content and sell your offer. You'll learn from feedback and iterate. Do people say "I love the topic, but I care more about this than that?" "Do you offer x?" Listen and keep working on your marketing channels. The key over time is to stay consistent and resilient. Learn from your customers' feedback.

Feedback is a gift. Constructive criticism helps you better understand how people interpret your work. When I was writing this book, I asked several people to read over sections. Feedback people gave me included "I didn't understand what you were trying to say in this section" or "Can you give more examples here?" or "I don't get how these ideas are connected." This was highly actionable and made the book better for you! I could rewrite, give more examples, and give more explanation to connect the dots. You also want to get feedback about your work.

In the same way, I strongly recommend getting constructive feedback from your target audience (ideal customers). Are you selling a yoga workshop in person and online? Get feedback from 20 yoga students about their interests and what they'd pay for. Do you want to teach online courses about building your online brand? Get feedback from people about the length and content of the course. You need to talk to your buyers. If you get consistent feedback about changes, improve your product. After the intensive first eight weeks, now stay the course for 96 more weeks to sell this product, or variations as you learn, across a span of 24 months, 2 years. If you are resilient, learn, and stay the course, you can definitely begin generating robust sales and get closer to that million-dollars in sales goal.

Note also that of the 96 weeks of this launch of your digital business, 95 are spent on sales and staying the course. Having an idea is not enough. Doing the work and executing the tasks it takes to get sales rolling may take up to 99% of the work having a profitable business. Sales and resilience are crucial! Rome wasn't built in a day!

Five Secret Sauce Tips of Entrepreneurship

Entrepreneurship isn't easy. I'm not a founder who has sold 10 companies yet, but I have built things from the ground up. Here, I present five secret sauce pieces of advice for you along this journey. As we know each other a bit better, you'll notice I love me some data.

Data: My first recommendation is to collect data, review it, and know the "what" of core parts of your business. For example, when I launch a new product, we set up analytics and watch how many people come to the website and how many people buy. On a checkout page for Your AI Bootcamp, our analytics indicated for our first launch that 281 unique viewers saw the site and 8 purchased the Bootcamp, roughly a 3% conversion rate to paid customers. My team says the number of views might be slightly higher than the real number of customers since our team did rigorous testing and tweaking with bugs on the website and may have counted them even though they are not customers. Overall, we can learn about which checkout pages are effective in getting sales, while others are less persuasive to buyers. This type of analytics data is helpful for finding "what" is going on but doesn't always give us high fidelity on "why" people aren't buying.

Constructive Feedback: My second recommendation is to talk to your customers. Interview 10 to 15 customers or potential customers and ask them about their needs, buying preferences, how they have solved this problem in the past, and what their goals are. Does your product help them with their problem and provide a transformation? Getting feedback directly from the horse's mouth is underrated! For example, when I asked customers who expressed interest in Your AI Bootcamp why they didn't buy, they emailed me back saying the time of the coaching was not good with their schedule, that they wanted only part of the Bootcamp, and other reasons. We learned from this "why" they looked at the checkout page but didn't buy, and we made new products! These customers purchased the "Your Personal Brand 101" course and coaching right away when we repackaged the offer! How would we have known to do this without this feedback? A guess? In my experience, people are more honest than you'd expect. Constructive feedback is invaluable. You need to learn both from your successes and growth opportunities.

For example, when I asked a customer why she purchased Your AI Bootcamp, she said that she really wanted a weekly thing she had to show up for to keep her momentum going. My team assumed it was about the content, but it wasn't the biggest factor in her decision-making! Another potential customer told me he couldn't do the bootcamp because he has a young daughter and his number-one priority is being there for her. He said he loved the content but would prefer downloadable resources to do on his own time when it fit his schedule. Again, how would I have known that if I didn't interact with customers and people who didn't buy?

Keep learning and iterating! If you are earnest, keep following up, and actively listen to people, I'm confident you can find a way to improve your products, understand your buyers better, and grow your business. If you are truly hearing that no one wants your product, ask them about issues that they *do* want support with. What products are needed and wanted? I can't promise you I know the right time to pivot (frankly I'm a serial premature-pivoter myself), but I do recommend you don't die on a hill of trying to sell one thing when everyone is far more interested in another adjacent product you could sell. Listen and learn!

Visibility: Make sure people can find your product. Where are your customers? Go make sure there are posters in those buildings and posts on those online platforms. I met a podcast producer once who told me about her work, but when I went to her website, I couldn't find material there. When I asked her, it was in a subheader's subpage you had to know about four clicks down. That was her main offer, and I was confused and didn't purchase it. Like bestselling author of *Atomic Habits* James Clear recommends about habit forming, make it obvious, attractive, easy, and satisfying.[6]

Competition: Look at other companies in your space. While there might be "competitors," chances are high there is plenty of market demand in your field for you and many others. What are other companies doing well? Where aren't they strong? Check Yelp Reviews, Glassdoor Reviews, G2 product reviews, and more. If you have a big factor no one else has, make sure it's clear and emphasize it! If customers continue to be annoyed about a factor two of your competitors are struggling with, how could you differentiate? Customers are usually tired and looking for the best deal. Tell them what makes you and your products different! For example, when people asked me how Women in Voice is different from Women in AI, I'd say we're a niche that still includes a whole field of conversational AI where people can find their people in our subdomain, which covers linguists, voice actors, and prompt engineers alike.

Product-Market Fit: Combining the first two recommendations will lead you to my third piece of advice, a factor called *product-market fit* (PMF). This is a term used in startup circles to define when your product is really hitting its stride in the market and clearly satisfies your customer for specific buyers in a specific market.[7] Typically, you can see this traction in your sales numbers and customers are gushing about how much they love the product.

An example of this is a popular hot sauce company in Florida called El Camino Green Sauce. Chef Carl Savino was previously a Tour Chef for the Rolling Stones and U2 and translated that culinary knowledge into a fresh green hot sauce. The hot sauce gets reviews from people who write five-star ratings like "The only problem with this sauce is that it doesn't come with a straw! Kidding, but I do quite literally put it on everything."[8] The color of the sauce is this vibrant green, and the logo is a smiling hot dog with a sombrero. They can't keep making enough products for all the customer demand wanting to

---

[6] https://jamesclear.com/three-steps-habit-change
[7] https://builtin.com/articles/product-market-fit
[8] https://www.trustpilot.com/review/elcaminogreensauce.com

buy this amazing hot sauce![9] The market loves their product, and they have either hit this magical PMF or are darn close to it. By listening to feedback from customers and tracking the numbers, your company can also grow and thrive to hit phenomenal heights.

Okay, time for a recap! The PSS Framework stands for Product, Sales, and Stay the Course and is a framework to help you get to your first $1 million in revenue. Now that you've seen the PSS Framework, how about you fill it out for yourself? Table 14.5 is a blank template of the PSS Framework. I recommend setting aside 45 minutes to really think this through. Write your answers here, on a sheet of paper, or online.

TABLE 14.5 Your PSS Framework: Scale to $1 Million in Revenue Starting with 8 Weeks

PSS Framework: First 8 Weeks			My Answers. Today's Date:___/___/_____
Week 1	Product	Choose a Product (41 ideas in Chapter 13!) Research Marketing Strategies	Product Choice to Start:_____
Week 2	Sales	Choose 3 Marketing Strategies	3 Marketing Strategies: _____ _____ _____
Week 3	Sales	Craft Offer and Transformation Statement Setup Signups How to Pay	My Offer is: _____ Transformation: Customers will go from _____ to _____ _____
Week 4	Sales	Launch Offer Tell the World	My Offer Launch Date is:___/___/_____ I will set up my 3 Marketing Strategies

(Continued)

[9] Learn more at **https://www.elcaminogreensauce.com**. I haven't tried it yet myself, but if you're in the area, try it out and let me know what you think!

TABLE 14.5 *(Continued)*

PSS Framework: First 8 Weeks			My Answers. Today's Date:___/___/_____
Week 5	Sales	Build the Company Rev up Marketing Batch Content Creation	I will work on the company and continue revving up marketing and get more efficient and making content. Ideas Include: _____
Week 6	Sales	Grow Your Leads and Sales Learn, Grow, and Iterate	I'll increase my leads by: _____ I'll get feedback from customers by: _____
Week 7	Sales	Bolster Your Knowledge of Sales Maximize Conversion	I'll increase my knowledge of sales by: _____
Week 8	Stay the Course	Stay Consistency Keep Going for at Least 22 Months	I'll stay consistent with my plan for at least 22 months. Final day of test: ___/___/_____

Now that you've filled out the PSS Framework for yourself, you've got a whole sprint in front of you! This may sound obvious, but you also need to set aside the time to do this.

A Note on Time

I dive in. I start new projects quickly. I become fascinated by something that when I wake I'm thinking about it, between every meeting or work thing I'm working on it, on a run I'm iterating it, and sometimes I even dream about things I want to tweak or review. I am passionate! But this may not fit where you're at.

You don't need to become obsessed with your venture, but you *do* need to set aside the time. Once you take 45 minutes or more to fill out your plan, you also need to set aside time in your calendar. When are you going to do the research? When are you going to set up the sales and marketing? Pull up your calendar and block out the time. Will it be on lunch break? After work? Across weekends? Make sure you make time for something as fabulous as bringing in more money!

Let your family and friends know so they can support you in your journey if you think they'll be supportive. When I wrote this book, I asked for more support than usual with cooking and dog care duties. It's hard to be typing this chapter for you while playing fetch with my dog. I set aside time for cuddles and remind myself that if she wants to keep living the princess life with trips to the park and excellent treats, then I better be making that money! If you don't make the time, I'm sad to say that even the most fabulous plans on paper most likely won't happen.

Similarly, you must stay the course. Resilience is key! Keep iterating, keep the faith, and make pivots if you need to. Maybe you originally wanted to sell bootcamps, but everyone is begging for a course on personal branding they can do on their own time. Great! Let's give them that to buy. Be flexible, but also true to your goals.

A Note on AI for Business

As mentioned earlier, it can be a good idea to use modern tools to grow your income streams. I recommend looking into AI tools during the time of AI. However, AI doesn't "make" you money on its own, at least not legal ways I've found!

AI is a tool you can use. For example, my team uses AI tools internally to generate images, reformat slide decks, provide strategy ideas, give tactical recommendations about how to effectively negotiate with partners, and find sample phrases for difficult work conversations that need to happen.

Additionally, you can use AI to build something you can sell. For example, you could use the famous ChatGPT to help you create a children's book and sell it online. You can build AI tools and sell them, also! This is what my company Clarity AI does for small to medium-sized businesses. At Clarity AI, we identify a revenue-boosting opportunity and price what we can build for companies and teams. For example, we have been asked to make AI tools that automate copying and pasting codes from PDF to PDF, to make a tool that optimizes water usage for an agriculture company, to make predictive analytics for the highest business margins, and to leverage text from a database to categorize businesses. Our customers buy these products for five to eight figures. We love to help companies boost their revenue and work more efficiently! There are plenty of awesome AI tools to consider that I recommend. Check them out at **YourAIRoadmap.com/Resources.**

The Goal of $1 Million in Revenue

As you stay consistent and work toward hitting a seven-figure or even larger goal, you can break it down into more manageable units. Though $1 million sounds like a big number, how many of a product do you need to sell to get there? Well, fancy that! I've made Table 14.6 just for you to see it. How much product do you need to sell? Depends on the price of the product.

TABLE 14.6	How to Get to $1 Million Revenue, Product Price Point, and Number of Products Sold	
Product Price	**Number of Products Sold**	**Product Price × Number Sold Is $1 Million in Revenue**
$100	× 10,000	$1,000,000
$200	× 5,000	$1,000,000
$500	× 2,000	$1,000,000
$1,000	× 1,000	$1,000,000
$2,000	× 500	$1,000,000
$5,000	× 200	$1,000,000
$6,667	× 150	$1,000,000
$10,000	× 100	$1,000,000
$20,000	× 50	$1,000,000
$50,000	× 20	$1,000,000
$100,000	× 10	$1,000,000
$200,000	× 5	$1,000,000
$500,000	× 2	$1,000,000
$1,000,000	× 1	$1,000,000

When you actually write down these numbers, they seem less scary to me. "$1 million in revenue" can sound so big and scary if you're currently making $62,000/year. But when you're an entrepreneur, this is a benchmark that people are commonly shooting for.

Well, in the beginning, it is likely that your product price might be low. I strongly recommend you increase it substantially. The fastest way to make substantial revenue is to have high product price points. Rachel Rodgers recommends women double their prices since men typically start with a higher price point. As you see at the very end of the $1 million revenue table, you need to sell only two products that cost one-half million to sell $1 million worth of revenue. I have closed six-, seven-, and eight-figure contracts. If the contract is $10 million, then you already have really high revenue! Spoiler, though! Your operating costs might also be quite high to deliver that product. Once you've created a stellar product, what you really need to do is sell, market, and sell the same product some more! This is what I mean by scaling.

Advanced Revenue Options

Before we end this hefty and I hope very helpful chapter, I also want to address the advanced readers here. Most people I speak with are working on their passion project and monetizing it. Many want to start something and get ideas that are easy to medium difficulty. If you are already well on your way and want to peruse some advanced options, Table 14.7 shows 16 advanced options for income streams. These typically require far more money to start, assume you already have real estate, expect you have executive knowledge of a domain, and assume you are prepared to scale a national franchise. These options aren't for everyone, but just in case you thought the examples in this book were too easy, these up the ante for you!

If these ideas aren't the right fit for you today, no sweat! You can at least read them over to dream of what further life chapters of yours could hold! Do you want to make your first millions and then publish a book and do paid public speaking? All of these are possible for you. In Chapters 13 and 14, we have covered 41 easy to medium income stream options and 16 advanced income stream options. That's 57 options! If you'd like to have these options for reference, you can download them at **YourAIRoadmap.com/Resources**.

TABLE 14.7   16 Advanced Income Streams[10]

	Income Stream	Description
1	Invest in real estate	Buy rental properties to generate income that exceeds mortgage and operating costs.
2	Rent out space	Rent out rooms or specific amenities (like pools) in your home on platforms like Airbnb or Swimply.
3	Real estate investment trusts (REITs)	Invest in real estate without having to buy, manage, or finance properties directly.
4	Royalties from intellectual property (IP)	Earn royalties from licensing your ideas, patents, or copyrighted works.
5	Advisory fee services	Assist companies in achieving specific goals, like getting their AI plan together at the company and preparing presentation decks.
6	Paid speaking	Engage in public speaking on expert topics and negotiate payment for speaking engagements.
7	ATM ownership	Place and maintain ATMs in strategic locations. Earn fees from transactions.
8	Laundromat	Operate a self-service laundry business. Expand to several locations.
9	Publish a book	Write and sell a book based on your expertise, either through traditional publishing or online sales.
10	Franchise	Find a really good company or product (restaurant, pet grooming business, hair salon, etc.) and franchise it. Document standard operating procedures, maximize the finances, and sell it nationally and internationally.
11	Fractional C-suite services	Offer fractional (part-time) chief-level services to companies. For example, be a fractional chief marketing officer (CMO) for five companies who all pay you $100,000 per year to help them roadmap their marketing. I've hired fractional chief financial officers (CFOs) and worked in fractional capacities for startups.

....

[10] If you'd like to download this list, go to **YourAIRoadmap.com/Resources**.

TABLE 14.7 (*Continued*)

	Income Stream	Description
12	Parking lot ownership	Purchase a parking lot and earn income from people paying to park there. This is especially great around sports stadiums where people pay a premium.
13	Private equity	Buy a company, and improve the company by increasing prices, cutting operational costs, and selling it or taking the company and its shares public.
14	Website flipping	Create or buy a website or other asset and sell it later (**Flippa.com, Acquisitions.com, Acquire .com**), similar to private equity but different types of products.
15	Broker mergers and acquisitions	Get a commission from connecting buyers and sellers for private equity deals.
16	Venture capital	Invest in companies and make money when the companies increase in value and sell via an acquisition or IPO.

Source: Adapted from [10]

Well, that was a content-dense chapter! Sounds like you might be ready for a break. Need a walk or tea break? Now is an excellent time.

To recap, in this chapter we reviewed how I founded UW French Club and Women in Voice from the ground up. We talked about how hard it can be to just start and how I recommend trying an online business. We reviewed in depth the PSS Framework for Product, Sales, and Stay the Course. We walked through what you need to do for the first eight weeks with eight product ideas, five marketing strategies to generate your fabulous flywheel, how to craft an offer with a transformation statement, and how to create a way for your product offer. We also talked about how constructive feedback is a gift, and we filled out your own PSS Framework (I hope! If not, go back and do it!). We talked about how important it is to set aside the time and hit that goal of at least $1 million in revenue. We finished with 16 advanced revenue options.

Whew! It was a lot. Well, I promised you practical, actionable, and data-driven advice. I hope I fully kept my end of the bargain! In the next chapter, we'll talk about what your life will be like with all that money. We'll talk more about financial freedom and a future-proofed life. Let's do it!

Questions for Reflection

Questions for You

- ☐ Have you ever created an organization or event? What was it? Why did you create it? What did you learn?

- ☐ Do you have experience with marketing? Sales? Do you know people around you who sell things well? Who do you respect and could learn from? Are there people online you follow you could learn from?

- ☐ What projects have you started but then not completed? Which projects might you want to pick up again? What went wrong? What was the obstacle (in the WOOP version of you getting to your dream outcome; see Chapter 14).

- ☐ Have you already tried monetizing a project? What worked, and what didn't?

- ☐ What prevents you from starting an income stream? Mindset? Fears? A friend doubting you? What will help you get past those obstacles and make a plan to get $1 million in revenue into your bank accounts?

- ☐ Does the PSS Framework make sense to you? Is there already a product in mind that calls your name? Are there ones you want to learn more about?

- ☐ Did you fill out the framework? What excites you? Scares you? Believe in yourself, you got this!

- ☐ Have you heard about sales funnels or marketing flywheels before? Have you experienced one by signing up for a webinar or training?

- ☐ When could you set aside three to five hours to begin your project? How can you block time in your schedule and make time for this?

- ☐ Have you already made a project and want to riff on ways to monetize it? Can you talk to friends or other stakeholders at coffee chats about this? Or how could you get more feedback to narrow down a specific product and launch it? Start small, iterate, and keep sharing your work!

- ☐ Have you already made a project and want to riff on ways to monetize it? Can you talk to friends or other stakeholders at coffee chats about this? Or how could you get more feedback to narrow down a specific product and launch it? Start small, iterate, and keep sharing your work!

- ☐ Which of the advanced options is new to you? Are there any you'd like to one day try?

CHAPTER 15

How Financial Freedom Feels: Fire Me, I Don't Care, My Income Is Future-Proofed!

In the previous chapter, we reviewed how you can generate quick cash, how you can make a simple offer, and how you can scale into the goal of your first $1 million in revenue. It might take time, but you can become a multimillionaire. For you to achieve financial independence, you need to know, grow, and be in control of your money. Imagine what that would look like. What would it feel like? How would your life be different? Imagine that you have scaled your income streams to over $3 million in the next few years. Your business is flourishing. You've figured out how to get through hurdles. Things that were once difficult, you got support for and found that you could figure things out. You watched your operational costs. You make good margins and robust revenue. What does this mean for your life? What expansive and rich life do you want? In this chapter, I'd love for us to dream together about financial freedom and stability.

Future-Proofing Your Income: On Wealth, Goals, and Values

When people talk about financial independence and future-proofing your income, the first thing that may come to mind is influencers. Social media is covered with influencers wearing designer clothes on yachts, walking through mansions, and driving fancy cars. You might think about billionaires, people with three houses and private jets. This certainly is a type of wealth. However, I define wealth as being financially secure and confident. It's not about a specific, universal number. To me, a rich life is about time, joy, freedom, agency, and having that delicious stability that comes from seven-figures or more in your own accounts in your own name that you can access at any time. It's less about showy external things. It's a deep inner calm.

Joan's Hot Take: Wealth Is Inner Peace

> For me, financial independence is about a deep inner calm more than a number on paper.

Wealth influencer Vivian Tu says the true mark of a rich person is that they don't feel the need to prove themselves.[1] If someone is continually talking about how "wealthy" they are, chances are *high* that they actually lack true stability emotionally and financially. They are looking for external validation, which means they aren't truly centered and financially sound. Another way to say it? The gentleman doth protest too much. Truly wealthy people do not give f*cks about what anyone else thinks. Prime examples of this are from Portland, Oregon, where I grew up.

People in Portland are notorious for not caring about fashion. Can you say socks, Birkenstocks, and baggy shorts for days? Despite their lack of fashion, these folks often have *plenty* of money to spend. A family friend owns a boutique and teaches her sales representatives

---

[1] https://www.cnbc.com/2023/12/27/i-became-a-millionaire-at-age-27-unpopular-rules-rich-people-follow-that-most-dont.html

not to judge anyone's appearances by how much they might spend at the company. "Treat everyone as though they could buy the most expensive things in the store!"

This is a good approach as some of the wealthiest people I know don't show their wealth outwardly. I can name five high net worth individuals off the top of my head that you'd *never* knew had millions in their portfolios from their appearances. Talk about stealth wealth! An example from my own family is that my grandpa dressed simply in gray sandals and cargo pants and drove a practical car. However, he was known to give huge tips and donations. In fact, his tips were so large that servers would ask if he made a mistake! Famously, he made a large donation to a service organization in his community. Their work spoke to his heart. When they asked the community for donations, he gave generously. The organization called him to ask, "Did he add an extra zero by mistake?" These people thought, "Could this older man dressed like this possibly have this much money? Can he safely make tips and donations of this size?" Indeed, he did and he could. Truly wealthy folks I know care most about their health, family, community, and passions that light them up. They don't care what *you* think! My grandpa certainly didn't. He cared about living into his values and spending his money accordingly.

Imagine if you could live your life the way you actually wanted to. Maybe for you, it's about finally feeling financially stable. Ahhhh. Or perhaps it could be about buying your dream home. It could be spending ample quality time with your kids and taking them on trips around the world. Maybe it's about continuing your education in a different country. Perhaps you want to pay for a premium education for a family member. Maybe you'd love to invest in projects to improve maternal mortality. Maybe you want to give to important causes in your community. Those goals and choices are your own. Is it clicking? That's what I'm saying! The choice is yours when you have financial freedom.

On vacation recently in Maui, I saw what appeared to be a happy woman at the beach. She was well-rested. She was healthy and toned from head to foot. This woman works out regularly! She was present. She was playing with her giggling toddler who was clean and happy. In her designer bathing suit with a full manicure, pedicure, and gorgeous jewelry, it was clear that this woman has financial independence. While this vision might be more femme and maternal than your goals, I hope you can visualize your version of your happiest, well-rested, vacationing self. I want this type of quality self-care, freedom, and connectedness that I saw on that beach for myself and you.

Side Effects of Income Expansion: Warning! Results May Include Happiness

When you have built robust revenue streams, you can future-proof your income. For me, even though I haven't hit my FI number yet, the work I have done toward future-proofing my career and income have changed my life. When I moved out of scarcity mode and expanded my income, I experienced the following:

- Felt more food security
- Let go of French tutoring students who didn't bring me joy
- Bought myself nicer professional outfits at thrift stores
- Ate healthy, fresh food
- Went to therapy to process the trauma of the past and become more the person I want to be
- Rented an apartment in a safe neighborhood
- Contributed the maximum amount to my retirement accounts every year
- Worked out regularly and hit my dance cardio classes weekly
- Made romantic decisions that were the right choice for me
- Quit a job after senior management screamed at me and my boss condoned it
- Turned down job offers that were too low, required relocation, and/or had long commutes
- Took risks in my career with more confidence

These are just a few examples of items that you might also want for yourself.

Future-Proofing Your Career

Now, let's connect the work on my finances to those of my career. Investments I've made via goal setting, personal brand, networking, and owning my story have accelerated some of my financial goals. Here are career highlights directly related to work I've done on my career, some past and some present:

- Buy books, courses, and tickets to conferences where I learn and level up professionally.
- Take naps when I need to. Rest is fundamental.
- Travel with friends and family.
- Got offered a job offer *hours* after I posted online that I was looking for one.
- Get flown to fancy conferences and get amazing opportunities in my DMs.
- Live where I want to.
- Have a robust emergency fund.
- Donate to causes and charities I believe in.
- Hire help for dog care, house sitting, groceries, and house cleaning. (A game changer! And the college student I hired is delighted about the extra cash. That was me needing that extra cash while getting my degree just a few years ago!)
- Hire help at work for projects, website work, podcasts, etc.
- Invest in startups I believe in, even knowing I could lose all my investment in a risky asset class.

These are how I have been building my career and finances. In the future, I have even bigger goals after I hit my FI number. I want more massages. More time away from screens and out in nature. I want to travel more and see the National Parks. I want to champion social justice causes. I want to invest more in female founders and founders of color! It's all possible. I hope you join me.

So back to *you*! What would you want your rich life to look like? What are your goals? What are the obstacles and steps to make your goals a reality? Goal setting? That sounds familiar! Let's call back to our WOOP method goal framework from Chapter 2.

WOOP Method Goal for Your Financial Independence

Let's check out what a WOOP method goal might look like for you to hit your financial independence:

Wish: I wish to future-proof my income and hit my financial independence (FI) number.[2]

Outcome: I can live the life I want without financial restrictions.

Carefree: I do not live in financial insecurity or layoff anxiety. I have enough money to be resilient through times of change, aging, medical emergencies, and more.

Time: I can structure my days how I want, travel, nap, rest, take care of myself, take care of my family, give back to my community, and live the life of my dreams.

No day job needed: I do not need a 9-to-5 job and paycheck. I don't have to try to climb corporate structures created by and for wealthy white men. I can keep working for money if I want to, but it's not a requirement.

Freedom: I have an abundance of agency and freedom because of my financial stability.

Obstacles: I need to address the obstacles that get in the way of my path to financial freedom.

Mindset: Sometimes the trauma of being laid off or having scarcity about paying grocery bills comes up. I feel anxiety and talk through those fears with my therapist and friends.

Persistence: It can take years to hit an FI number. I have to stay persistent, resilient, and steadfast in pursuing my goal. There are fancy, shiny things nearby about cars and trips that are alluring, but hitting milestones yearly toward my FI number is more important in the long run.

Plan: To get past the obstacles, I need to address each one. I follow Joan's *3-Part Financial Freedom Recipe*. For a more detailed refresher on this, head back to Chapter 9.

---

[2] And beyond, perhaps? You can always want more. That's totally fine. I have goals beyond my FI number also! If you want to review content on FI numbers, check out Chapter 12.

Know: Money in, money out, and money left over, I know where my money is and what is going on with it.

Grow: I know how to grow my income and income streams. I continue to invest in a diversified portfolio and use the 4% drawdown method to keep my overall portfolio robust.

Be in Control: Just in case there is huge turbulence in my life, I have 6–12 months of living expenses in an HYSA. I have periodical check-ins to review my finances. I make changes if necessary. I have my life insurance set up to take care of my loved ones. My will is up-to-date and squared away. I am building legacy wealth for myself and my family.

As I review this WOOP goal for financial independence, big emotions bubble up for me. I'm nervous and also excited. For you, there might be some big emotional hurdles to tackle. You may have a new mountain of clerical work! That's okay! It took me a while to get my financial house in order when I began uncovering all the optimizations I could do for my finances.

Financial Freedom Power Hour: Make the Time

I recommend setting aside a few hours here and there and blocking them on your calendar. You could label the time block "Financial Freedom Power Hour." In those time chunks, you can set up accounts, tidy legal things, and fill out the spreadsheets and frameworks in this book. The only way you're going to make this happen is if you set aside the time and do it.

Are some of these tasks you may need to do boring? Yep! Annoying? For sure! Sometimes accounts are pesky to set up. Companies may put roadblocks in your way to paving your way to financial independence for their own reasons. But it is worth it. You may want and need support from supportive friends and family (and reminder there's NO obligation to inform your pesky, condescending uncle[3]).

---

[3] Or whoever else is a hater or doubter for you. Lucky you if you don't! If you do have people like this in your life, you know what I'm talking about. Boundaries, my friend! Boundaries. If your doubter is you, it might be time for therapy!

Ideally, I've helped to make them easier for you throughout this book! Reminder, you can download the frameworks and resources from this book at **YourAIRoadmap.com/Resources.**

From Food Stamps to Multimillionaire

One of the things that might be coming up is doubting that this is possible for you. You might be thinking, "Well, Joan, you're a privileged, educated, white chick. Is this really possible for me?" I'd like to speak directly to those doubts and fears. In Chapter 2, I shared Arlan Hamilton's story. She previously lived on food stamps. She did not go to college. She is a Black, gay woman. She has raised more than $30 million and is a multimillionaire. Was it hard work? Yes. Did it take years? Also, yes. But if it was possible for this amazing Black, gay, woman from the South, then I bet it's possible for you. On Hamilton's podcast *Your First Million*, she speaks about the connection between money and options:

> *The reality was I didn't have cash flow. And because I didn't have cash flow, I didn't have options. And because I didn't have options, I didn't have freedom. And I believe that every single one of us, every single one of you listening, has incredible ability, enormous ability to be not only where I am but way beyond where I am, without question, to do laps around what I've done, laps around the sun. I want that for you so desperately. I want that for you so bad because I just know we all have the ability to get there.*
>
> *I was so hungry and I don't mean in a good way. I was so physically hungry most days. I was so down and out. I'm 42 today, and for 35 years I was broke, poor, I had really rich experiences along the way, and I'll always treasure those."[4]*

Hamilton was physically hungry and broke for 35 years but was able to build cash flow, have options, and get her freedom. It is not

---

[4] Shortened version. Episode here: **https://open.spotify.com/episode/08aPYNXc6X VcRrjijZoVcU**

lost on me how powerful and revolutionary it is to use the word "freedom" when talking about a Black woman in the United States who has built her own wealth and path through a racist and sexist world. She believes that "every single one of us" has the ability to be not only where she is but "way beyond." That's pretty powerful evidence.

Hamilton is spectacular but not the only Black woman to achieve the extraordinary. In Chapter 10, I shared the story of Rachel Rodgers, a multimillionaire Black mother of four children. She previously had a credit score of 480,[5] a mountain of student loan debt,[6] and a car that was repossessed twice.[7] But from this instability and financial insecurity, she has built a multimillion-dollar company that employs 25 people.[8] In her book, Rodgers writes about how people can craft their offer and scale their businesses to become a millionaire within three years.[9] Again, Rodgers is not an anomaly either! Rodgers' *Hello Seven* podcast has more than 100 episodes[10] of her interviewing women entrepreneurs and many female and male entrepreneurs of color about creating seven- and eight-figure businesses. I'm talking $10 million in revenue and above! Slogans on her website include "Goodbye, financial stress. Hello, seven figures!"[11] and "It's not impossible. It's doable."[12]

Hamilton, Rodgers, and I are on the same page. All of this is possible for you. You can definitely check out their podcasts and books. Much of their work is synthesized and referenced throughout this book, especially in Chapters 13 and 14. With all that said, I'd like you to make this journey your own. I know you did a WOOP goal in the career section. I'd now like you to make one for your WOOP financial independence. What does it look like? What obstacles are in your way? What is your plan to use the frameworks, checklists, and resources in this book to create your own roadmap?

---

[5] *We Should All Be Millionaires*, p. 241
[6] https://rachelrodgers.com/press
[7] https://helloseven.co/podcast/leadership-skills
[8] https://helloseven.co/about
[9] (p. xii)
[10] https://open.spotify.com/show/5Z94TrOMD5mnhldQjeD9Rr
[11] https://helloseven.co/about
[12] https://helloseven.co

Your AI Roadmap: Future-Proofed Career and Income Framework

Ready? Let's do this! Let's write your future-proofed career and income roadmap to thrive in the age of AI:

Wish: I wish in my career: _____

_____

I wish in my finances:_____

_____

Outcome: The outcome would look: _____

_____

The outcome would feel:_____

_____

Obstacle: Obstacles in my way are: _____

_____

_____

_____

Plan: If the obstacles _____ happen, then I will _____

_____

Spend the time to fill out Your AI Roadmap: Future-Proofed Career and Income Framework. It will be worth it. I'm confident you can do this. Go back to specific chapters if you need to. Reminder that you can download this resource and others from this book at **YourAIRoadmap .com/Resources.**

Questions for Reflection

Questions for You

☐ How did it feel to imagine your life with financial freedom?
☐ What emotions came up for you while reading this chapter?
☐ What are new learnings from this book you incorporated?

☐ What are obstacles that you might have been struggling with for years? What can you do differently? Do you know what your specific obstacle is? How can you get help with it?

☐ Do you resonate with parts of Hamilton and Rodgers' stories about hard times? Both of them increased their income, got in control of their finances, and now are living the lives of their dreams.

☐ What doubts do you have? Why do you not believe in yourself? Is there a reason you don't believe you could live your biggest, rich life? Why do you think your situation is so much worse or impossible compared to these stories? You're special, but you're not unique. I'd let go of the excuses, make the time, and tackle the action items.

☐ How are you going to navigate through these waters differently from the past? Do you need to ask for support? Would getting support from a therapist help you?

☐ How much happier and freer could your life be? Let's go!

CHAPTER 16

Haters Gonna Hate: Let's Say I'm Wrong

I n this short chapter, I want to address the doubters. If you've made it this far in this book, it's hard to imagine you really can't stand my advice, but maybe you've got serious doubts. You really aren't down with my data-driven evidence. Let's say you do *not* want to get to know more people, invest in your personal brand, expand your network, get your finances in order, or expand your wealth. I hear you. You might be tired, worn-out, feeling sad, and still questioning whether any of this would help you.

In this chapter, I would like to speak directly to those with serious doubts. This chapter will review the counter examples. In the United States, we teach the five-paragraph essay method. You explain a concept and argument, three reasons you're right, and then a conclusion. In the French educational system, you explain a concept and an argument, then you explain a counter argument, and then you explain why the counter argument is wrong. Let's go a little European in this chapter.[1]

Let's review the advice from this book in concrete and specific terms from this hallmark, and then the contrarian perspective. There is plenty of advice in here, but you are welcome not to agree with me. Let's review where those choices of inaction might lead you. In Table 16.1, I'll review counter choices to the recommendations I make in this book, the result of them, and the topic overall referenced. Get ready for some contrarian content!

---

[1] Are you a European reader reading my American-centric book? You rock, you! Bienvenue!

TABLE 16.1 Counter Argument, Result, and Topic in This Book[2]

Counter Choices	Result	Topic	From Where in the Book
You never question the things you think and do mind work.	You get stuck in patterns and let the ideas of others shape your path without reflection.	Thought Work	Chapter 1
Never reflect on the meaning of your life.	You do not know your meaning or why you get out of bed in the morning.	Ikigai	Chapter 2
No desire to make a job or career path.	Stay in one job forever, lose a job easily with a layoff, do not grow your paycheck.	Finances	Chapter 9
No online presence.	You do not have the ability to be seen online by others.	Personal Brand	Chapter 5
You have no LinkedIn; people don't see a profile there.	You do not get known beyond a small group of people.	Networking	Chapter 4
No goals.	No ambition, stagnate.	WOOP Method	Chapter 2
Do not define obstacles to your goals.	Hit the same obstacles again and again and get stuck there.	WOOP Method	Chapter 2
Don't make a plan.	Unable to hit goals without knowledge of obstacles and plans to overcome them.	WOOP Method	Chapter 2
Don't measure your successes.	Do not document your successes for future use and celebration.	STAR method	Chapter 8
Never strive in your career and do the same job for life.	Be underpaid and overworked for life, CEOs make 400% the average employee.	Systemic Oppression	Chapter 9

(Continued)

[2] https://docs.google.com/spreadsheets/d/17vMTYUycKp0ziPFBHDMJgGC2ogvAiHK-R372A9ytrSM/edit?usp=sharing

TABLE 16.1 *(Continued)*

Counter Choices	Result	Topic	From Where in the Book
Never talk about your successes.	People do not necessarily know your work or successes ever.	STAR method	Chapter 8
You hide under a rock.	People cannot find you or know you exist. You may perish in silence.	Networking	Chapter 4
Have little to no network.	Cannot leverage your network when you need support.	Networking	Chapter 4
Hope people give you credit for your work without you showing them.	People sometimes do not see your work, take your work as their own.	STAR method	Chapter 8
Never take the first step and choose the "nothing" option of "all or nothing."	Never make steps toward goals you don't even know whether you have.	Prototyping	Chapter 8
Dive into plans (i.e., expensive degrees, moves to other states, jobs) you haven't researched.	Unsure if it fits your goals, could incur huge amounts of debt, not sure if it's a good fit.	Prototyping	Chapter 8
Be unaware of your finances.	Not know how much you spend a month regularly and have an emergency fund.	Finances	Chapter 9 and 10
Talk to no one about your finances.	You live in a world where money is taboo and you don't learn amazing skills to be effective and build your wealth.	Taboo	Chapter 9
Not know your net worth.	Be unaware of the overall financial health of where you are and where you want to go.	Finances	Chapter 12
Not know your financial independence number.	Not know how much money you need to one day retire.	FI	Chapter 12

TABLE 16.1   *(Continued)*

Counter Choices	Result	Topic	From Where in the Book
Never consider how to expand your wealth.	Think your wealth is restricted for life based on what 9-to-5 job you can get.	Expansion	Chapter 9
Never invest in the stock market and make money while you sleep.	Never grow the money you have and live in a scarcity mindset of frugality.	Investing	Chapter 11
You make more money, but spend more and have no money left over.	Never grow your wealth and have financial security.	Lifestyle creep	Chapter 10

Source: Adapted from [2]

Gosh, the emotions bubbling up for me writing this table weren't great. I felt sad and frustrated. Some of my friends feel this way and don't work on making changes. Maybe some of these are pieces you believe. I'm not saying you need to do all of these things starting today, but I strongly recommend you begin your journey.

Results of Inaction: Unaware of Your Goals

You don't know what your goals are. You don't succeed at things you're interested in. You stay lost. Honestly, this one breaks my heart, and I want to move on because it hurts. I hope this book supports you in becoming more and more aware of your goals and the possibilities around you.

Results of Inaction: Don't Take the Next Small Steps

You don't take action. You don't set aside time. You watch your favorite K-drama and scroll Instagram instead. You get too overwhelmed even to take the next step. Good news! If you've read to this point in the book, you know that you can prototype. You can take the next small step to validate your choices and move to bigger steps. The only way to know if it's the right direction is to go a few more steps down the path!

Results of Inaction: No Network, Not Landing a Job, Not Bringing in Income

My friend Harrold lost his job during a layoff. He has been on the job market for over a year and a half. I have seen jobs that he could be good at but when I ask him to send me a résumé so I can make an introduction, he does not follow up. One time when he did send a résumé, it was such a poor résumé that I couldn't possibly send it to anyone for consideration. It would be embarrassing for him, and it would tarnish my reputation. I know he's a smart and hardworking person! As of the writing of this book, he still does not have a job. He has told me he has significant debt. I'm truly worried for Harrold.

Results of Inaction: No Research on Compensation or Negotiation, Being Underpaid

My friend Marcel got a new job recently. He is a lot older and wealthier than me and in the last chapter of his career. When he was offered a new job, they asked him how much to pay him. He did not do the research or ask around. He asked for $190,000 per year. They approved it right away and mentioned in passing that they would have approved $200,000 per year easily. Marcel accidentally left over $10,000 on the table. That amount of money could be an amazing trip and much, much more.

Joan's Hot Take: Take Action

If you want to future-proof your career and income, you must take action.

I have seen the results in their lives where big things have happened, and they have no network to rely on. They do not know the goals in their life. They do not take action. They doomscroll social media. When I look at all the actions I'm taking and those of folks who don't take action, months to years later, our careers and financial situations are in different places. I mentioned the story where my friend has $150,000 less in her retirement than I did. I have a different amount of confidence, friends, and opportunities in my inbox. These differences in actions have big effects in the short and long term.

Results of Inaction: Living in Fear and Financial Insecurity

To be able to future-proof your career and income, I strongly recommend you take action on the gaps in your network and brand as the exercises in this book explore. I have provided the counter arguments and seen the results. I want the best for you and cannot recommend them.

Bleh! This chapter was horrible to write. I hope you can see from these counter arguments to my advice where those choices could lead you. Not great places! Please take my advice and future-proof your career and income, my dear reader. That is what this book, *Your AI Roadmap*, is all about. Let's move on to more optimistic and powerful waters. Let's talk about what's on the horizon for you as we work to make the world a better place for all.

Questions for Reflection

Questions for You

- ☐ What advice in this book has surprised you?
- ☐ What mindset isn't serving you? Where are you finding obstacles?
- ☐ What parts of this book have opened your mind? Writing this book I learned things!
- ☐ What are the aspects of inaction that you are participating in? Things your friends and family have gotten stuck in? Share this book with them! Or at least consider how they might have gotten there and have empathy for understanding where they are coming from.

CHAPTER 17

Beyond AI's Horizon: Mindset and an Irresistible Revolution

Like you, Jennifer had big dreams. After only one semester of college, she dropped out and began working as a dancer. Gigs and music videos paid her $25–50. Not that momentous a start, but Jennifer had hustle. She was hired to work on Broadway and beat out 2,000 other applicants for a key role as a dancer. That's the top 0.05%. Wow! Jennifer then said she also wanted to go into acting. People said, "You're a dancer; you can't be an actor."[1]

Wow, she proved them wrong. She landed a lead role in the movie *Selena*. Jennifer was paid $1 million for the role, shattering a glass ceiling for Latina actresses. Then she decided she also wanted to be a singer. Her first music album *On the 6* was a smash hit in 1999. Next came her leading roles in the hits *Maid in Manhattan* and *The Wedding Planner*. Jennifer has an incredible work ethic.[2] She goes after her goals unabashedly!

That's right, Jennifer is Jennifer Lopez, J.Lo. From music videos paying $25 back in the day, J.Lo now has an estimated net worth of $400 million.[3] Can I tell you how much I *love* knowing that J. Lo. owns a $20 million penthouse in Manhattan?[4] Today, J.Lo is "a dancer, who

---

[1] https://www.netflix.com/title/81031929
[2] https://www.billboard.com/music/pop/jennifer-lopez-on-the-6-if-you-had-my-love-interview-8513788
[3] https://www.celebritynetworth.com/richest-celebrities/singers/jennifer-lopez
[4] https://www.architecturaldigest.com/story/jennifer-lopez-returns-her-manhattan-penthouse-to-the-market

became an actor, who became a singer, who became a global icon. She's a woman of color who had the audacity to pursue her dreams," said Elaine Goldsmith-Thomas in J.Lo's documentary *Halftime*.

I'd like to highlight for you J.Lo.'s incredible mindset. There were plenty of doubters in her life, but she kept going. What if Jennifer had given up? What if she had not gone after her dreams? We wouldn't have her amazing work in our lives! We are constantly in reinvention. We do not fossilize and just "become" a dancer, actor, lawyer, AI entrepreneur, caretaker, or side hustler. It is incredibly rare anymore that anyone holds the same job for 30 years.[5] The questions we ask kids and *ourselves* are powerful. In the seminal book *Becoming*, former First Lady Michelle LaVaughn Robinson Obama posits that the common societal practice in the United States of asking young children what they want to "be" when they grow up is unhelpful. Why unhelpful? As humans, we are perpetually in a state of evolution. We change, grow, and do not keep just one job or identity as the primary or only forever. That reinforces the 30-year one-job career that is no longer the norm.

Growth Mindset

Through this whole book, you've seen me talk about healthy striving in our professional lives. Go for it! You rarely get things you didn't go for, even if at first they don't succeed. You need to provide for yourself, unless you're truly a trust-fund baby. Even then, the money could dry up. As the world around us changes rapidly, we must cultivate a curious and growth mindset.

Leading with curiosity is something I'm still growing in. Being curious is asking questions before diving in. It acknowledges boundaries, learning more, and getting buy-in. For example, I employed a dog sitter to take care of Luna while I was on a river rafting trip. He lived minutes away from the rafting company. An ideal business partner for folks rafting who need dog care! I wanted to tell him to get in touch with the company to expand his business asap! However, I led with curiosity. I asked the dog sitter about his dog business and whether he had interest in expanding it. When he said, "Yes," I asked, "Could I offer an idea about expanding your business?" I again got a "Yes" and

---

[5] https://www.ft.com/content/4104612a-e423-11e4-9e89-00144feab7de

shared my idea! But boundaries need to be respected if he instead had said, "No thanks."

Similar to curiosity, a "growth mindset" is the belief that one's abilities and intelligence can be developed through effort, learning, and persistence. The concept was documented by Dr. Carol Dweck in her 2006 book *Mindset: The New Psychology of Success*.[6] Whether you think "while I haven't accomplished my dream yet, I can learn and grow" or "I didn't get the thing I wanted on my first try," your mindset is crucial. As you saw from my recent career journey, I pivoted several times as my goals and opportunities evolved. Just like the title of Pinky Cole's book, *I Hope You Fail*.[7] Pinky's story of resilience and grit via years of hard work, she learned that "Failing is not failing at all. It's about finding the aspirations and the losses and about rising above it. [...] Everything in life is modifiable."[8]

Democratization of Wealth and Power

This book talks about wealth. Wealth is a form of power. By being in control of our wealth, we have more power in our lives. In a world where you can make tremendous money from a smartphone and laptop, why would you work a 9-to-5 job for $62,000 while the white male CEO makes $17 million?[9] You can opt out of these corporate structures and situations that don't serve you. Rest is a form of resistance. When we don't have financial freedom, we might spend our whole lives in a grind. White men typically decide if we get hired or fired. When we are healthy, wealthy, and stable, we don't have to work for companies and people who don't serve us. We can nap and rest when and how we want. We can shape our lives to be the ones we envision.[10]

An amazing example of how earning your own money helps your agency and power, I want to share with you the story of Liz Fong-Jones.[11] At a young age, Fong-Jones learned how to code and began

---

[6] https://hbr.org/2016/01/what-having-a-growth-mindset-actually-means
[7] https://www.amazon.com/Hope-You-Fail-Statements-Everything/dp/1400242851
[8] https://www.youtube.com/watch?v=8VWwhQ7XVL8
[9] https://fortune.com/2023/08/04/ceo-worker-pay-gap-ratio-afl-cio-report-highest-paid-ceo-america-tim-cook-sundar-pichai-apple-live-nation
[10] Again, I hope you're not a psycho killer and that's the life you want. Going to go forward here with the idea that we're on the same page about a more equitable, peaceful world.
[11] https://open.spotify.com/episode/4zBfbAwp5srNjmcGFbXocR

working in computer science. When she ran away from her abusive family at the age of 16 for being trans, she had a paycheck coming in that was more than minimum wage. Fong-Jones eventually worked at Google for more than 10 years and now works as a Field CTO at honeycomb.io.[12] She lived frugally, maxed out her 401k matching, and built a huge amount of wealth. Today, she is an investor and philanthropist. She has put up fundraising matching campaigns of $100,000[13] to fight gender and racial discrimination. She sits on the Board of the National Center for Transgender Equality and has given six-figure donations to that organization and others like Trans Lifeline. Fong-Jones has a seat at the table, makes decisions, and advocates for people like her. In a podcast episode with Arlan Hamilton, Fong-Jones discussed how she wants trans communities and trans communities of color to not only survive but also thrive.[14] When we have economic freedom, we can work to change policy and funding causes that are meaningful to us. This is the definition of financial freedom.

I hope throughout this book you noticed I shared stories of many other amazing people. Anyone can future-proof their career and income. I'm inspired by entrepreneurs and investors from many different backgrounds, some of whom have been featured in these pages:

- Punjabi entrepreneur, mother, model, and influencer Diipa Büller-Khosla[15]
- Muslim female AI entrepreneur, author, and investor Dr. Rana el Kaliouby[16]
- Black gay female investor at Backstage Capital, author, and millionaire Arlan Hamilton
- Jewish female brand guru, author, and podcaster Aliza Licht[17]
- Black female entrepreneur and Slutty Vegan restaurant owner Pinky Cole

---

[12] lizthegrey.com

[13] https://www.fastcompany.com/90275462/meet-the-google-engineer-getting-its-workers-ready-to-strike

[14] https://open.spotify.com/episode/4zBfbAwp5srNjmcGFbXocR

[15] https://www.vogue.in/beauty/content/motherhood-social-media-and-the-true-business-of-beauty-with-diipa-buller-khosla

[16] https://www.linkedin.com/in/kaliouby

[17] https://www.linkedin.com/pulse/being-jewish-activist-wasnt-brand-me-aliza-licht-jjpse

- Black, female self-made millionaire, born in 1867 to parents who had formerly been enslaved, Madame C.J. Walker[18]
- Chinese female AI entrepreneurs co-founders Demi Guo and Chenlin Meng[19]
- Black, female, hard of hearing, AI entrepreneur Eyra Abraham[20]
- White gay female multi-millionaire entrepreneur and author Dorie Clark
- Transgender female and field-CTO, investor, and philanthropist Liz Fong-Jones
- Black, female, mother of four, multimillionaire, and best-selling author Rachel Rodgers
- Filipina animal farming entrepreneur Aileen Suy[21]
- Latina, singer, dancer, actor, and real-estate mogul Jennifer Lopez

Anyone can build phenomenal wealth. Entrepreneurship can be a great equalizer. The people in this list and thousands more have navigated unclear waters across years to tremendous successes. You have the ability to future-proof your income.

With the advent of the digital age, making money is easier than ever. Why? Because we have access to a ton of people online through smartphones. These days you need time, a computer, and Wi-Fi to make money in ways that weren't possible just a few years ago. You can use your smartphone and connect to people around the world in the blink of an eye. The age of AI is a time of great volatility where there is tremendous opportunity to democratize power and wealth for people previously excluded from wealth. Lucrative opportunities are now readily available to anyone with a computer, Wi-Fi, and time enough to take action. That might be a job in the AI sector, and it might not be. I recently saw an influencer named Emily Van Hoff with more than 213,000 followers. Her colorful textile art sells for $2,000 per piece.[22] Wow, there is money to be made! Then imagine if Emily used AI and automation tools to make her operations even more profitable.

---

[18] **https://madamcjwalker.com/about**
[19] **https://venturebeat.com/ai/pika-labs-raises-55m-launches-new-ai-video-platform-to-take-on-runway**
[20] **https://eyraabraham.com**
[21] **https://www.bworldonline.com/top-stories/2022/11/15/487100/born-and-bred-for-business**
[22] **https://www.emilyvanhoff.com/shop**

The Power of Yet

"Yet" is one of my favorite words. As you can probably tell by now, I love to be a tad bit of a contrarian. When people say something doesn't exist, I say "yet!" We are all in stages of growing and becoming. I hope your ambition means you are striving for things across your whole life long. During the writing of this book, I've been building my wealth and my career. I hope the fact that I do not yet have a net worth of $100 million doesn't deter you from taking the data-driven advice in this book. I wish I already had more than $10 million in my financial portfolio. I want to close my first eight-figure deal before this book goes to press. I wish I could promise you that my career and finances will never have ups and downs. Yes! I've had ups and downs before.

Even with all the resilience in my story and all I've learned, I don't want you to have doubts in your potential because of my story and journey. Who knows what my next stages of my life and career hold for me? Your journey is your own! I wish I could promise you a career and financial path full of smooth sailing and a cloudless sky. That's just not the way of the world. Most of us have ups and downs. You've got to keep at it.

"Your personal goals need a long-term strategy," writes Dorie Clark in her book *The Long Game*.[23] Exactly! You need a long-term strategy for your goals. For your life! Resilience is key. When we get out of the struggle-bus of future-proofing our career via a big and robust network and our income with multiple revenue streams, we need to dream beyond hours and days, to months and years. I've begun working on dreaming in *years*. What do I want for myself? My family? My team? My legacy? We all need to make goals and continue to shoot for them. We can continue to learn and grow.

You saw that through the stories in this book. Does this sound familiar to aspects of your life? What have you had to be resilient through? Do you feel you've already peaked? Do you see where that powerful word "yet" could apply to your goals and dreams?

---

[23] **https://www.barnesandnoble.com/w/the-long-game-dorie-clark**

Joy and Meaning

I want to be a positive force of change in this world. I want more joy for you and me. When we zoom out, what is the meaning of our lives? Poet Mary Oliver writes, "Tell me, what is it you plan to do with your one wild and precious life?" In the beginning of the book, we talked about Ikigai, and I'd love to revisit the topic of meaning and building a meaningful life. I love the concept of making the world a better place. One of my favorite phrases is "We pay it forward, we pay it back." When you have the ability to help open doors for someone, do it. Remember the people who opened doors for you. The best things in my life have been reciprocal and paid dividends.

Joan's Hot Take: We Pay It Forward, We Pay It Back

> Pay it forward. Pay it back. Make the world a better place.

Today, when I think about my plan for my life, my answer is to strive toward financial independence for myself and my family and live into my values through more investing, building, and education. Clarity AI can build impactful AI solutions. This book can help you in your career and financial journeys. The *Your AI Roadmap* podcast can connect people with leaders actually building AI and stop so much fluffy hype. As I grow in my career and wealth, I fund women and Black and Brown founders working in femtech, climate action, and AI for social good. In investor lingo, that is my thesis as an investor. This is one of the key reasons I am a founder and investor. I want to live into my values. One of the most powerful ways to do this for yourself is to be an entrepreneur and business owner. If you're interested in working with me on fabulous projects, reach out! Here are some example projects

- **Public Speaking:** I do a lot of public speaking about AI, careers, and future-proofing income.
- **AI and Data Work:** At Clarity AI, we build custom AI solutions via automations, data ingestion platforms, sophisticated mobile app data tracking systems, and more. You can get an intro to our team via our website: **hireclarity.ai**.

- **Bootcamp, Courses, and Workshops:** My team has courses for people who want to upskill you can find at **YourAIRoadmap .com/Courses.**

- **Investing:** In the future, I hope to making investing a bigger part of my life. I'm eager to build a fund to invest in companies who lead and build products with my shared values. Want to see my investments beyond my stock portfolio? Learn more at **Your AIRoadmap.com/Invest**

Excited to potentially partner on a project? Feel free to reach out. While not all projects and partnerships are the right fit, you rarely get opportunities you don't ask for. Send an email! Okay, let's reflect on this book and what we covered in this tome.

Conclusions and Opportunities for Change

As we wrap up our journey together, we began by acknowledging the pesky truth of the age of AI: everyone's day job is at risk, but we all still need money. We have explored the answers to the following questions:

Resilience in the Age of AI: How do we bolster career resilience during the turbulent and opportunity-filled times of AI?

Careers: How do we future-proof our careers? How do we pursue careers in AI if we want?

Income: How do we future-proof our income more broadly?

I hope this book provides you robust answers to many of these questions. You need to ensure that you continue to evolve your skill sets and income stream to remain relevant and stay robust regardless of what wild tech advancement is around the corner. I'd recommend having a healthy distrust for the status quo. Question the status quo. "That's just how it has always been" is a phrase that is one of my CTO's greatest pet peeves. The phrase is a relatively meaningless justification. Upholding the status quo without questioning it could mean that you are unquestioningly upholding norms shaped for and by white supremacy and patriarchy. Yikes!

Black innovator and entrepreneur Steven Bartlett[24] states "Most of the obstacles that we stand in front of us are self-imposed."[25] Sounds similar to this quote from Rachel Rodgers: "Eliminate all the fictitious obstacles."[26] The obstacles might be mindsets and outdated social constructs. "Most of our experience is a bunch of social myths, a bunch of doors that we just haven't tried pushing on yet. And I, at a very young age, started pushing on those doors. And when you start pushing on all of them and you realize there's nothing behind them, that they lead to nowhere, I think it develops into a habit where you start questioning all the norms and assumptions around you a lot more. You start questioning social norms about, you have to do this at this age, and you have to go to university, and you have to pursue a career, and quitting is for losers, and all of these narratives. Turns out most of them are BS."[27] I agree with Steven in large part. Regardless of our age, we have the opportunity to question what is the norm, where those norms came from, and who they serve.

My parents and grandparents' generations have lived with the 9 to 5 being the norm: "The 40-hour, five-day workweek has been the norm in the United States for almost 100 years."[28] So if you're one of my beloved older readers, you might feel more alarmed and shocked that I suggest paths beyond a 9-to-5 job. Documenting the norm is just a data point. "That's how it's always been" is inaccurate across the board. Status quo changes have been sweeping across my grandparents' lifetime.

The term "Baby Boomer" comes from the almost 20% increase in the number of babies born in the United States after World War II.[29] These are folks born from 1946–1964.[30] In 1965, 42% of the U.S.

[24] https://www.theguardian.com/lifeandstyle/2023/dec/16/steven-bartlett-this-much-i-know
[25] We could question this statement as folks with debilitating illnesses might not fully agree. Quotes from podcast episode: https://podcasts.apple.com/us/podcast/the-mel-robbins-podcast/id1646101002?i=1000644585201
[26] We Should All Be Millionaires, p. 233–234
[27] https://podcasts.apple.com/us/podcast/the-mel-robbins-podcast/id1646101002?i=1000644585201
[28] https://www.kqed.org/education/536039/why-do-we-still-work-40-hours-a-week
[29] https://www.census.gov/library/publications/1960/dec/population-pc-a1.html
[30] https://www.usatoday.com/story/news/2023/03/01/baby-boomers-age-range-years/11151270002

population were tobacco cigarette smokers.[31] Today, that number is around 12%.[32] The first commercially available birth control pill was approved by the FDA in 1960. By the late '60s, it is estimated that it was used by around 9 million Americans, representing about 4% of the population.[33,34] By 2017, the number had increased to 65% of the U.S. population.[35] This is an increase by an order of magnitude of 16x. In other large societal changes, the year 1965 ushered in the Voting Rights Act to protect the voting rights of Black Americans.[36,37] In 1974, women were allowed to get credit cards in their own name.[38] That wasn't that long ago. You most likely have a parent, grandparent, or coworker who lived through that time. The Americans with Disabilities Act (ADA) was signed in 1990.[39] Gay marriage was legalized in 2015.[40] There are now wide sidewalks, designated bathroom stalls, and other ADA-compliant aspects normalized in American workplaces.

So, what type of impact do you want to have in this world? What impact do you want to have through your work, through your wealth? What stability can you bring to yourself, your family, your friends, your community, and the world?

An Irresistible Revolution

"The role of the artist is to make revolution irresistible," is one of my favorite quotes from social activist Toni Cade Bambara.[41] At the beginning

---

[31] https://www.infoplease.com/math-science/health/substance-abuse/smoking-prevalence-among-us-adults-1955-2013

[32] https://www.cdc.gov/tobacco/data_statistics/fact_sheets/adult_data/cig_smoking/index.htm

[33] https://www.washingtonpost.com/lifestyle/2021/11/06/lesser-known-history-birth-control

[34] https://nces.ed.gov/programs/digest/d19/tables/dt19_101.10.asp

[35] https://www.cdc.gov/nchs/products/databriefs/db327.htm

[36] https://www.loc.gov/classroom-materials/elections/right-to-vote/voting-rights-for-african-americans

[37] There are still many ridiculous and unethical hoops in place attempting to prevent Black Americans from their ability to vote and participate in the democratic process.

[38] https://www.forbes.com/advisor/credit-cards/when-could-women-get-credit-cards

[39] https://www.britannica.com/topic/Americans-with-Disabilities-Act

[40] https://www.history.com/topics/gay-rights/gay-marriage

[41] https://www.npr.org/2020/12/19/948005131/i-want-us-to-dream-a-little-bigger-noname-and-mariame-kaba-on-art-and-abolition

of this book, I told you the sage advice of my PhD advisor Mike, "If you lead with bias, people shut down and won't listen. If you lead with money, opportunity, or something else that everyone wants to listen to, then you might be able to talk to them about bias." If you did indeed read this book, I hope that it was immensely helpful to you to learn about career, income, and expansive opportunities. I hope you also resoundingly heard about the unjust systems at play that shape our world today. As your artist, I hope you got the full message.

The age of AI has the potential to democratize wealth and power. You can be part of it. I believe in you. I know that you can effectively take this roadmap to chart your next directions with more hope, data-driven tactics, an expanded perspective, and zest for life, liberty, and the pursuit of stability and resilience.

My dear reader, if you have read the end of my heartfelt roadmap for you, I am truly honored. I am so proud of you. You read through some modern, playful, data-driven, weighty, and sometimes emotionally difficult content. I am so impressed by you! The advice in this book can change your life for the better. I am so happy for you and your next steps. I believe in your abilities to future-proof your career and income. I've given you the best methods and strategies I know. Now, it's your turn to put them into action and make your life and the world a better place. If you're interested in working with me on fabulous projects, reach out! Here are some ways to collaborate:

- **Public Speaking:** I do a lot of public speaking about AI, careers, and future-proofing income. Email my team at **hello@ hireclairty.ai.**

- **AI and Data Work:** At Clarity AI, we build custom AI solutions via automations, data ingestion platforms, sophisticated mobile app data tracking systems, and more. You can get an intro to our team via our website: **hireclarity.ai.**

- **Bootcamp, Courses, and Workshops:** My team has courses for people who want to upskill you can find at **YourAIRoadmap .com/Bootcamp** and **YourAIRoadmap.com/Courses.**

- **Investing:** If you're interested in investing with me and in the next stages of my career, I'm eager to build a fund to invest in future companies who lead and live into my shared values. There is a contact for at **YourAIRoadmap.com/Invest.**

- **Podcast:** Listen to my podcast! I interview folks who are building in the AI field who work at Microsoft, Google, Intuit, Adobe, and more about their work and career trajectories. We're on Apple Podcasts, Spotify, and more: **YourAIRoadmap.com/Podcast**.

- **Newsletter:** We have a killer newsletter you can join at **Your AIRoadmap.com/Newsletter**.

Excited to potentially partner on a project? Feel free to reach out. While not all projects and partnerships are the right fit, you rarely get opportunities you don't ask for. Send an email! **hello@hireclarity.ai**.

Go forth with this roadmap of tools to be resilient and live in joy, freedom, wealth, and fulfillment!

With love,

Joan

PS: Got tons of resources for you to grow your personal brand and network with me!

Want to get personalized your AI roadmap ideas?

Take the Your AI Roadmap Personality Quiz: **YourAIRoadmap .com/Me**

Resources: Download frameworks and resources from the book: **YourAIRoadmap.com/Resources**

Let's make it easier! Scan the QR code to these resources:

Resources from the Book	Your AI Roadmap Podcast

Joan's LinkedIn	**Money Tools**

Podcast: **YourAIRoadmap.com/Podcast**
Book Recommendations: **YourAIRoadmap.com/BookRecs**
Your Personal Brand 101: **YourAIRoadmap.com/Brand**
Money Tools: **YourAIRoadmap.com/Money-Tools**
Your AI Roadmap Website: **YourAIRoadmap.com**
Instagram: @YourAIRoadmap
X (Formerly Twitter): @YourAIRoadmap
TikTok: @YourAIRoadmap
Newsletter: **YourAIRoadmap.com/Podcast**
Women in Voice Website: **https://www.WomenInVoice.org**
Clarity AI: HireClarity.AI

Book Reflections of the Entire Book

Questions to Reflect on the Whole Book

- [ ] What is Ikigai? Why is this important?
- [ ] What is the WOOP method versus STAR method? Why are they important?
- [ ] What's Joan's rule about how much time in which buckets?
- [ ] What's the difference between a job and career?
- [ ] What's the difference between a paycheck and income?
- [ ] What are a few reasons people hate networking?
- [ ] What's a silly slogan about weak ties? Randos?
- [ ] What's the difference between a job and career?
- [ ] What are three tips to making your LinkedIn profile better?
- [ ] Who does the taboo about not talking about money help? Who does it help?
- [ ] What are living expenses? What is lifestyle creep?
- [ ] What is an FI number?
- [ ] What are your favorite easy to medium income stream options I proposed?
- [ ] What is the PSS Framework?
- [ ] What does financial freedom and stability look like to you? What does it feel like?

☐ What doubts have you had about my advice? Do you know others who are struggling from inaction? Struggling from not prototyping and validating their decisions?

☐ Have you heard about the growth mindset? Do you believe that you can always be improving?

☐ What advice did my PhD advisor Mike give me? Did you notice the discussion of social justice and inequities in this book?

☐ How did you feel reading about the fact that some people get wildly underpaid simply because of their race, gender, sexuality, etc.? Are these new ideas to you? What can you do to make the world a more equitable place?

☐ As you know, grow, and are more in control of your finances, how do you want to help shape the world to be a better place?

☐ Who do you want to share this book with? Who could use this type of support in your life beyond you?

Download the questions for reflection and resources from the book: **YourAIRoadmap.com/Resources**.

Scan the QR to go directly there:

Epilogue

At lunchtime today, I took a break and ate in the sunshine of my front yard. My dog frolicked in the grass. I threw the ball for her, and she spun around and jumped to catch it in the air. I was wearing a colorful striped top and chased her back and forth across the yard. Gentle spring breezes sent cherry blossoms from the trees in my neighborhood all around us like a living painting. The cherry blossoms dotted the yard with pink and white. A frenzy of pink and green and joy! My morning was full of business calls and talking with my team. In the afternoon, I'll work out and then go to a happy hour event to chill with friends. I feel happy and free.

My romantic partner and I spend tons of time together. We travel regularly and are excited for more. I love being part of a team. Slow dancing. Eating amazing food. Having someone who helps me be the best and most wholehearted version of myself. I am grateful to have someone deeply kind, brilliant, and loving in my life. We talked about ambition and life goals from the first time we met. We're aligned about the realities of our today and the optimism of the path into tomorrow. I love charting our roadmap together. Thank you, my love, for living through this wild journey of life with me.

Acknowledgments

No one completes a book alone. Common sense would tell you there is a village helping this book get to you. Here is a long list that I'm sure isn't even complete! If I missed you, my sincere apologies. I appreciate you.

Wiley: Thank you to my team at Wiley for the support with publishing this book. Thank you to Danielle Curtis who championed the contract for this book getting over the line. I'm grateful that when I thought I'd been too "out there" that those were the same factors that helped the proposal stand out and get approved! I'm not sure this book would have happened without your support. I was a tad incredulous you approved a manuscript that talks about white supremacy, and I'm grateful it got over the line.

Special thanks to my Wiley team, Jim Minatel, Sara Deichman, Navin Vijayakumar, and Adaobi Obi Tulton. Big kudos to Jim for project management and to Adaobi for thoughtful and generous structural edits.

Thank you also to the wider Wiley team who supported work who I wasn't directly in contact with!

Business community: Thank you to Rachel Rogers and the HelloSeven Club for support and inspiration. Thank you to Arlan Hamilton. The way you change the world via your leadership has changed the trajectory of my life.

Author community: Thank you to the authors in my circle who gave me advice about the writing, publishing, and promotion process: Rebekah Bastian, Tracey Spicer, and Shelmina Babai Abji.

Early readers: Thank you to those who read and gave early feedback including Bonnie B. Daneker, Gabby Bajorek, Kira Sidhu, Meera Patel, Maddy Apple, Kimfer Flanery-Rye, Kassel Galaty, Rebecca Evanhoe, Dr. Charisse Iglesias, Dr. Sara Bly, Dr. George Smith, and a few folks who requested not to be named. Love you!

My home team: Thank you to the Clarity AI team for their support as I wrote this book in addition to my duties as a CEO.

Thank you to my extended family who supported me along my journey.

Thank you to the Women in Voice community, board, ambassadors, members, team, and sponsors who embraced me and shared my mission with open hearts and minds.

Thank you to Kat Dowrey my instructor at my gym, Community Fitness, who helped me do ample amounts of cardio, dancing, and squats while writing this book. I needed exercise to feel strong while writing this heartfelt book. I'm grateful for the inclusive, celebratory gym environment with good parking.

Friends and family: Thank you to my mentors, friends, and network for your support, inspiration, and doubts that have fueled me. Thank you to my friend Dr. Charisse Iglesias who helps me navigate through this wild ride of a life.

Thank you to my mom, dad, sister, and brother-in-law for their love and support along with the journey. My dear parents, I dedicated my PhD dissertation to you, and I again thank you here for your support in this new journey that is far less comfortable for you, but also potentially so impactful for many more folks.

Thank you to my partner and my dog. I love you so! I cherish our time together, and writing this book has only fueled my recognition that life is very, very short and I deeply wish to spend it with you. This writing process for the past few months has been career therapy. It helps bring to center stage what is most important to me in my career today and my goals for tomorrow. It also centers what I love at home, my great fortune of a modern, ebullient family.

To my dear readers, this book is truly for you. It was your questions online and the impact of these resources that were in my beating heart to make sure this book crossed the finish line! Your support means the world, and I am so delighted to see and hear from you. Reach out on social media. I provide tons of free advice, tips, events, and more; I hope you'll see that I practice what I preach in this book and continue to grow and evolve!

About the Author

AI entrepreneur, investor, and influencer, Dr. Joan Palmiter Bajorek is ranked as the #4 Voice AI Influencer by Voicebot.ai. She is the CEO of Clarity AI, driving innovative AI and software solutions that boost revenue for scaling small and midsize businesses. She hosts the popular *Your AI Roadmap* podcast, featuring top AI experts from Google, Microsoft, Upwork, Adobe, Rev, Latimer.ai (Black-GPT), and more.

Dr. Bajorek's career is a dual fusion of social impact and technical innovation. As the founder of Women in Voice, a 501(c)(3) nonprofit with more than 20 chapters and 56,000+ followers, she champions diversity, equity, and inclusion in the AI field. With 10+ years of technical experience in data and AI development for Fortune 500 clients, she has held senior roles at Nuance (acquired by Microsoft for $16B), Netavox, and VERSA Agency. Her business acumen is demonstrated by closing six-, seven-, and eight-figure contracts. She has invested in 12 startups and advises companies like CleanAI, Agria, and various enterprise companies.

As a public speaker, Dr. Bajorek has spoken at CES, Voice Summit, and VentureBeat. Her work is featured in publications including Harvard Business Review, Adobe XD, Cambridge University Press, and UXmatters, as well as at Google i/O. She holds a PhD in multimodal AI from the University of Arizona and an MA in linguistics from the University of California, Davis. Her BFA and BA degrees are in photomedia and French from the University of Washington. She lives in Seattle, Washington.

Download your free Your AI Roadmap resources and money tools at **YourAIRoadmap.com**.

Index

A

Abraham, Eyra (entrepreneur), 224
academic performance, WOOP
method and, 22
Actionable, in SMART goals, 20
adjectives, in personal brand, 58
advisory fees, as an income
stream, 111, 200
affiliate commissions, as an income
stream, 112
affiliate marketing, as an income
stream, 172
aging, caregiving and, 152–153
Alma, 131
Amazon, 52–54
Americans with Disabilities Act
(ADA), 229
Angelou, Maya (poet), 11
annual percentage yield (APR), 113
app creation, as an income stream,
172
Apple, 141
artificial intelligence (AI)
about, 5, 74–77
for business, 197–198
future jobs and, 80–81
job salaries, 77–80
products, as an income stream, 172
volatility and opportunity in the
age of, 3–14
work in, 226, 230
ATM ownership, as an income
stream, 200
Atomic Habits (Clear), 194
attending, prototyping and, 92
auto loan debt, 132

B

B corps, 184
"Baby Boomer," 228–229
bad debt, 116
Bajorek, Joan Palmiter (author)
founding of UW French Club
by, 182–183
founding of Women in Voice
by, 183–185
on income, 104–105
income streams of, 111–115
LinkedIn, 231

personal brand of, 58–60
professional opportunities of, 38–41
Bambara, Toni Cade (social activist),
229–230
Bartlett, Steven (entrepreneur), 228
Bastian, Rebekah (VP), 165
Be in Control, in 3-Part Financial
Freedom Recipe, 109
Becoming (Obama), 221
Belong, as a Blue Zones Power 9 factor, 16
Big Earner, 165
Blakely, Sara (Spanx founder), 165
blogs, as an income stream, 172
Blue Zones Power 9, 16
boasting, networking and, 44–45
Bolles, Richard Nelson (author)
What Color Is Your Parachute?, 50
bond portfolio, as an income stream, 113
book deal, as an income stream, 112
book publishing, as an income
stream, 200
bookkeeping, as an income stream, 172
books, prototyping and, 92
bootcamps, 227, 230
Born into Wealth, 165–166
Bowie, David, 11
"Brag Sheet," 91
bro-culture, networking and, 45
broker mergers and acquisitions, as an
income stream, 201
Buettner, Dan (author), 15
Büller-Khosla, Diipa (entrepreneur), 223
Burnett, Bill (professor)
Designing Your Life, 41
business
AI for, 197–198
ownership of, as an income stream, 112
buy and sell items, as an income
stream, 112

C

call to action, for networking, 48–49
Canva, 61
career building
80% networking rule for, 33
people-first, 33–35
careers
about, 28–29
author's tips for, 20